SELECTED WORKS OF

D. I. KACHENOVSKII

Ukrainian International Lawyer

PUBLISHED BY
TALBOT PUBLISHING/THE LAWBOOK EXCHANGE, LTD.

By William E. Butler

EDITOR

Selected Works of D.I. Kachenovskii (2014)

On the Freedom of the Sea by Gerard de Rayneval (2013)

Adventures in Internationalism: A Biography of James Brown Scott by George A. Finch (2012)

The Nakaz of Catherine the Great: Collected Texts (with Vladimir A. Tomsinov) (2010)

On the History of International Law and International Organization: Collected Papers of Sir Paul Vinogradoff (2009)

INTRODUCTION

The Illustrious Hugo Grotius Of the Law of Warre and Peace by Hugo Grotius, Clement Barksdale, transl. (2013)

The Most Excellent Hugo Grotius, His Books Treating of the Rights of War & Peace by Hugo Grotius, William Evats, transl. (2013)

De Jure Belli et Pacis by Hugo Grotius, William Whewell, transl. (2012)

A Treatise on the Laws of Commerce and Manufactures by Joseph Chitty (2012)

On the Origin, Nature, Progress and Influence of Consular Establishments by David B. Warden (2011)

The Syllabi: Genesis of the National Reporter System (2011)

The American Institute of International Law by James Brown Scott (2010)

A Manual of the Law of Maritime Warfare by William Hazlitt (2009)

The Catholic Conception of International Law by James Brown Scott (2008)

A Treatise on the Law of War by Cornelius van Bynkershoek (2008)

Pennsylvania Blackstone by John Reed (with Mark Podvia) (2006)

SELECTED WORKS OF D. I. KACHENOVSKII

Ukrainian International Lawyer

Edited by WILLIAM E. BUTLER

John Edward Fowler Distinguished Professor of Law
Pennsylvania State University
Foreign Member, National Academy of Sciences of Ukraine
and National Academy of Legal Sciences of Ukraine

TALBOT
PUBLISHING
Clark, New Jersey

ISBN 978-1-61619-406-2

TALBOT PUBLISHING

AN IMPRINT OF

THE LAWBOOK EXCHANGE, LTD.

33 Terminal Avenue
Clark, New Jersey 07066-1321

Please see our website for a selection of our other publications and fine facsimile reprints of classic works of legal history:
www.lawbookexchange.com

Library of Congress Cataloging-in-Publication Data

Kachenovskii, D. I. (Dmitrii Ivanovich), 1827-1872, author.
[Works Selections]
Selected works of D. I. Kachenovskii : Ukrainian international lawyer / compiled and edited, with an introduction by William E. Butler, John Edward Fowler Distinguished Professor of Law, Pennsylvania State University, Foreign Member, National Academy of Sciences of Ukraine and National Academy of Legal Sciences of Ukraine.
pages cm
Includes bibliographical references and index.
"The present volume contains what are believed to be all of the works published by Dmitrii Ivanovich Kachenovskii in the English language."--Acknowledgments.
ISBN 978-1-61619-406-2 (hardcover : alk. paper)
1. International law. I. Butler, William Elliott, 1939- editor, compiler, writer of introduction. II. Title.
KZ2943.K33A2 2014
341--dc23 2014007919

Printed in the United States of America on acid-free paper

CONTENTS

WORKS BY D. I. KACHENOVSKII

ACKNOWLEDGMENTS

The present volume contains what are believed to be all of the works published by Dmitrii Ivanovich Kachenovskii in the English language. Some are completely unknown to Russian and Ukrainian international legal doctrine; all are uncommon; most have been inaccessible to western international legal doctrine, although their existence and importance have been acknowledged from time to time.

Kachenovskii was among the most illustrious Ukrainian/Russian international lawyers of his time, a status acknowledged during his lifetime, for decades following, and again in the post-Soviet era. His interest in England and in the United States, and his command of the English language, were most unusual. Apart from F. F. Martens and V. E. Grabar, who came along later, it is difficult to name another international lawyer from the Russian Empire who had so thorough a command of Anglo-American doctrinal writings on international law.

Locating these materials has been a challenge. I am grateful to Jeri Fitzsimons and Mark Podvia of the Law Library at the Dickinson School of Law, Pennsylvania State University, for their resourcefulness in assisting in this matter and to Dr. O. V. Kresin, at the V. M. Koretskiy Institute of State and Law, National Academy of Sciences of Ukraine for help in obtaining materials from Ukraine.

W. E. Butler
Newville, Pennsylvania
February 2014

ON THE LIFE AND WORKS OF D. I. KACHENOVSKII

W. E. Butler

The world of public and private international law in the Russian Empire was, in the mid-nineteenth century, still in its formative stages. When Moscow University was founded in 1755, lectures on the law of nature and nations[1] were an integral part of the curriculum but delivered by continental European professors (Austrian and Prussian) of a natural-law orientation.[2] As faculties of laws were embedded in the expansion of Russian higher education during the nineteenth century (St. Petersburg, Kazan, Kharkov, Kyiv, and others) and the Baltic universities (Tartu), now within the Russian Empire, reinvigorated, young Russians succeeded to the Chairs previously held by

---

[1] A Memorandum issued in 1765 to the professors of Moscow University reminded them that "in the law class or faculty they study Russian laws, and in so doing also laws of other countries and universal public law ...". Quoted in T. N. Neshataeva and V. L. Tolstykh, «Зарождение науки международного права в России (вторая половина XIX – начало XX в.» [Origin of the Science of International Law in Russia (Second Half of XIX and Early XX Centuries)], in Золотой фонд российского науки международного права [Golden Fund of the Russian Science of International Law] (2007), I, p. 16.

[2] See W. E. Butler, "F. G. Strube de Piermont and the Origins of Russian Legal History", in id, *Russia and the Law of Nations in Historical Perspective: Collected Essays* (2009), pp. 129–144.

foreign imports. In one of the wiser decisions adopted by Russian authorities at the time, it was considered to be essential in most disciplines for Russians aspiring to the professoriate to spend a year or two in western Europe, usually at State expense, in order to attend lectures and pursue dissertation research, sometimes even to acquire a foreign learned degree.

Kachenovskii was fortunate in being able to undertake his European visits at all. The tides of revolution in Europe during the late 1840s could not fail to produce a reaction in Russia, where nationality relations were sensitive. A Manifesto of Emperor Nicholas I dated 27 February 1848 observed that "The West of Europe has suddenly been rocked by sedition and the threatened overthrow of lawful authorities and the social system". This destructive trend, the Manifesto said, must be stemmed. The editors of journals in Russia were instructed to assist the "Government in protecting the public against the contagion of ideas harmful to morality and public order". A number of measures limited the autonomy of universities and constrained the freedom of university instruction. Rectors and deans were no longer to be elected. The rector was appointed by the minister from among persons who had scholarly qualifications and was confirmed by higher authority. Deans were appointed by a minister from professors available to undertake this position. The academic curriculum and the content of what was taught were strictly regulated. Pursuant to a Circular of 1 January 1850, professors were obliged to submit to the dean details of their lectures, specifying the manuals and textbooks which they proposed to use. The deans had to "ensure that the syllabi did not conceal anything incompatible with the teachings of the Orthodox Church, with the form of government, and with the spirit of our institutions". As part of this campaign, measures were introduced to limit the previously free contacts with the scientific thought of Western Europe. Foreign visits were suspended; professors no longer had the right to receive uncensored foreign literature. It was prohibited to teach the State law of foreign powers. It was in this environment that Kachenovskii proceeded to complete his University education and magister dissertation.[3]

In the discipline of law, the most popular destinations for aspiring professors were the Prussian and Austro-Hungarian universities, followed by the French, with the Italians, Dutch, and others lagging well behind. England and Scotland, the original destinations of Russian law students under Empress Catherine the Great in the 1760s, were not frequented for these purposes again until the nineteenth century. One must speculate that Russian postgraduate students found the proximity, excellence, and intellectual congeniality of the adjacent Germanic school more to their liking and more relevant to their future professorial careers. In many instances these episodes of study abroad resembled an academic "Grand Tour", during which the young Russians perfected their foreign language skills, visited numerous academic and private libraries, attended lectures and seminars, received personal tutelage and supervision from obliging German professors, and immersed themselves in the cultural experience of European travel.

Each postgraduate traveling for these purposes was required to submit a substantial Report upon returning to his University and to the relevant Russian ministries. Often these were published in journals of the Ministry of Justice or the Ministry of Enlightenment; some appeared as

---

[3] On these events, see V. E. Grabar, *The History of International Law in Russia 1647–1917*, transl. W. E. Butler (1990), pp. 281–282.

separate publications, either offprints from a journal or a slender monograph. This is a body of literature, in the instance of jurists, which has yet to be explored for the insights that may be obtained into the development of international and comparative law in Russia.

One early pioneer in the "Legal Grand Tour" was the Ukrainian jurist, Dmitrii Ivanovich Kachenovskii[4] (1827–1872) — remarkable for his early contributions to the development of international legal doctrine in the Russian Empire, but the more so because he visited England twice to this end and, moreover, published original works of scholarship in the English language. Kachenovskii possessed that commodity most rare amongst lawyers in the Russian Empire of his day — a command of the English language. In the present volume we collect his English publications, all of them uncommon and never before assembled in one place.

The Author

Dmitrii Ivanovich Kachenovskii was born in Karachev,[5] Orlov Province, Russia, on 8(20) December 1827 into the family of a Chancellery clerk.[6] Primary

[4] Spellings of his surname in English are sundry: Katchenovsky, Katchenoffsky, Katchenowsky, among others. We follow the Library of Congress transliteration of his name, which in Cyrillic, of course, has Russian and Ukrainian variations.

[5] Some sources report his place of birth as Kharkov, which is incorrect. He was a distant relative of Mikhail Trofimovich Kachenovskii (1745–1822), a professor of Moscow University.

[6] For biographical data on Kachenovskii, see V. E. Grabar, note 3 above; Grabar, «Каченовский Д. И.» [Kachenovskii D. I.], Энциклопедический словарь [Encyclopedic Dictionary], XIVA, p. 808. Grabar, «Каченовский Дмитрий Иванович» [Kachenovskii

education was initially in a public school. His father's death left the family destitute. His mother placed Kachenovskii in the Orlov School for children of chancellery personnel at treasury expense. A gifted young man whose abilities displayed themselves early on, he was transferred to the fourth grade of the I Kharkov Gymnasium at treasury expense. Something of a prodigy, he graduated in 1842 at

---

Dmitrii Ivanovich], Новый Энциклопедический словарь [New Encyclopedic Dictionary], XXI, cols. 335–337; «Каченовский Дмитрий Иванович» [Kachenovskii, Dmitrii Ivanovich], Русский биографический словарь [Russian Biographical Dictionary] (1897; reprint ed., 1994), pp. 575–577; S. I. Posokhov and O. N. Iarmysh, «Каченовський Дмитро Іванович» [Kachenovskii Dmitro Ivanovich], in Iu. S. Shemshuchenko (ed.), Юридична енциклопедія [Legal Encyclopedia] (2001), III, pp. 68–69; V. N. Denysov and K. O. Savchuk, «Каченовський Дмитро Іванович» [Kachenovkii Dmitro Ivanovich], in Iu. S. Shemshuchenko (ed.), Антологія української юридичної думки [Anthology of Ukrainian Legal Thought] (2004), VIII, pp. 73–76; V. A. Iastrzhembskii, «Каченовский Дмитрий Иванович» [Kachenovskii Dmitrii Ivanovich], in M. P. Chubinskii and D. I. Bagalei (eds.), Юридический факультет Харьковского университета (1805–1905). История факультета. Биографический словарь профессоров и преподавателей [Law Faculty of Kharkov University in the First 100 Years of Its Existence (1805–1905): History of the Faculty. Biographical Dictionary of Professors and Lecturers] Kharkov, 2007), pp. 242–247 (reprint of the 1908 edition with a new preface). See, in general, V. Denysov and K. Savchuk, «Розвиток науки міжнародного права в Україні у XIX – першій половині XX сторіччя» [The Development of the Science of International Law in Ukraine in the XIX-First Half of the XX Centuries], Український щорічник міжнародного права 2008 [Ukrainian Yearbook of International Law 2008] (Kyiv, 2010), pp. 264–317; K. Savchuk, «Дмитрий Иванович Каченовский: один из фундаторов отечественной науки международного права» [Dmitrii Ivanovich Kachenovskii: One of the Founders of the Fatherland Science of International Law], Международное право [International Law], no. 2 (2013), pp. 219-229.

the age of 15 with the gold medal (first in his class) and enrolled, with the special authorization of his guardian, in the Law Faculty at Kharkov University. Completing his University degree in 1847, he was invited to remain in the Faculty as a professoriate stipendiary. In 1848 he passed his magister examination, whereupon the Law Faculty petitioned to have him appointed as a junior scientific assistant in the Chair of All-People's [общенародное] Law (then a term widely used in the Russian Empire for international law). The petition was declined; Kachenovskii was appointed to the position of privat-docent only after defending his magister dissertation, at the age of 22, in 1849: a historical survey of the provisions of international law on dominion over the seas.[7]

At Kharkov the Chair of Natural and Political Law and the Law of Nations had not been filled after the death of Professor B. O. Reith (1770–1824). The Professor of Roman Law, Konstantin Pavlovich Paulovich (1782–18?), lectured temporarily in the Chair of Political Economy and Diplomacy from 1824 to 1832. In 1832 Tikhon Fedorovich Stepanov (1795–1847) was appointed to the Chair of Diplomacy and from 1835 until his retirement in 1845 Stepanov held the Chair of the Law of Nations. He was succeeded by Sergei Nikolaevich Ornatskii (1806–1884), who in 1848 removed to Moscow University to the Chair of the Encyclopedia of Laws. Lecturing on the law of nations during the academic year 1848/49 was entrusted to the Professor of Criminal Law, Gavriil Stepanovich Gordeenko (1805–1849), who was succeeded by Kachenovskii.[8]

---

[7] The magister dissertation was not published and remains in manuscript, being at one time in the ownership of the former librarian of the University. Its whereabouts are unknown today.

[8] Grabar, note 3 above, p. 286.

Commencing his lecturing duties, Kachenovskii offered, in addition to international law, a course on “State Institutions” to students of the Law Faculty. In the next academic year (1850–1851) he was appointed Secretary of the Law Faculty. His course load was enlarged to include the standard introductory course on the “Encyclopedia of Jurisprudence and State Institutions”, as well as lectures on the basic laws of the Russian Empire and the institutions and laws regulating State service. He quickly “became a star of the first magnitude”.[9] The international law topic set by Kachenovskii for students participating in medal competitions during the academic year 1851/52 was: “A Critical Evaluation of the Work by Hugo Grotius *De iure belli ac pacis* Showing the Influence of Works by this Publicist on the Development of the Science of the Law of Nations”.[10]

In 1855 Kachenovskii defended a dissertation for the degree of doctor of political sciences at Moscow University on the law of prize, which in expanded form was published at London in 1867 and is reproduced in the present volume. While in Moscow, Kachenovskii became involved in intellectual circles frequented by Timofei Nikolaevich Granovskii (1813–1855) and other “Westernizers” who engaged in passionate disputes with the “Slavophiles”. Whether he encountered the life and works of the American statesman, Daniel Webster (1782–1852), in Moscow or Kharkov remains obscure. Sometime in 1855 he acquired the fourth edition of Webster’s collected writings

---

[9] M. F. De-Pule, «Харьковский университет и Д. И. Каченовский: Культурный очерк и воспоминания из 40-х годов» [Kharkov University and D. I. Kachenovskii: Cultural Survey and Recollections from the 1840s], Вестник Европы [Herald of Europe], XLV, no. 1–2 (1873), p. 86.
[10] Grabar, ibid., p. 289.

introduced by Edward Everett (1794–1865) and wrote a lengthy review for the new literary and political journal founded by Mikhail Nikiforovich Katkov (1818–1887).[11] This he enlarged into a more substantial piece, relying, he said, on some additional articles about Webster. Kachenovskii evidently completed his manuscript in London and sent it to the publisher from there. This book is probably the first biography of an American political figure by a Ukrainian author, and, moreover, in the French language.[12]

Kachenovskii was sent abroad in 1858 on his first academic visit, touring widely throughout Western Europe, including Prussia and England, for eighteen months. The "purpose of my journey", he said, "from the very outset was determined firmly and clearly": to "familiarize myself with the contemporary state of international law" and "to add to my knowledge of the State sciences in general". To this was soon added a third objective: "in March 1858 the Council of the University informed me that the teaching of the State law of European powers would be assigned to me upon my return from abroad". It was necessary for Kachenovskii to expand his horizons into the field of comparative public law and study "the political life abroad and make observations concerning the institutions of at least the leading peoples of the Western world".[13] While in England he made the

---

[11] Русский вестник [Russian Herald], no. 3 (May–June 1856), pp. 385–416: "Of the public figures of North America, no one enjoyed recently such a wide reputation as Webster" (p. 385). The article is widely recorded as having been in a French journal, *Messager russe*, a reference taken from the Preface to the Brussels edition in book form of the Webster biography, because Kachenovskii in that publication had translated the Russian title of the journal into French.

[12] Kachenovskii, *Daniel Webster: étude biographique* (Brussels, 1858).

[13] A. N. Stoianov, Воспоминание о Д. И. Каченовском: Биографический очерк [Recollection of D. I. Kachenovskii: Biographical

acquaintance of John Westlake (1828–1913), Sir Robert Phillimore (1810–1885), and Sir Travers Twiss (1809–1897) and spoke at the Antislavery Society.

In Prussia he met frequently with Professor C. F. Wurm (1803–1859), and in London visited the Houses of Parliament and attended various public lectures and meetings. There is no doubt that his foreign travels had precisely the impact that was intended — they greatly influenced his approach to the discipline of international law and initiated his involvement in matters European.

Upon his return to Ukraine, Kachenovskii delivered his inaugural lecture at the Imperial Kharkov University on 24 September 1859. In substance the lecture was a report on his travels abroad and his assessment of the state of teaching and research on public international law at the leading universities in England, Germany, France, and, to a lesser extent, Italy and Austria — a mixture of gossip, conjecture, opinion, and fresh information. He drew interesting analogies between Russia and the United States:

> … there is much in common, and I am not alone in seeing this, in the attitudes of America and Russia towards the Old World. In the United States, just as in our fatherland, the need for spiritual communion with Europe was created at virtually the same time … Americans to be sure have read and are reading no less than we are everything that emanates from Europe, but their own writers differ little from the English. In science one also cannot say that they have overtaken the English … Russian literature, subject to the routine French,

---

Essay], (Kharkov, 1874), p. 22. Stoianov had access to two volumes of manuscript notes which Kachenovskii left of his visit to Europe.

German, English influence, has acquired incomparably greater autonomy and weight than the American ...".[14]

He made a strong plea for comparative jurisprudence, although he did not use those words:

> A young people should not be too afraid of their receptiveness; only by reason of this quality do they find in themselves the power to overtake mature peoples and surpass them. If the experience of one nation is not passed on to another, if each is forced to begin everything anew, what should one expect from the successes of mankind. So-called progress is achieved precisely through economies of time and labor, succession in the development of ideas.[15]

Kachenovskii decided to offer a series of open public lectures. Given widespread interest at the time in the possible emancipation of Russian serfs, he decided to devote the lectures to the relations of Europeans with negroes, giving particular attention to the British and French colonies. This suggestion encountered resistance in the Council of Kharkov University as being "inappropriate" because "much would relate also to our fatherland". Nonetheless, the Council approved the suggestion, observing that "censorship does not prohibit articles on the trade in negroes and abolition thereof at all". In the end, the public lectures never

---

[14] D. I. Kachenovskii, «Вступительная лекция по международному праву» [Inaugural Lecture on International Law], Русское слово [Russian Word], no. 4 (April 1860), p. 6.

[15] Ibid., p. 5. No doubt similar sentiments contributed to Kachenovskii being instructed, when making his visit abroad, to study the State law and institutions of the countries that he visited, that is, the domestic public law aspects of foreign countries, upon which he would subsequently lecture.

happened because the Ministry considered them to be "untimely". Nonetheless, Kachenovskii devoted twenty to thirty hours in his course on international law to a historical survey of the origins, development, and decline of slavery in the West. Without saying a single word about Russian legislation on serfdom, he convinced his students of the need to abolish that institution in Russia, which predisposed their later activities when they served on committees to improve the lot of peasants.[16]

Kachenovskii was appointed professor *ordinarius* in 1859 at the Chair of International Law and assigned to lecture on the State law of European powers. Being an unapologetic proponent of constitutionalism and human rights, Kachenovskii embodied these opinions in his course on comparative State law. Here he used his visits abroad to advantage, drawing upon his personal experiences in witnessing the operations of Parliament in England, the Sejm in Hungary, and French, Prussian, and Austrian parliamentary bodies. When Russia become interested in local self-government and justices of the peace, Kachenovskii enriched his lectures with examples of English and other European experience. A "Westernizer" often accused of Anglomania, Kachenovskii was described by his students as a "patriot in the best sense of the word" who sought to eliminate shortcomings inherent in Russian society by references to relevant foreign examples.[17]

---

[16] So the students recalled. See M. M. Kovalevskii, «Моя жизнь» [My Life], История и историки [History and Historians] (1975), p. 281; P. Leibin, «Памяти Д. И. Каченовского» [In Memoriam D. I. Kachenovskii], Санкт Петербургские ведомости [St. Petersburg Gazette], no. 15 (15 January 1873), p. 2.

[17] Kovalevskii, «Характеристика Д. И. Каченовского в связи с личными о нем воспоминаниями» [Characterization of D. I. Kachenovskii in Connection with Personal Recollections About Him],

By all accounts his lectures were popular and attended by students from throughout the University, not merely the Law Faculty.[18] His popularity extended beyond his formal lecturing, though. He encouraged students to meet informally with him, supplying students with recent publications, inviting them to his home, and involving them in conversations on contemporary issues, both academic and social. These conversations "were often no less important than the lectures, because Kachenovskii was a rarity of a talented and multi-dimensional individual. He was seriously interested in painting, not a bad pianist, knew ancient languages, and had an excellent command of French, German, and English. Preferring to read the best works in their originals, he began to study Italian and Spanish".[19]

In Faculty affairs he was well regarded by all colleagues for his fairness in administering matters, but as a

---

in Д. И. Каченовского: Торжественное заседание Юридического Общества при Харьковском университете 22 ноября 1903 г. Характеристики и воспоминания В. А. Ястржембского, Максима Ковалевского, А. Н. Фатеева, Н. Ф. Сумцова, Л. Л. Гиршмана, А. П. Шимкова [In Memoriam D. I. Kachenovskii: Solemn Session of the Law Society attached to Kharkov University on 22 November 1903. Characterization and Recollections of V. A. Iastrzhembskii, Maksim Kovalevskii, A. N. Fateev, N. F. Sumtsov, L. L. Girshman, and A. P. Shimkov] (Kharkov, 1905), p. 25.

[18] Among his students who later achieved renown as international lawyers were M. M. Kovalevskii and A. N. Stoianov. For recollections of student impressions, see the essays by L. L. Girshman and A. P. Shimkov, in note 17 above.

[19] V. Iu. Ivashchenko, «Профессор Д. И. Каченовский в воспоминаниях современников» [Professor D. I. Kachenovskii in the Memoirs of Contemporaries], Проблеми періодизації історії та історіографічного процесу: Харківський історіографічний збірник [Problems of the Periodization of History and the Historiographical Process: Kharkov Historiographical Collection] (Kharkov, 2002), V, pp. 91–92.

"Westernizer" he was in constant conflict with the "Slavophiles" in the Faculty, especially P. A. Lavrovskii (1827–1886) and N. A. Lavrovskii (1827–1899). Partly fueled by personality conflicts, partly by differences of view on individual issues, these disputes sometimes negatively affected the instructional process. Kachenovskii, for example, opposed the introduction of the History of the Slavonic Peoples in the syllabus for the magister examination on the grounds that this subject-matter was an "unnecessary embellishment".[20]

A man of principle, Kachenovskii vigorously opposed a practice at Kharkov University under which university professors would accept students as boarders in their homes, charging high rents for accommodation, on the understanding that these boarders would most certainly be successful on the examinations. Ultimately, Kachenovskii's view prevailed, such that by the end of the 1850s this academic abuse had all but disappeared — an outcome that Kachenovskii's students attributed mostly to his efforts.[21]

A second visit abroad, undertaken principally for reasons of personal health, although academic interests were pursued, occurred from June to October 1861.[22]

---

[20] See A. Voronov, «Воспоминания бывшего студента Харьковского университета 60-х годов» [Recollections of the Former Student of Kharkov University of the 1860s], Русская старина [Russian Antiquity], CLIV, no. 6 (1913), p. 575; D. I. Bagalei, N. F. Sumtsov, and V. P. Buzeskul, Краткий очерк истории Харьковского университета за первые сто лет его существования [Concise Survey of the History of Kharkov University During the First Hundred Years of Its Existence] (Kharkov, 1906), pp. 202–203.

[21] See A. Shimkov, «Воспоминания о Д. И. Каченовском» [Recollections of D. I. Kachenovskii], in note 17 above, pp. 84–87.

[22] See Kachenovskii, Краткий отчет о занятиях профессора Императорского Харьковского университета Д. И. Каченовского за границею с июня по октябрь 1861 г. [Concise Report on the

Kachenovskii spent time in Austria and Italy, followed by some days in France and Dublin, Ireland (the Irish visit was to attend the fourth Annual Meeting of the National Association for the Promotion of Social Science). During three weeks in Austria, principally in Vienna, he spent time at the Reichsrath — primarily a waste of time, he said, as there were no interesting parliamentary addresses to be heard. He criticized the Austrian system of elections to the Reichsrath — candidates were mostly appointed by provincial assemblies without the direct participation of the people. The candidates for deputy, he said, were mostly tools of the Austrian Government.

Of greater interest to him were the disputes between Hungary and Austria over the constitution. Kachenovskii arrived in Vienna shortly after a memorable parliamentary address by Ferenc Deák de Kehida (1803–1876), the "Wise Man of Hungary", and followed the polemic which the address generated. In his view, the resolution of what he called the "Danubian question" was closely connected with the future of the "Slavonic tribes" and deserved the special attention of Russian publicists. Although he professed himself to lack the "special preparation and especially a knowledge of Slavonic languages" necessary to become fully acquainted with the issues involved, he did make the acquaintance of representatives of various political parties and peoples who were destined, he believed, to play a role during what he called the Austrian "crisis'. In his view a "coup" was imminent in the Danubian area whose results would be felt "in all of southeastern Europe".

Occupations of the Professor of the Imperial Kharkov University, D. I. Kachenovskii, Abroad from June to October 1861] (Kharkov, 1862), pp. 1–12.

While in Vienna, Kachenovskii visited lectures offered by Robert Edler von Zimmermann (1824–1898) on the philosophy of law, Leopold Freiherr von Neumann (1811–1888) on international law, and Lorenz von Stein (1815–1890) on the theory of finances. He came away persuaded that the Austrian Government had granted greater scope for university instruction in the post-1848 period. In general he believed the situation at the University Law Faculty was quite satisfactory. Neumann lectured to students on international law who were primarily being trained for positions in the Austrian diplomatic or consular service. Other Austrian institutions had introduced international law to the curriculum, notably the law of war in military schools.

Venturing into Italy, Kachenovskii visited Venice, Padua, Milan, Turin, Florence, Pisa, Bologna, Parma, but omitted Rome because of considerations of time. He took the occasion to visit parliamentary sessions in Milan and chat with local lawyers. In Florence he used the San Lorenzo Library and State Archives. Bologna was a disappointment. The University had moved to new quarters, leaving few traces of the Glossators ("even their works and manuscripts had been moved elsewhere").

Kachenovskii had a special interest in penal institutions, which he visited as occasion permitted during both his first and second tours of Europe. During the second visit he went to Austrian prisons near Vienna and in France visited asylums, crèches, and school for poor children, lamenting the absence in Russia of societies and institutions similar to those operated by the Catholic sisters in Europe.

Kachenovskii's visit to Ireland was occasioned by an invitation from the National Association for the Promotion of Social Science, founded in England. For three decades until its dissolution in 1886, the Association brought together "an inchoate body of social reformers, social workers, lawyers, educationalists, economists, doctors and business men",[23] including international lawyers. The Society held annual congresses of a week or so in duration. Kachenovskii had been elected a Foreign Corresponding Member by the Council of the Association on 14 July 1859.[24] In 1860 Kachenovskii sent from Kharkov a communication to the Secretary of the Association, George W. Hastings (1825–1917), urging that an "international department" be created. The Letter was read out at the Glasgow Congress and served as the initiative for the formation of a "Department of Trade and International Law" attached to the Association (reproduced in the present volume below).

The first sessions of the new Department were opened at Dublin on 14 August 1861. The initial discussions

---

[23] See B. Rodgers, "The Social Science Association, 1857–1886", *The Manchester School*, XX (2008), p. 283. The *Transactions* published by the Association deserve the attention of international lawyers, for they contain much material on matters of public and private international law, including neutral trade, belligerent rights, legal status of foreigners, general average, international copyright, trademarks, and the like. The Association held 28 congresses before winding up its activities.

[24] George W. Hastings (ed.), *Transactions of the National Association for the Promotion of Social Science 1859* (1860), p. xxxiii. The status of Foreign Corresponding Members was highly selective. In all during the early years of the National Association only twenty or so individuals were chosen. Kachenovskii was the sole individual from Russia. The sole American was William Beach Lawrence (1800–1881), the international lawyer and politician, who was elected after Kachenovskii and sent several substantial communications to the National Association on the subject of belligerent rights and neutrality. Kachenovskii published an extensive review article of the first three volumes of the *Transactions* that will have given the Russian reader a substantial introduction to the issues and personalities engaged in the Association annual meetings. See D. I. Kachenovskii, Русское слово [Russian Word], no. 4 (1860), pp. 59–80, no. 5 (1860), pp. 46–69.

concentrated on the Treaty of Commerce between England and France, recently concluded. One of the architects of the treaty, Michel Chevalier, was elected President of the newly-formed Department. Discussions then turned to international law proper: the acquisition of immoveable property by foreigners; bankruptcy; belligerent rights; literary property, and others. In the absence of the newly-elected President, who was needed elsewhere, Kachenovskii was invited to take the Chair. He also spoke during the plenary sessions, setting out in concise form the essence of the history of Russian legislation on foreigners.

Kachenovskii was recorded as being among those who spoke in support of a resolution proposed by Mr. W. S. Lindsay, M.P., which was unanimously adopted by the Department on Trade and International Law:

> That in the opinion of this Department, it is most desirable that the principles laid down by the Congress of Paris in 1856, with respect to maritime warfare, should be extended to the length of exempting the private property of citizens of belligerent nations, not being contraband of war, from capture at sea.[25]

These were not his only visits to Europe. Italy especially attracted his presence, in 1864, 1866, 1868, 1870, and in May 1872 he traveled to Austria upon the advice of his doctor.

Kachenovskii served several terms as secretary of the Law Faculty (1850–1853, 1867–1870). He was elected Dean of the Law Faculty in 1870, but resigned in September 1872 because of poor health. He died of consumption three months later (21 December 1872/2

---

[25] George W. Hastings (ed.), *Transactions of the National Association for the Promotion of Social Science 1861* (1862), p. 794.

January 1873). A bachelor, he lived with his mother throughout his life. In the volume published in commemoration of the thirtieth anniversary of his death, both his own portrait and that of his mother appear, together with a facsimile of a manuscript in his hand. Although his financial resources were modest, he bequeathed the sum of 973 rubles, the interest from which was to be used to establish the Kachenovskii Prize for an outstanding work in the field of international law. Laureates of the Kachenovskii Prize included Vladimir A. Iastrzhembskii (1866–19?), who wrote several works on maritime law and capitulations.

During his years of declining health, Kachenovskii became increasingly critical of political life in Russia and the West. By the mid-1860s, his political and cultural values were no longer in tune with the intellectual trends of the time. His students were attracted by radical views popular at the time propagated by Alexander I. Herzen, N. A. Dobroliubov, and N. G. Chernyshevskii, or by the nationality issue, especially pertinent in Ukraine. Kachenovskii retreated towards idealism and poetry while remaining constant to his belief that social progress could be achieved in Russia solely through the dissemination of Western European culture. Attendance at his lectures fell off; critics in the learned journals of the day criticized his dogmatism and doctrinaire opinions. Kachenovskii sought consolation in art history, an interest which he pursued during his later European travels and as a collector of engravings and drawings. A fully-fledged study of Michelangelo was contemplated; although never finished, substantial portions were published during his lifetime.[26]

---

[26] Kachenovskii, «Флоренция и ее старые мастера (Из путешествия по Италии)» [Florence and Its Old Masters (From a Journey About

The Works

The materials in the present volume would appear to be among the first, if not the very first, substantial works by a Ukrainian/Russian international lawyer published in the English language outside the frontiers of the Russian Empire. As modern doctrinal writings express the position, "… D. I. Kachenovskii became the first Russian specialist in the field of international law to be well-known abroad".[27]

These materials are fully reflective of, and fall within the period of, Kachenovskii's principal contributions to international legal doctrine. During his lifetime, he was the only international lawyer in the Russian Empire following closely and reporting on the major developments in legal works by continental European and English publicists. He intended, but never brought to fruition, to write a general work, a *cours*, on public international law. At one time collaboration with M. N. Kapustin on this project was envisioned, but abandoned, allegedly, said Grabar, because of "their divergent outlooks and dissimilar scientific methods". Whereas Kachenovskii treated the postulates of reason as the basis of international law, Kapustin was an adherent of positive law.[28] Of Kapustin's inclination to positivism, there can be little doubt. Kapustin wrote: "At the present time, the science of international law finds

---

Italy)], Вестник Европы [Herald of Europe], IV, no. 8 (August 1869), pp. 634–683; V, no. 10 (October 1869), pp. 678–750. N. F. Sumtsov, Художественные интересы Д. И. Каченовского [Artistic Interests of D. I. Kachenovskii], note 13 above, pp. 57–62; N. F. Sumtsov, «Труды Д. И. Каченовского по истории искусства» [Works of D. I. Kachenovskii on the History of Art], Южный край [Southern Territory], Nos. 6905–6906 (1901).

[27] Note 1 above, p. 23.

[28] Grabar, note 3 above, pp. 371–372.

firmer support in the mémoires and notes of State officials than in the speculations of the schools". As quoted by Kachenovskii, "the 'realm of law' does not admit arbitrary fabrications; metaphysics and metapolitics should be alien to the jurist".[29] Actually, upon closer examination, this explanation of their differences is unconvincing, for Kachenovskii was deeply influenced by the positivism and empiricism of the English approach to the law of nations and made extensive use of treaties and case reports in his works on the law of prize.

Although his efforts to write a *cours* were confined to an introduction (1863) and a historical survey (1866)[30] and, contrary to a widely-shared view, were not the first in Russian international legal doctrine (T. F. Stepanov and M. N. Kapustin were before him), they were nonetheless a valuable step forward. Part One consisted of remarks introducing the volume and two prefatory lectures, followed by a section on the significance of the science of international law in the system of jurisprudence which included persuasive passages refuting those who denied the existence of international law. Part Two addressed the history of international law from Antiquity to the Middle Ages. The promised Part Three never appeared. V. P. Danevskii, reviewing the *cours*, described Kachenovskii as an "admirer of the French school … His style is picturesque,

---

[29] See Kachenovskii, «Успехи науки международного права в Германии и Англии» [Successes of the Science of International Law in Germany and England", Русский Вестник [Russian Herald], II (March 1856), Contemporary Chronicle, p. 32.

[30] Kachenovskii, Курс международного права [Cours of International Law] (Kharkov, 1863–1866). 2 vols; Part One is reprinted in note 1 above, pp. 43–166. Fragments of Part One are published in Iu. S. Shemshuchenko (ed.), Антологія української юридичної думки [Anthology of Ukrainian Legal Thought] (2004), VIII, pp. 77–108.

lively, and light … He is devoid of German pedantry … the tone of the work, although not pedantic, is persuasive in the manner of a popular textbook", although inevitably guilty of "French prolixity and repetitiousness".[31]

Read carefully, Kachenovskii was coy about whether international law actually existed during the period of Antiquity. Rather he referred to the "development of international links" among ancient communities and about the "foreign relations" of those communities. He did not actually use the term "law of nations" or other equivalents. Being greatly influenced by the writings of Laurent, Kachenovskii evidently shared Laurent's skepticism about the existence of international law in Antiquity. Adapting a translation of an article on the international law of the ancient Greeks, he expressly declared in speaking of the foreign relations of Rome that "one seeks in vain for principles of international law in Roman policies".[32]

---

[31] Danevskii, note 20 below, p. 204.

[32] The article is Kachenovskii, «Международное право древних греков» [International Law of the Ancient Greeks], in Пропилей: сборник статей по классической древности [Propilei: Collection of Articles on Classical Antiquity] (1856), kn. 5, otd. 1, pp. 225–256. The article was in fact a combination of summary and translation from F. Laurent, *Histoire du droit des relations internationales* (Ghent, 1850), vol. II. However, volume 2 of Kachenovskii's *cours*, although greatly indebted to Laurent, does "not slavishly follow Laurent, although it would be difficult not to subject oneself to the colossal material, attractive exposition, and profundity of views of the Belgian scholar, but Kachenovskii, using his material, succeeded in preserving his scholarly independence and, thanks to recent investigations of scholars, could even correct certain ambiguities and fill gaps in Laurent's *Histoire de droit des gens*". See Iastrzhembskii, «Д. И. Каченовский как ученый и преподаватель » [D. I. Kachenovskii as Scholar and Teacher], note 17 above, p. 14.

The primary source of law Kachenovskii considered to be the "legal consciousness of peoples". Many jurists, wrote Kachenovskii, "describe all the monuments and forms in which law is expressed as its sources. This is untrue and ambiguous. Legal consciousness and the beliefs of mankind … are the principal, highest, single source of written and unwritten law".[33] The subjects of international law, in Kachenovskii's view, included, in addition to States, their organs and their citizens.

Law of the Sea

In his preface, Kachenovskii indicated the importance of the subject-matter of his book, its scope, the method of research, and a periodization of the history of privateering and relevant sources:

> At sea, civilization has still not succeeded in overcoming the harsh customs of the Middle Ages … the efforts of belligerent States at sea are directed towards the destruction of mutual trade. Finding regular fleets inadequate for their purpose, they invite private individuals into the struggle … These voluntary entrepreneurs, known since ancient times as sea pirates, are also termed privateers … Privateers do not limit themselves to the pursuit of the enemy: they are charged in addition with supervision over neutral subjects … Deciding cases concerning the legality of booty also appertains to belligerent States … Deciding cases concerning the legality of booty also appertains to belligerent States; they institute prize or admiralty courts for this purpose …

[33] Quoted in Grabar, note 3 above, p. 480.

> It is evident from what has been said that the science of all-nations law may consider privateering as a custom of warfare at sea from two aspects: (1) in its immediate consequences for the belligerent powers; [and] (2) with respect to neutral trade. … [The first issue is simple and clear; the second, complex and confusing]: in treaties and decrees there are sharp contradictions and inconsistencies; and in science, disagreements. Few publicists arrive at calm conclusions … almost everyone has his favourite theory or system accepted in a certain State. (pp. iii–xvi).

Kachenovskii investigated privateering in its second aspect, but given the close link between privateering and procedures in prize courts, he could not avoid giving some attention to prize court proceedings. His intention was to demonstrate:

> … the boundaries within which the activity of privateers and admiralty courts had been confined by international law with respect to neutral trade, to find generally recognized principles which should govern such activity, and finally to trace the gradual application thereof in the practice of States …
>
> The author chooses the historical-critical method … the so-called philosophical school of all-nations law now has no outstanding representative. Almost all publicists refrain from construction derivative theories … and begin to search for the legal foundations of the international community within the essence of the State itself, in the consciousness and age-old convictions of civilized man. The new orientation has appreciably enlivened the scholarly of the last ten years. Heffter, Oppenheim, Pütter, Wheaton, Müller-Jochmus, Laurent, C. F. Wurm, Hauteville, Reddie, and others have long overtaken the pupils of Martens …

In a necessarily condensed account, but clear and precise, with detailed footnote references to treaties, prize court decisions, and doctrinal writings, Kachenovskii developed the following periodization of the history of privateering and admiralty courts (the pagination references are to the Russian edition of 1855):

> 1. In the Middle Ages warfare at sea was virtually indistinguishable from piracy and, because of the inadequacy of the regular fleet, it was carried on by private individuals (corsairs). The institution of responsible privateers was the first step toward curbing anarchy … Neutral trade was not on a large scale and the activity of privateers before the end of the sixteenth century was directed primarily against the enemy … (pp. 1–20);
>
> 2. From the end of the sixteenth century a mercantile orientation was predominant in warfare at sea: belligerents promulgated decrees limiting neutral trade; privateering took on broad dimensions and obstructed the intercourse of nations; abuses took root in prize courts. Such a state of affairs gave rise to struggle: the neutral endeavoured to mitigate the medieval system of prize legislation … Freedom of the flag was asserted and certain abuses of the admiralty courts were eliminated … (pp. 21–46);
>
> 3. After the Treaty of Utrecht, England, then paramount, endeavoured to restrain the development of international law at sea and to make her own prize laws binding upon all Europe. The continental States consequently formed the opposition and … struck determined blows against privateering. Thanks to Russia's energetic intercession new principles of neutral trade gained the upper hand … (1780–1793) … (pp. 47–72);
>
> 4. But with the disturbance of the political system (1793–1815) … arbitrary decrees and regulations dominated over the norms of the law of nations; the

autonomy of prize courts grew, and privateering intensified … (pp. 73–129);

5. Since the Congress of Vienna, the development of the international law of the sea has been uninterrupted; the principles of armed neutrality have acquired the force of a universal law; the autonomy of prize courts has weakened and privateering has declined … the long desired reforms of warfare at sea have approached realization … (pp. 130–174).

The original dissertation was a candidate for the Demidov Prize and earned a favorable review from Professor Ignatii Ioakinfovich Ivanovskii (1807–1886), who held the Chair of International Law at St. Petersburg University.[34] In Ivanovskii's view the issue of maritime neutrality "has been virtually exhausted from the dogmatic point of view, but its history affords much scope for study" He welcomed Kachenovskii's account in the book of "how pirates who acknowledge no one's authority are transformed into national privateers" as a question that "up to now has been virtually ignored". The most important part of the book in his view was the survey of the period from 1793 to 1815, where the author directed special attention to the relevant domestic legislation of England and France.

Ivanovskii, just as Kachenovskii himself, emphasized the "advantage of freedom of neutral trade and to its being exempted from all constraints which do not flow from a reasonable view of war". But he contested Kachenovskii's view that "prize courts are international institutions":

---

[34] For Ivanovskii's extensive review, see Двадцатьпятое присуждение учрежденных П. Н. Демидовым наград 26 мая 1856 года [Twenty Fifth Awarding of the Prize Founded by P. N. Demidov on 26 May 1856] (1856), pp. 321–331.

> International practice is more logical than Mr. Kachenovskii in this respect. Its rules are more in conformity with the idea of neutrality. Never, in no instance, does a belligerent have jurisdiction over neutrals. In the eyes of a neutral prize court the belligerent is merely a State institution of that power to which the privateer belongs.

Kachenovskii believed the privateer "to be the plaintiff in a prize court, and the neutral to be the defendant". Ivanovskii did not concur:

> In general, the author is too indulgent towards English prize practice and sees the decisions of William Scott [Lord Stowell – WEB] as the application of principles of international law … [whereas that] noted judge never seriously adhered to either the *consolato del mare*, or other sources of positive international law, or the requirement of justice, and his entire theory of prize jurisdiction is based on a pathetic sophistry and is directed towards the complete destruction of neutral trade.[35]

A second substantial review of Kachenovskii's treatise was published by M. N. Kapustin (1828–1899), who had acted as the official opponent at the dissertation defense. Kapustin wrote:

> We have before us virtually the entire literature of international law; to subject it to criticism, to find the correct independent view of certain phenomena of European public life, having traced their historical development — these are the tasks which Mr. Kachenovskii has resolved so successfully. It is pleasant to record that his services to the science of international

---

[35] Quoted in Grabar, note 3 above, p. 336.

> law have already been noted by European scholars: the German writer, C. F. Wurm, well-known as an authority in the field, has published a review of Kachenovskii's work in the *Allgemeine Zeitung* which is very flattering to our author. [36]

Kapustin considered Kachenovskii's treatise to be "… one of the best additions to our legal literature".[37] That view of the dissertation was shared by Kachenovskii's successor in the Chair of International Law at Kharkov, V. P. Danevskii (1852-1898):

> [Kachenovskii's dissertation] is rightly considered to be the finest work on privateering not only in our literature, but also in the foreign literature … His study is rich not only in treaties; many internal regulations and ordinances of various States are cited which relate to privateering and prize proceedings. The procedure for prize proceedings was developed by Kachenovskii in great detail, although somewhat confusedly … the author very conscientiously expounds the doctrines of the celebrated English judge, William Scott, on judicial evidence, military contraband, and the delivery of

---

[36] Русский вестник [Russian Herald], I (February 1856), Contemporary Chronicle, p. 144. Kachenovskii's treatise is discussed as part of Kapustin's general survey of Russian legal literature published during the calendar year 1855. For the review by Wurm, see *Allgemeine Zeitung*, no. 349 (15 December 1855), pp. 5578–5579.

[37] Brief passages from the dissertation were published as «Морская война и каперство в средние века » [Naval Warfare and Privateering in the Middle Ages], Московские ведомости [Moscow Gazette], no. 24 (24 February 1855), lit. otd., pp. 85–86; no. 25 (26 February 1855), lit. otd., pp. 89–90.

dispatches by neutral ships to the enemy, and also his doctrine on blockade and sabotage and colonial trade.[38]

The doctrines of William Scott, Danevskii observed, were juxtaposed by Kachenovskii with those of the French prize judge, Jean Etienne Marie Portalis (1746-1807) and both subjected "to a critical analysis which has no parallel in the Russian literature on the subject". Kachenovskii in his account, Danevskii said, does not separate history from theory nor treaties from doctrine. Danevskii concluded:

> The thread that runs throughout Kachenovskii's study is that the history of privateering in connection with the question of private property gradually and decisively declined in the natural course of its development to the benefit of the destruction of the former and recognition of the complete inviolability of the latter … [This work is characterized by] the unusual erudition of the author and the liveliness of his exposition of the subject-matter: … in some ten or eleven of his printed signatures one can find more material and ideas than are to be found sometimes even in a multi-volume English or German work.

Kachenovskii's treatise in the law of prize, reproduced herein in the revised and expanded English version,[39] never

---

[38] See V. P. Danevskii, Очерк новейшей литературы по международному праву [Survey of Recent Literature on International Law] (St. Petersburg, 1876), pp. 253–256.

[39] For many decades the English translation of Kachenovskii by Pratt was considered to be the "… first instance of the translation of a Russian book on international law into the English language". Grabar, note 3 above, p. 353. That distinction is now known to belong 155 years earlier to the *Discourse* by P. P. Shafirov (1673–1739), published at London in 1722 and identified by the present writer. See W. E.

appeared in the Russian language in this form, that is, with the benefit of taking into account the fruits of the 1856 Declaration of Paris. Russian legal doctrine takes the view that the dissertation recommended certain reforms, set out in the dissertation as postulates that flowed from the basic principles of international law and its historical development, partially realized in the 1856 Paris Declaration.[40]

International Legal Jurisprudence

Kachenovskii's lecture in London on the contemporary state of international jurisprudence attracted considerable attention.[41] Many routinely credit Kachenovskii with the idea concerning the need to unite those working in the field of international law in an organization of some sort; eventually this notion found resonance in a number of other countries and was eventually achieved through the creation in 1873 of the Institute of International Law.

His London lecture, it should be noted, actually explicitly encouraged the creation of a specialist periodical on international law; one wonders whether his London lecture on international legal jurisprudence has been confused with his communication to the National Association for the Promotion of Social Science (below), sent in 1860. The communication was among the catalytic factors in persuading the National Association to establish a

---

Butler, "P. P. Shafirov and the Law of Nations", in Butler, note 2 above, pp. 207–250.

[40] See note 1 above, p. 22.

[41] The lecture was translated by K. Savchuk and made available to a Russian-speaking audience for the first time in Международное право [International Law], no. 2 (2013), pp. 230-258.

Department of Trade and International Law, but very possibly the communication, especially upon publication in the *Transactions* of the National Association, had a more enduring resonance. Even more plausible is the likelihood that Kachenovskii pressed his ideas on the need for institutional collaboration among international lawyers in Europe at every opportunity and regarded his success in the National Association as merely one step in the right direction. As for the idea of a specialist periodical, those too began to appear in Europe.

Personalia

Kachenovskii had the highest possible regard for his mentor in Germany, Professor Christian Friedrich Wurm (1803–1859), whom he mentioned on numerous occasions in his Reports on the visits made abroad and in his scholarly publications. His obituary assessment of Wurm's contributions to the science of international law appeared in Russian[42] and English, the last of which appears in the present volume.

Wurm wrote extensively on, *inter alia*, neutral and belligerent rights at sea.[43] Without question his views were a significant influence upon Kachenovskii and, through him, upon Russian naval policies.

---

[42] Kachenovskii, «Христиан Фридрих Вурм: некролог» [Christian Friedrich Wurm: Obituary], Русский вестник [Russian Herald], xx, kn. 2 (March 1859), pp. 136–144. Also see A. Wohlwill, "Wurm, Christian Friedrich", *Allgemeine Deutsche Biographie*, XLIV (1898), pp. 326–332; H. Dvorak, *Biographisches Lexikon der Deutschen Burschenschaft* (2005), VI, pp. 386–388.

[43] See especially C. F. Wurm, *Von der neutralität des deutschen seehandels in kreigszeiten* (1841).

Perpetual Peace

While in London in 1859, Kachenovskii came into contact with the organized peace movement, whose origins dated back to the Napoleonic wars. He took the occasion to draw the attention of his audience to a Russian diplomat inspired to write on the subject of peace and war while in England and eventually publish his work in Russia upon returning home. The diplomat was Vasilii Fedorovich Malinovskii (1765–1814), a graduate of the Faculty of Philosophy at Moscow University in 1781, sometime archivist in the Moscow Archive of the College of Foreign Affairs, adept in matters of literature, and possessing a sufficient command of English to secure a diplomatic posting abroad. His first assignment was as interpreter to the Russian Mission in London, where he spent two years, some if not most of his days at Richmond. There while assisting on diplomatic matters he prepared in his spare time a treatise on war and peace and a translation of Alexander Hamilton's report on the use of manufactures. Returning to Russia in late 1791, Malinovskii served in Romania and eventually was appointed Consul General in Moldavia. Recalled home in 1803, Malinovskii continued to write and translate, helped found the Russian Bible Society, was active in philanthropic affairs, and ultimately became the first director of the Tsarskoe selo Lycée — a tenure that provided to be brief, for Malinovskii died in 1814.

Although Malinovskii's name does not appear on the title page of his *Discourse on War and Peace* (1803), the author made it clear that part one was completed at Richmond in 1790 and part two at "Belozerka near Petersburg in 1798", followed by the initials "V. M.".

Malinovskii's authorship also is confirmed by collateral correspondence.[44]

Kachenovskii's account of Malinovskii in 1859 to the Peace Society in London was a major occasion, even reported in the Russian press. He referred to this in his Report on his foreign tour in 1859 and 1859: "… to the Peace Society I communicated excerpts from the interesting proposal for perpetual peace written at the end of the last century by the Russian publicist Vasilii Malinovskii. They printed it in the *Herald of Peace* in July 1859. The book itself is not well known even in Russia, but deserves attention for the thoughts and sentiments that run through it".[45] The American Peace Society is said to have reprinted Kachenovskii's account in the same year, but a search of its journal *Advocate of Peace* does not confirm this.

Associations of International Lawyers

As noted above, Kachenovskii was accorded the honor of being the sole Russian to be elected a Foreign Corresponding Member of the National Association for the Promotion of Social Science in 1859. Unable to be present at the Fourth Annual Meeting held at Glasgow in September 1860, he wrote a long letter to the General Secretary of the Association, G. W. Hastings, which was read aloud to those present. Whether Kachenovskii's letter had been orchestrated with other foreign colleagues has not been determined, but apparently foreign participants in the Annual Meeting had been outspoken in recommending to their British colleagues the formation of a sixth Department

---

[44] See W. E. Butler, "Law and Peace in Prerevolutionary Russia: The Case of V. F. Malinovskii", in note 2 above, pp. 282–295.

[45] Русский инвалид [Russian Invalid], no. 131 (17 June 1861), p. 538.

within the National Association dedicated to "Trade and International Law". That suggestion was accepted in the Glasgow proceedings, partly in response to Kachenovskii's eloquent plea for a forum in which international lawyers could assemble to pursue objectives of mutual interest. The letter was printed as a lengthy footnote in the annual proceedings of the Association.

Either Kachenovskii's proposal had enduring resonance, perhaps reinforced by the publication of his letter, or he regarded the creation of the new Department within the Association as merely a first stage in a more ambitious undertaking. Kachenovskii is widely regarded as one of those who inspired the eventual formation of the Institut de droit international. Although he did not live long enough to see the Institut come into being, the founders of that organization recalled his contributions to the initiative many years later. Grabar referred to Kachenovskii as "one of the initiators" of the Institute.[46]

The Translator

The translator of Kachenovskii's treatise on the law of prize was Frederic[k] Thomas Pratt (1799–1868), the third son of John Pratt, of Lambeth, Surrey. He became a scholar of Trinity College Cambridge in 1820, B. A. 1821, M. A., 1825. On 8 December 1836 Pratt was incorporated at St. John's College, Oxford, where he received the degrees of B.C.L. in 1836 and D.C.L. in 1837. He was called as an advocate at Doctor's Commons on 2 November 1837, where he achieved the offices of Steward (1840–1842),

[46] Grabar, note 3 above, p. 469.

Librarian (1842–1844); and Treasurer (1847–1850).[47] Pratt's arms, painted on a panel in an oval frame, hung in Doctors' Commons and later in the chambers of Sir Anthony Wagner, Garter King of Arms, in the College of Arms.[48]

Unduly obscure in English legal history, he was a distinguished practitioner of the law of Admiralty and the author of several treatises on the subject.

He followed United States admiralty practice closely, being responsible for bringing Joseph Story's writings to the attention of a British audience at the outset of the Crimean War.[49] This was followed by a collection of cases and materials on war contraband,[50] a subject close to Kachenovskii's heart. These case reports drew upon the papers of Sir George Lee (1700–1758), also a member of

---

[47] See Frederic Boase, *Modern English Biography containing many thousand concise memoirs of persons who have died between the years 1851–1900 with an index of the most interesting matter* (privately printed, 1897; reprint ed., 1965), II, col.1620. The privately printed edition was limited to 250 copies. Pratt's Christian name appears in various sources as Frederic and as Frederick.

[48] See G. D. Squibb, *Doctors' Commons: A History of the College of Advocates and Doctors of Law* (1977), p. 74, 201.

[49] See Joseph Story (1779–1845), *Notes on the Principles and Practice of Prize Courts; with a Selection of Documents and Forms as Used in the High Court of Admiralty in England*, ed. F. T. Pratt (1854). This book was reviewed by M. N. Kapustin in the third article of a series of four published as «Английские призовые решения 1854 и 1855 годов» [English Prize Decisions of 1854 and 1855], in Московские ведомости [Moscow Gazettes], no. 67 (4 June 1855), lit. otd., pp. 267–268.

[50] F. T. Pratt, *Law of Contraband of War: With a Selection of Cases from the Papers of the Right Hon. Sir Geo. Lee and an Appendix, Containing Extracts from Treaties, Miscellaneous Papers, and Forms of Proceedings. With the Cases to the Present Time* (1856). The book is dedicated to John Lee, LL.D., a descendant of Sir George Lee, who made his ancestor's papers available to Pratt.

Doctors' Commons. The cases and materials were revised and enlarged to take into account the American Civil War.[51]

Pratt's other books dealt with the law of navigation and sea lights, of which there were three different titles.[52]

When and how Pratt came to become acquainted with Kachenovskii is unknown, but they most certainly met during Kachenovskii's visits to London after 1857. Kachenovskii's interests in the law of the sea and admiralty law would have encouraged an acquaintanceship. That they remained in correspondence is evident from the revisions introduced into the English edition of Kachenovskii's treatise on prize, for Pratt clearly supervised their incorporation into the volume after receiving them from Kharkov via post or by safe hand.

Pratt, however, figures on the title page of the volume as the translator. How he came to have a command of the Russian language remains to be determined, if that was

---

[51] Pratt, *Law of Contraband of War: With the Reported Cases to the Present Time, and a Selection of Unreported Cases from the Papers of the Right Hon. Sir Geo. Lee LL.D, Formerly Dean of the Arches, etc., etc. Together with the Foreign Enlistment Act and the British and French Proclamations Respecting the Observance of Neutrality in the Present War in North America* (1861). This book is substantially the 1856 edition with the addition of new materials, including reliance upon additional doctrinal writings. Kachenovskii, if available to Pratt by then, is not cited.

[52] See Pratt, *An Essay on the Use of Lights by Sea-Going Vessels: and the Rule of the Road at Sea: With Numerous Cases and an Appendix, Including Foreign Ordinances, with Translations* (London, 1857); Pratt, *The New Admiralty Regulations Respecting Lights and Fog Signals: With Notes and References* (1858); Pratt, *A Treatise on the Law Relating to Sea Lights, and the Rule of the Road at Sea: With Numerous Cases to the Present Time: Foreign Ordinances and Translations: With an Appendix Containing the New Admiralty Regulations Respecting Ship Lights and Fog Signals* (1858).

actually the case. It seems likely that Kachenovskii, who had a sound if not superior command of English, may have produced drafts that Pratt edited, at a minimum, and perhaps did indeed translate from the Russian text. Kachenovskii will assuredly have given Pratt a copy of his original dissertation published at Kharkov in 1855.

Pratt died at Upper Norwood, Surrey, on 13 April 1868.

WORKS BY
D. I. KACHENOVSKII

PAPERS READ BEFORE THE JURIDICAL SOCIETY

VI.

THE PRESENT STATE OF INTERNATIONAL JURISPRUDENCE

PART I.

BY PROFESSOR KATCHENOVSKY

[Read 21st June, 1858.]

Whatever different opinions may be held concerning the progress of Europe during the last fifty years, it can hardly be denied that international relations have received, during that period, a great extension. If we compare the age we live in with the eighteenth century in this respect, we shall observe the most important improvement. Until the end of the revolutionary war, the European powers had seldom any repose from mutual discords; maritime commerce was in constant danger of being interrupted; diplomacy rather nourished than mitigated the national jealousies; the Christian world felt but little the common interest of peace. The treaties of 1814–15 open a new era in history. The warlike spirit been subdued by its own excesses, the pacific and commercial spirit became the prominent feature of the age. It would occupy us too long to go into all the causes of this wonderful change, brought about by the combined action of many material and moral forces. It is sufficient for our present purpose to say that the great inventions of modern science, as railroads, electric telegraphs, and steam navigation, have chiefly contributed to produce this revolution. The nations, formerly separated by distance, and by the various difficulties of communication, are united now, and form a great Christian commonwealth, or a *civitas maxima*.

In this state of things, the science of international law has acquired great and practical importance for the present generation. We can now, with better reason than ever before, repeat the words of Grotius, that the cultivation of this branch of knowledge, "*interest humani generis*." "The mere existence of this science," says Robert Mohl, in his last work on the history and literature of politics, "is yery gratifying. It gives us a satisfactory proof of the superiority of our manners and of our ciyilisation over the ancient world." The Greeks, the most enlightened people of their time, considered the other nations as barbarians, destined for slavery; the Romans saw in a foreigner their natural enemy. In the middle ages, the general feuds, and the prevalent ideas of universal monarchy, prevented the diffusion of a humane spirit in the mutual relations of Christian communities. It was not before the last two centuries that the term *international law* came into general use, as expressing the laws of peace and war (*jus gentium sensu moderno*). Those laws were constructed into a science by Hugo Grotius. He published his immortal work *De Jure Belli Pacis* in 1625, during the most bloody war that ever desolated Europe; and with great force proclaimed, in the face of the world, the general principles of justice and of' civilisation. His influence on public opinion was wonderful. His work found its way into the cabinets of princes and statesmen, into the libraries of students, and even into the tents of military men. After the death of Grotius, his successors continued to cultivate this science as far as their respective talents allowed them to do it. None of them, it is true, can be compared with him in reputation and success; but, if we consider their works taken as a whole, we shall find in this mass many valuable contributions to this *nobilissima pars jurisprudentiæ*. Eyery successive age, almost every country, has produced its great international jurists. Coming to the present time, we can say without exaggeration that the science of Grotius is now more generally known and better understood than in his times. International questions are discussed in the nineteenth century, not only by statesmen and by philosophers, but by the press and by public opinion. The study of this branch of jurisprudence is promoted, more or less, by all the European universities.

In stating these facts, I have no intention to affirm the science of international law has attained, in our time, its utmost development and perfection. I am aware, on the contrary, that there is much to do for this part of knowledge. It seems to me, also, that international jurisprudence is less appreciated by our contemporaries than it deserves to be. There exist still in the minds of men prejudices against it. From time to time we read and hear the most violent attacks against the tendency and method of publicists; the most abusive language is held even against international law itself. I shall now call your particular attention to this subject. It is highly important to determine how far the attacks of sceptics can be justified, and in what degree the science is responsible for the faults of its temporary organs.

The first class of sceptics consists of men who deny altogether the existence of international law. We find in their number men most distinguished in science, as Hugo, Puchta, Rossi, Quetelet. In their opinion, the regulations of international law are a dead letter; governments acknowledge, for their conduct in external policy, no other law but selfish interests. It is hardly possible to deny that there is some truth in these assertions. Modern history is full of atrocious wars, of unlawful conquests, of perjury, and of other international crimes and offences. But the same facts can be cited against every human law and institution. There exists no community on the earth where offences are not committed, where punishment strikes every offender, where the accused can find no means of evading the severity of justice.

But there is a great difference between civil and international law, say the sceptics; civil law has its legislators, on the contrary, international law does not acknowledge a head for independent communities. This is true, but their *common will* or mutual consent takes the place of a lawgiver, and performs legislative functions. The existing relations of nations are always a *status quo*, which cannot be changed by the arbitrary will of one opposed to that of all the others. Europe has no dictator; so much the better. If the skeptics could prove that the application of international law is dangerous, or contrary to the true interests of independent communities, that would establish their opinion. But it would be difficult to prove such an absurdity. What are the first principles of international law? The independence of nations, the inviolability of their respective territories, the maintenance of their honour, &c. Under the sanction of this law stands every human being in a foreign country. One of the best statesmen of our time (Daniel Webster) proclaimed, with better reason than the sceptics, the truth, that the existence and application of international law, in all its force, is as advantageous for states as the existence of private law for citizens of the same country.

Modern scepticism goes, then, too far in this point. However numerous the transgressions of international law which may occur, and unfortunately do occur, even at the present day, *the law exists still in the conscience of humanity*. This one fact is sufficient reason why we should not despair for justice. While nations hold in their breasts the feeling of their common origin, while the civilisation of mankind stands unimpaired, we can hope for improvement in the mutual relations of different states. If we compare enlightened Europe with the Asiatic world, we see the difference between states acknowledging international law, and states governed by mere force and cunning. The existence of Asiatic states is unsafe; the independence of nations is not there secured; the conqueror there finds no check to his path of rapine and murder; violence effects with impunity the most bloody revolutions. The Christian world, on the contrary, presents to us quite a different character. Here the selfish policy of different states has its limits; *their interests* are governed, in the first place, by the common interest; or, in other words, *subjected to the law of general security*; the most despotic governments acknowledge and perform mutual duties. It is true that the existing state of things (*status quo*) has its imperfections; that some anomolies occur here and there in the conduct of states; that they are yet far from following invariably the dictates of universal justice. But on the other wise, hardly any one but a pessimist can say that Christian communities are governed only by Machiavellian principles in their mutual relations. By those principles they could not have mitigated the cruelty of war, or abolished the slave trade and privateering, as they have done, acting in. conformity with the conscience of humanity. This conscience appears to gain ground more and more. Only two centuries have passed since the practical foundation of international law by the Westphalian congress, and important results have been already obtained by it. We may expect yet greater blessings from the enlightenment of future times.

I come now to the second class of skeptics — Rousseau, Bentham, Kant, and others — who do not deny the existence of international law, but think that it is *uncertain* and wavering (*chancelant*); because nations have no general code, no common judge, and no other means of deciding their disputes but war. These imperfections of practice, in the opinion of skeptics, deprive order of stability, and make the *status quo* of every age precarious and liable to be subverted. These doubts and fears seem to me very exaggerated. We have no sufficient grounds for adopting the opinion that the non-existence of a code is a great evil in itself. The Roman law, in its best times, consisted of incoherent rules and customs, but was administered more successfully than in the period of its codification. This free country also has no code; its constitution is established on the basis of the common law; but there is no doubt that the law is more solid, more respected, and better administered, here than elsewhere. The codification of international law is even less necessary for the present age than the codification of its public and private law is for any particular country, because that law is not complicated. It can be ascertained and interpreted in almost every doubtful case. Most treaties are framed with great exactitude; the customs to which international law appeals are known to all the world. some parts of it the codification of which would be of great value, as the so-called private international law; but all doubtful and uncertain points of its properly public branch can be determined by mutual agreement, as we have seen was done by the Vienna (1815) and Paris (1856) congresses, on the disputed questions of the rank of diplomatic agents, of the navigation of rivers, of the commerce of neutrals, &c.

With respect to the question of a supreme court for states, it is true that nations often feel the want of an impartial judge for the settlement of their disputes; but it is no less true that they have in their hands sufficient means of preventing unnecessary wars. Those means are — good offices, mediation and arbitration, also congresses and conferences. That all these means are used successfully, nobody can doubt who is acquainted with the history of the last fifty years. The Paris congress of 1856 laid down the general rule, that all disputes in Europe should be submitted to the impartial mediation or arbitration of third powers. For those who think that a supreme court would be more efficacious in settling European disputes than any or all of the means used in present practice, I submit the following observations: — Considering the state of Europe, it would be difficult to prove that this court would be more obeyed than mediators or arbiters; in fact, resistance to its opinions is as possible as refusal of submission to the impartial advice of those powers; the authority of the supreme court (if ever instituted) would be no less dependent on the mutual consent of parties. It is hardly possible to give to such a court compulsory powers against independent states without dangerous consequences for all nations.

I come now to another class of sceptics, who, without denying the existence or the practical efficiency of international law, think that it is difficult, almost impossible, to reduce it to general principles, or to give to it a scientific character. The difficulties which, in the opinion of these sceptics, stand in the way, are the following: — International relations arc governed; not by general laws, but by particular treaties and customs very variable and discordant. The customary rules are most vague and uncertain; as to treaties, they form but mutual compacts between the parties, and have no character of law. To refute this important objection, it is necessary to explain, in a few words, the nature, objects, and sources of international law.

International law can have no other object in view but universal justice. With the idea of this law we combine the ideas of order and of general security for independent communities. Under international law we understand, not this or that treaty, but such rules or principles as are necessary for the mutual benefit of all states, and the observance of which is prescribed by the conscience of the civilized world. This conscience is, then, the principal source or fountain of that law. It may be objected against this, that the conscience of humanity is rather uncertain — that it is easy to misunderstand its dictates. But we speak here of such a conscience, or general will, as is expressed in an obligatory form. In this case it is not difficult to find in it the general principles of law.

1. If we observe the international relations of the present time, we find that there exist some rules recognized by all civilized states as necessary condition of their coexistence. The authority of those principles cannot be denied. Grotius speaks of them as *jus gentium necessarium, ab ipsâ naturâ profectum*. It is true that they are established only by reason, but there is no government which would not give them practical efficiency by all means in its power; no government can repudiate them without isolating itself from all other communities. I mean here, such principles as the independence of nations, the sanctity of ambassadors, and even many general principles relating to war.

2. The general will of nations is expressed in congresses, as I mentioned before. There is no doubt that the rules prescribed in them for the mutual conduct of governments have all the force and validity of international law.

3. We come now to treaties. It is true that a publicist should be very circumspect in founding general rules upon treaties, because many of them have a. special character, and are of value only for the contracting parties. But we cannot adopt this opinion unconditionally, and say the same of all treaties: they often contain general rules: it is necessary to consider and compare them with attention,

before we come to any conclusion as to their authority in a particular case. In studying history, we find that some articles of international law were established and adopted in *successive treaties* by civilized governments, with the evident intention of making those articles obligatory for all the world. Many customary rules of barbarous ages were abolished in this manner — as the *droit d'aubaille* and the *droit de naufrage*; in our time, also, improvements in practice are obtained usually by treaties. The particular treaty, according to its value and importance, extends its authority when third powers accede to it, or when it is put under the guarantee of other states. We can find, even in special treaties, some analogy or resemblance to one another.

4. The rules adopted *mutuo consensu* are to be found in international customs or usages. Almost all the laws of war, and the privileges of ambassadors, are sanctioned in this manner. But we should be careful in distinguishing national from international customs. *The essential quality of the latter is reciprocity*; and, we should add, that the rules adopted only in cases of retorsion cannot be called customary rules.

These are the principal forms in which international law is brought to evidence and general knowledge. If all the rules mentioned above are taken as a whole, and considered from the point of view of universal justice, there is no serious difficulty in constructing the science. If treaties do not accord with customs, then we should ascertain whether nations desire to abolish the customary rule, or to retain it with some modifications. The conscience of humanity cannot be misunderstood in this case. Some usages are in arrear of the improvement of the age, and, when found so, are abrogated by treaties; while; on the contrary, treaties are very seldom superseded by customs, because customs of which the validity is once undermined cannot be called customs, since they have lost their obligatory force.

I shall not enter here into all the details of scientific method, and beg to offer but a few general remarks, important for judging of the present state of international jurisprudence. But before I enter upon this subject, I feel the duty of giving brief historical sketch of the different schools which, from the death of Grotius to the present time, have cultivated in Europe the science of international law.

In the eighteenth, and even at the end of the seventeenth century, we find all the publicists divided into two schools, independent and inimical; the one called itself the *philosophical*, the other was named the *positive* or *practical* school. The difference between them consisted in this: The *philosophical* school considered international law as one of the branches of the *jus naturæ*; in their opinion, the rules of private law were to be applied to the mutual conduct of states. It is hardly necessary to say that that method is erroneous. The relations of states undoubtedly are governed by the principles of justice, as well as the relations of men; but the nature of a state or community is as different from the nature of man, as the juridical person differs from the physical person; the confusion of their qualities leads to the obscurity and perversion of all the general principles of jurisprudence. We must not wonder, then, that the philosophical school contributed but in a small degree to the improvement of science, and fell into great errors; it was unable to give an explanation of many international questions, because it could not find for them any guidance in private law. Intervention, neutrality, and all similar phenomena, never occur in the life of individuals, and find no place in private law. This school stood completely apart from practice; its professors cared not about state papers or diplomatic history; they studied the law as a dead letter in their lecture-rooms. We must not be astonished that their study seemed sterile, dull, and unprofitable, in the general opinion; and that they even discredited the science of international law in the eyes of statesmen.

The *positive* school (established. by Moser, in Germany) fell into another extreme. The adepts of that school thought that international law consists of the rules observed by the diplomatists and courts of Europe. Now, if we recollect what were those rules in the eighteenth century, we shall be able to appreciate how lax were the moral principles professed by that school. It never separated law from policy, and was not inclined to criticise diplomatic documents from the juridical point of view. This indifference to universal justice is the greatest accusation against that school. .There was but one man in the eighteenth century whose opinions were independent of both schools; and his works have more value, even for the present age, than the voluminous compilations of all the German professors of that time. I speak of the celebrated Dutch jurisconsult, Cornelius Bynkershoek. In his opinion, international law consists only of rules founded on reason, and approved by the consent of nations. He said, *ratio est juris gentium magistra*, and followed its dictates in all his conclusions, criticised the laws even of his own country with an impartiality not often to be found even in our own times, and explained with great force the most difficult points of international law — *de dominio maris, de foro legatorum, de jure belli.* His practical genius and erudition claim the next place in our esteem after Grotius. It is to be regretted that Bynkershoek lived in an age so unfavourable to the study of international law, and that his judicial occupations allowed him so little time for his scientific pursuits.

We come now to the present age. In the beginning of the nineteenth century, Professor Martens of Göttingen published his valuable work on international law. There is in it a tendency to amalgamate the two different schools, and to combine the philosophic and the practical methods.

The chief merit of Martens lies in the construction of international rules, founded upon the mutual compacts of nations. He compiled treaties, compared them, and contributed by this to the elucidation of many historical and practical points of law. His successors in this mode of cultivating the science were Saalfeld, Schmalz, and Klüber. To the same school belongs the American publicist Wheaton, whose works are known and much appreciated in this country.

But there are many errors and imperfections in the method of Martens. He is too much occupied with the classification of treaties, and gives them an exaggerated importance. His views are of limited scope; he seems to be more compiler than jurisconsult. I do not contest his merits, but I do not rate them so high as they were appreciated by his immediate successors.

During the last twenty years a new movement of ideas is observable in the science of international law. Publicists found the compilation of treaties not sufficient for their purpose: parliamentary debates, state papers, and the memoirs of celebrated diplomatists, of which the publication came into general use after the congress of Vienna, opened new problems for jurisprudence. The scientific method was changed for the better. Casuistical and critical investigations, neglected before, became more and more predominant. I have no room for reviewing here all the works that have appeared since 1839; it is sufficient to enumerate the best of the general treatises on international law, and to appreciate their character in general terms. One of the most remarkable books published in Germany, and written with a critical tendency, is "Heffter's Modern International Law:" this is a concise digest, adapted more for students than for practical men. The same may be said of an inferior work by Bernard Oppenheim, published in 1845. The casuistical tendency is exhibited more in the English works of Oke Manning, and

Robert Phillimore. On the contrary, Pando, the Spanish publicist, is more inclined to philosophical views. But, to observe better the influence of the new method, we should turn our attention not so much to the general treatises as to the dissertations and essays, in which are treated some doubtful topics of international law. The best of them have for their authors, Dr. Wurm of Hamburgh, Professor Mohl, the French jurists Ortolan and Hautefeuille, and some Dutch publicists. I hope to give a more detailed account of them in another work destined for general circulation, and shall conclude this paper, perhaps already too long.

In studying these various works, the idea suggests itself of a *Periodical for international jurisprudence*. The necessity of it seems to me beyond dispute. We find in other branches of juridical and political knowledge more unity and harmony than in international jurisprudence. The professors and practitioners of civil and criminal law, political economists, and statisticians, have their organs, interchange their opinions, and even hold congresses for the discussion of unsettled questions. On the contrary, international jurists, who have a common work to do for the benefit of the civilized world, have no means of communication. It is very difficult even to collect all their works; they hardly know each other by name, and cultivate separately a science destined for general use. The effects of this isolation are felt by all who take an interest in international law. A periodical published in England, or in France, would be a circulating medium for the diffusion of the most useful and practical knowledge, promote the interests of peace, and contribute largely to the general civilisation of the Christian world.

I think that these desires have nothing utopian or visionary in them, but are honest opinions inspired by the science itself, of which the destination is to promote and diffuse the principles of law and of justice in the world. The improvement of this science, says Robert Mohl, one of its celebrated supporters, cannot be indifferent even to those who think that the practical efficiency of international law is imperfect; because the conduct of government and of nations, sooner or later, undergoes the influence of ideas. This influence is perhaps little felt or observed by the ignorant, but is hardly disputable. We live now under the rule of public opinion. If a certain action is thought unlawful, if a certain practice seems to be barbarous, its continuance is impossible.

I can add to this an illustration drawn from history. When Grotius published his immortal work, who could foresee that it would become an authority in the eyes of kings and of nations? A bloody war raged without the least hope of pacification; but the time came when the father of international law was respected as a. general legislator and instructor. We men of the nineteenth century should be encouraged by this example given by the father of the science. We have brighter prospects before us; we live in an enlightened and pacific age. We should promote, then, as far as possible, the spirit of justice, and contribute by this to the work of civilization.

(*To be Continued.*)

PAPERS READ BEFORE THE JURIDICAL SOCIETY

XXVIII.

ON THE PRESENT STATE OF INTERNATIONAL JURISPRUDENCE

PART II.

BY PROFESSOR KATCHENOVSKY

[Read 5th May, 1862.]

In the first part of this paper I tried to refute the erroneous opinions of sceptics about international law, and to prove, by reasoning and facts, its real existence and authority. I have now another task to perform. I come to the principal subject of our discussion; namely, to the question — Is international jurisprudence much improved and extended in Europe at the present time? In answering this important question, I will rely chiefly on my personal observations. It is not unknown to your Society, that I visited many countries of Europe with the special view of ascertaining the progress of international jurisprudence. The results of this long excursion, unsatisfactory as they may appear, I feel it my duty to submit to your impartial judgment. It will afford me great pleasure if you find in them new matter for thought. But you must not suppose that I exaggerate the value of my own researches and impressions. Facts collected even by the most conscientious traveller have but a fragmentary character. The progress of any branch of human knowledge cannot be rightly appreciated without the careful study of the best works written upon it. You will, then, kindly allow me to add here some critical remarks concerning the literature of international jurisprudence.

I will speak first of Germany, where I expected to find international law more successfully cultivated than elsewhere. My expectations, I am sorry to say, were but partially true. The Germans themselves are not satisfied with the present state of this branch of knowledge in their country. The most impartial of them say unanimously, that the study of international law has rather declined than improved during the last thirty years, with the exception of Berlin, Heidelberg, and Vienna, where it is still flourishing. Formerly, some of the German universities were reputed to be the best diplomatic schools in Europe. At the present time, there are few professors in them seriously inclined to cultivate international jurisprudence. Even those who write occasionally books and pamphlets on it, are for the most part engaged in the special study of some other branch of law. In fact, the great impulse given to the cultivation of diplomatic knowledge by Professor Martens of Göttingen has subsided, and is followed by a retrograde movement. Lectures on international law have gradually ceased to attract the attention of students. Looking on it as jurisprudence of secondary value, they have left it for Roman law, or turned their attention to criminal jurisprudence. This general neglect of diplomatic education is easily explained, if we take into consideration the present state of the diplomatic service in Germany and some other countries of Europe. Patronage still reigns there to the exclusion of merit. Even subordinate diplomatic posts (as secretary of legation, *attaché,* &c.) are distributed generally among the members of the aristocracy; a young man of the middle class can hardly enter the fashionable and exclusive circle of the Ministry of Foreign Affairs; he must have extraordinary talents, and the most powerful protection, in order to rise there to any distinction. In short, diplomacy is an ungrateful vocation for a German university man to enlist in, and he acts very prudently in preparing himself for the bar, or for any other branch of public service, in the hope of further advancement.

With all my deference for the erudition of German professors, I must say also that their lectures on international law contain but elementary principles. They are for the most part devoid of practical illustration, and by this alone lose much of their utility. The academical youth of our present age is little inclined to abstract researches. Modern students of politics feel a. very natural aversion to mere philosophical speculations. The questions occurring between different states and governments are questions of life, not of pure reason. International law, considered as theoretical knowledge, has little value. If it does not serve for practical purposes, it serves almost for nothing. The time of its scholastic construction is gone for ever. A publicist of the nineteenth century has nothing to do with the method of Grotius or of Pufendorf. State papers should be the principal subject of his study. It is useless to stir the dust of forgotten dissertations. I am happy to say that the best of the German professors had already left the traditions of their predecessors, long before any body dared openly to condemn the old school of international law. Our lamented member Dr. Wurm was, as you know, one of the greatest defenders of the practical method in this branch of jurisprudence. In the university of Heidelberg, Dr. Macquardsen belongs to this class of publicists. The same can be said of Dr. Neumann, professor in the university of Vienna. As I have not visited all the German universities, it is possible that I may have omitted here the name of some other public teacher unknown to me. But, as far as I am able to judge, by my own observation and from general opinion, the decay of diplomatic studies in the German universities is considered as a general fact.

The indifference to international jurisprudence is visible not only in the lecture-rooms, but also in the literature of Germany. From the middle of the eighteenth century up to the epoch of the congress of Vienna, the activity of the German mind in this branch of knowledge was very great indeed. It appears to the best advantage in the stupendous works of both Mosers, father and son, in the instructive volumes of Gunter, and in many other publications. To them succeeded Martens, with his numerous followers. At the present time, on the contrary, a German school seems hardly to exist. During the last thirty years, few general works on international law have been published in that country. Even dissertations (or, as they are called there, monographs) do not appear as often as formerly. The chief, if not the only, peculiarity of the international jurists of modern Germany is their mutual independence. None of them is acknowledged as the founder of a new scientific dynasty; every body is inspired by ideas of his own, or by his philosophical creed, rejected of course by others. Neither Savigny nor Gans, by whose controversy on juridical methods the German scholars were divided about thirty years ago, has left any disciples in international law. Its living expounders have no common teacher, and have forgotten old traditions. It is difficult to find between them any connection or approximation of views and principles; and still more difficult to form a conjecture as to the future. In short, the actual state of international jurisprudence in Germany is less satisfactory than could be imagined. The school of Martens has ceased to exist, but is not superseded by a new one; old methods are abandoned as erroneous, but in their place reigns confusion.

The best elementary work on international law published during the last twenty years is, undoubtedly, that of Heffter, professor at Berlin. It was undertaken in concert with Gans, but finished principally by Heffter himself. The double origin of this work can be traced in its features: they bear the impress of philosophical ideas belonging to the great disciple of Hegel, and at the same time reflect the image of another mind. Hence the eclectic character of the book. But, if it wants unity, it abounds in good details. Here the great merits of the learned author cannot be contested. Unfortunately, he gives us but general principles; their practical illustration lies beyond his scope and purpose. True to the German character, Heffter appears to have cared more for systematic regularity than for the fulness of his work. He gives much space to abstract reasoning, and very little to casuistry. State papers and memoirs of diplomatists are seldom, if ever, criticised by him; it seems as if he were better acquainted with the academical literature of international law than with its living history. For this reason, perhaps, Heffter will never be an authority in the eyes of practical men. He is too concise, and not clear enough, to be understood and appreciated by the general public. Vattel is still an oracle of statesmen, though his scientific value does not stand above mediocrity.[1]

Heffter's work is the last effort of German learning embracing the whole of international law, and having the character of a compendium. The book of Oppenheim *(System des Völkerrechts,* 1845), treating the same subject from the point of view of elementary principle, seems to be greatly inferior when compared with it. Since that time the tendencies of German publicists have taken another direction. They have declared war against old methods, and tried to reconstruct international jurisprudence upon a new basis. This critical spirit gave the first signs of life about

---

[1] The work of Heffter has had four editions in Germany, the last in 1860; and has lately been translated into French. It fully deserves to be better known in England.

twenty years ago, and has become more and more predominant. Gagern, a literary diplomatist of 1815, was the first man who formed the opposition party against the school of Martens and his followers. His aphoristical work, *Kritik des Völkerrechts,* though insignificant; was received by the public very favourably. In the essays of Fallati, late professor at Tübingen, Hälschnor, Püttor, and Kaltenborn, the new tendencies are supported and promoted. Whether this powerful party will give new life and soul to international jurisprudence, and what will be its ultimate success, it is impossible yet to judge: time must show. What is done by the new publicists is very promising; of course, their aspirations are lofty, and for the most part good; but between aspirations and execution there is a wide difference. Unfortunately, the leaders of this party do not agree much in their opinions. Every one of them holds firmly to his own programme, and rejects the amendments proposed by others. Their mutual polemics grow endless, and seem often to be a mere logomachy, serving little to the extension of our knowledge in international law. The projected reforms in it have rather a vague character, and would bring but scanty results. For instance, the merits of Kaltenborn's criticism *(Kritik des Völkerrechts,* 1847) consist, not so much in the invention of a new juristic method, as in the partial revision of the existing methods. This work is reputed to be the best yet produced by the school. As to the large book of Bulmerincq *(Die Systematik des Völkerrechts:* Dorpat, 1859), I consider it as perfectly useless. The learned author gives us nothing but a repetition of what we know already from Ompteda and Kaltenborn.

The best path for critical inquiries in international law was opened by the late Dr. Wurm. His essays, fragmentary as they are, contain more precious gems of thought than all the discussions about sovereignty and the communion of nations promoted by Pütter, Kaltenborn, and *tutti quanti.*

As to the, practical value of Dr. Wurm's researches, it cannot be contested, and, as far as I know, has never been doubted. But you know more of this talented publicist. I revert to him only in remembrance of his services, and to express my desire of seeing his works collected and reprinted in Germany.

I cannot leave that country without mentioning the last essay of Dr. Robert Mohl, which enriched the subject of my paper with new truths. This eminent man contributed many useful works to every branch of political knowledge, and paid, during his laborious life, great attention to international law.[2] In 1860, appeared at Tübingen the first volume of his dissertations *(Staatsrecht, Völkerrecht und Politik),* including a new plan for improving this branch of jurisprudence. Robert Mohl is perfectly right in saying that jurists have made great omissions in their systems of international law. There are many questions of a social character scarcely known to the reigning school, but extremely important in practical life. The international relations of former centuries concerned principally governments, and but in an indirect way individuals. We live, on the contrary, in a period of universal contact. The communications between the different countries of Europe grow more and more frequent and easy. The time is approaching when the civilised world will form one indivisible community. The interests of this new society should be protected and defended every where. It is impossible to regulate them by following old precedents. When all the conditions of life are subjected to such a change, when human activity is so prodigiously extended, new principles of law must be sought, and necessarily will be found, in universal justice. In bringing to light the

[2] In the first volume of his *History of Political Knowledge*, we find a treatise on the literature of international law. He published also an interesting essay on the extradition of criminals (*Asylrecht*).

existence of international society in Europe, Robert Mohl opens a large field of inquiry. In his opinion the international law of the future should embrace the domain of private law, and reform many institutions of it. Its actual state is more suited to the restriction than to the extension of human intercourse. Under the influence of an exclusive spirit, intellectual, commercial, and other relations are left, without sufficient protection, to the free will of individuals and companies. Even contracts, when concluded between the subjects of different states, are not sufficiently enforced.

In agreeing with Dr. Robert Mohl, I am happy to say that his honest desires find great support in public opinion. The present age is not indifferent to the interests of general civilisation. The necessity of fixed and uniform rules of private international law is much felt in Europe, and expressed by some distinguished jurists. Some reforms in it are already projected, and seem likely to be realised in a short time. Insurance, patents, trade marks, copyright, bankruptcy, remain among the subjects to be regulated for the common benefit of all nations. May this new cosmopolitan tendency bring forth good results for present and future generations!

I conclude here my account of Germany, and come to Belgium. I shall not speak of the universities of that country; international jurisprudence seems not to be much studied at them. But it is impossible to pass by a work now in course of publication in Belgium — I mean the *History of International Relations,* by Professor Laurent of Ghent (Gand: 1850–62, 7 vols.). The genius and the erudition of this distinguished man excite general admiration. Even those who do not agree with all his conclusions are obliged to admit his superiority over all his predecessors. None of them ever embraced the immense field of knowledge with such a powerful hand. The works of Ward, Wheaton, Pütter, and Müller-Jochmus, on the history of international law, good as they are, stand far behind his wonderful work. It would take too long to give here a critical analysis of it. I will but tell you, in a few words, what problem Laurent has undertaken to resolve. From the title of his work, as indicated above, you see the comprehensive nature of its subject. To write a history of international relations is to write a history of humanity. These relations, as you know, have various characters; they are warlike or pacific, intellectual or commercial, religious, moral, or purely material, &c. It is not a light task to explore their origin and gradual extension; but Laurent's erudition is as large as his field of inquiry. He feels himself at home in every country, in every age. We find him never obscure or confused in his various researches. Beginning from the most ancient times, he describes the wars and treaties, the commercial intercourse and geographical discoveries of nations, with the same masterly hand. His principal aim is to delineate the moral and intellectual progress of human society under the influence of different nations. He looks on religion, philosophy, and literature, from a cosmopolitan point of view, as instruments of general civilisation. Mankind, according to the opinion of Laurent, is led by Providence to final harmony and unity; mutual jealousies, wars, and conquests, are to disappear — universal peace will reign between nations. He proves, by facts, the gradual and incessant application of this providential law. Such is the general character of his work. You will say, perhaps, that it is rather historical than juridical. To this I answer that both elements are mixed in it, and that Laurent himself would be unable to determine whether he gives more importance to the first or to the second. Some volumes of his work may be called even philosophical and theological. But, whatever opinions may be held on the limits of a history of international relations, it is impossible to deny that Laurent has contributed very largely to the development of this branch of human knowledge. With his aid we are enabled to trace the origin of the international feelings and ideas by which humanity was governed during its past ages, the influence of wars on the destiny of the world, and the successive attempts to mitigate their pernicious effects. I do not doubt that all impartial and enlightened men will look on the work of Laurent with sympathy and gratitude. The tendency of his mind is of the most elevated character. He is inspired by the noblest enthusiasm for his subject, and is free from common prejudices, grand in his ideal conceptions. He has made discoveries where superficial observers of human events had passed by without understanding the meaning of important facts. The social qualities of our nature are rightly appreciated and deeply explored by him in their full scope and activity. The learned professor has carried his work to the seventh volume. The first three, and in my opinion the best, embrace the history of the international relations of antiquity; in the fourth he speaks of Christianity and its international influence; the last three give the description of the middle ages. May M. Laurent live to terminate his labours! There are few men in our age who are so prepared as he is to accomplish a work of that character. It is to be regretted that controversies with the Catholic party in Belgium have disturbed the tranquillity of M. Laurent's mind. He has given, during the last three years, so much of his time to theological controversies, that I may express a legitimate apprehension for the continuance of his work. Its interruption would be indeed a very great calamity. Let us hope, also, that the usual impartiality of the author will never leave him in his difficult researches.

From Belgium we proceed to the country of Hugo Grotius. It is gratifying to find here the noble traditions of an ancient glory still existing. In fact, the cultivation of international law in the Dutch universities has never, up to the present time, been interrupted. Though the period of eminent jurists ended with the death of Bynkershoek, yet, amongst their successors, appeared some distinguished and laborious men. During the first half of the nineteenth century the best works on international law were published by De Wal and Den Tex, professors at Leyden and Amsterdam. Professor Vreede, of Utrecht, may be mentioned as their able and learned follower. His *Introduction to the History of Dutch Diplomacy* is a book of great merit. I could notice here many other works, if that would not make this general sketch too long. It is sufficient to observe that they consist of dissertations and pamphlets on international questions, and that some of them, though written by young students, are of considerable historical value.[3] May this activity of the Dutch universities long continue to promote the progress of knowledge!

On the contrary, in the universities of France, we find few good interpreters of international jurisprudence. Even at Paris, where there exist so many colleges and a central school of law *(l'école de droit),* this branch of study is neglected. But that fact certainly does not arise from any general decay of this knowledge there. I know no other country in Europe where international questions are as generally understood as in France, and so widely judged by public opinion. French periodicals are full of able essays on international law. A great number of political pamphlets issue every month from the principal publishing houses of Paris. Some of them are published anonymously, and even by order of government; these have, of course, a purely official character. But there are others which bear the stamp of an independent and honest opinion. Whatever may be the cause, it is impossible to deny the activity of the French

[3] The best of them are criticized by Robert Mohl in his Literature of international law (Geschichte der Stautswissenschaft, 1 vol.)

mind in the study of foreign policy. The neglect of international law in the universities of that country, I explain but by temporary or fortuitous circum-stances. Great international jurists are not wanting in France. In their number may be counted Fœlix, Hautefeuille, Ortolan, whose profound works are too well known in Europe for any criticism of them to be necessary here. We should not forget also that the Parisian academy for the promotion of moral and political philosophy, *Académie des Sciences Morales et Politiques,* has rendered, and still renders, great services to international jurisprudence. Under its protection are made valuable researches in diplomatic history. The annual prizes for the best works in jurisprudence, fostered by this Academy, are a very good institution indeed. They offer a noble remuneration to useful men, who hardly receive any other profit from their intellectual labour, and bring to the knowledge of the public the best books published in the French language.

Now let me say a few words on the state of international jurisprudence in Italy and Spain. As to the first-named country, its political condition up to the most recent times was unfavourable to the mental activity of the people. International law was for a long time either banished from the Italian universities, or cultivated in them very imperfectly. Even now in the Austrian dominions, for instance at Padua, the restrictions on its study amount almost to prohibition. The first independent chair for this branch of jurisprudence was founded in 1849, at Turin, and held by Professor Mancini, the author of the celebrated doctrine of nationalities. It is but natural that this doctrine should have received general applause in Italy. May it contribute to the unity of that country!

I am glad to say that the knowledge of international jurisprudence is now much improved in Spain. After consulting the works of Bello, Ferrater, Riquelme, I do not doubt of this fact.·I admire even more the posthumous treatise on international law by Pando, published in 1852. This is one of the beat books I have ever read upon the subject. When we consider the wonderful fate of Pando's manuscript, seized by banditti, and then unexpectedly restored, *(cosas de España!)* and the adventurous life of the author, who, when living in South America, was cut off for many years from all communication with the world by blockades, sieges, and civil war, we come to the conclusion that he who could finish his work under such unfavourable circumstances was one of the most extraordinary men in the world; and his book is not only worthy to be consulted, but fully deserves a European reputation. It is imbued with a liberal and philosophical spirit, vast erudition, and an astounding knowledge of history. As Spanish literature is little known in Europe, I will mention to you some minor works recently published in that country. Here, namely, belong the lectures of Goñi on the *History of Spanish Diplomacy* (1848), and the curious little book of Corsini on the *Laws and Usages of War* (Corsini, *Las Leyes de la Guerra.* Madrid: 1858.) Mr. Corsini, being a military man, deserves our peculiar notice. His protestations against cruelty in war, and his struggles with the ancient habits of a fanatical people, are very remarkable indeed. I do not find his book Quixotic, but admire it sincerely; it is full of good sense and honest convictions. May his example serve other men of his profession! In our time it is not useless to preach loyalty and justice in war; the effect of good works is never lost upon humanity. As far as I can judge, we may expect now from Spain other contributions to the literature of international jurisprudence. The universities of that country are not deficient generally in able professors of law; the central university I have found even in a flourishing state. In 1859 an Academy for the promotion of political philosophy was established at Madrid; and, as I have heard since, has already entered upon its functions. The first volume of its memoirs has now issued from the press *(Memorias de la Real Academia de Ciencias Morales y Politicas, Tome I., Parte Prima.* Madrid: 1861).

Shall I speak before your Society on the state of international jurisprudence in England? Why not? I know that I approach a subject familiar to every one of you, but I will not be long. Perhaps you may be interested in hearing the opinion of a foreigner on the works of English jurists. Being aware of your love of truth, I hope that you will correct my views if they should be erroneous.

International law was cultivated in the universities of England earlier than in those of continental Europe. Even before the great work of Grotius was published, Alberico Gentili, an Italian refugee and professor at Oxford, wrote his treatises, *De Legationibus, De Jure Belli, De Justitia Bellica Romanorum,* in which he attempted to trace out this branch of jurisprudence, and to give it an independent existence. One of his successors, Professor Zouch, published the first elementary book on international law *(Juris et Judicii Fecialis, &c. Explicatio*). In the Scotch universities its knowledge seems to have been diffused later, under the influence of the celebrated philosophers of that country who flourished in the eighteenth century. I do not know whether any work on international law appeared in Scotland before Rutherford's lectures. As to the proper English school of jurists, it cared little for theory and philosophy, and retained from the commencement of its existence a practical character. This tendency grew more and more exclusive, and led English publicists to exaggerated views. Some of them, as Selden in the seventeenth, and Jenkinson in the eighteenth century, in defending the interests of their country against the continental states, distinguished themselves by blind partiality and misrepresentation of facts. Selden's *Mare*

Clausum was considered on the continent as a book written by order of government, and paid for by it. The pamphlet of Jenkinson, *On the Conduct of Great Britain, &c.,* had also an official character. Thus its polemics on questions of maritime law brought upon the English school a great deal of invective; the public opinion of Europe looked on it with suspicion and mistrust, doubted its sincerity, and even accused it of dishonesty. This general condemnation is unjust, of course; but it is true that, up to the end of the eighteenth century, international law employed very few independent minds in England.

We come now to the times of Sir J. Mackintosh and of Sir W. Scott (Lord Stowell). These two distinguished men are considered as the best interpreters of international law in England. Their scientific views (I do not speak here of their practical life) are of more elevated character than those of their predecessors. They searched for principles, not for facts alone; and viewed foreign policy as much from the point of duty as from that of right. Animated by the noblest feelings of justice, and imbued with a philosophical spirit, Sir J. Mackintosh contributed largely to the enlightenment of his countrymen in their dealings with other nations, and combated with success their insular prejudices. His opinions were received throughout Europe with great respect, and inspired all honest hearts with confidence in England. It is, however, to be regretted that his lectures on international law were never published; nothing but an introduction to them has appeared in print. The exertions of Sir W. Scott for his country's honour are no less deserving of praise. Acting us judge in the Court of Admiralty during the time of a most cruel war, he tried to be just and impartial to neutrals, as far as his powers allowed him. Unfortunately he did not adhere strictly to the principles of international law, even as understood and expressed by him in many of his learned decisions. He lived in the time of paper blockades and the continental system, and was obliged to submit to the inconstant policy of the belligerents. So, after having proclaimed his opinion, he often retracts it from no other motive but practical necessity. When compared with his predecessors, Sir W. Scott is far superior to all of them taken together; but, great as he stands in history, his opinions are not those of our age. He defended to the utmost the medieval practice of maritime war against modern civilisation. According to Sir W. Scott, belligerent rights are immutable; he never admitted their relaxation, and punished the infraction of them by neutrals with all the rigour of law. It was but natural to expect from him the same impartiality to the parties engaged in war. Unfortunately, in 1806 came the continental system of Napoleon, and the celebrated orders of council of a most repressive character. The belligerent powers proclaimed the general destruction of neutral commerce, the existence of which, as founded on international law, was never contested by the learned judge. The effect of these arbitrary measures is known; they shook all the principles proclaimed in the most solemn way by Sir W. Scott. His juridical edifice lost its ground; laws, usages, and precedents, respected by him, were torn to pieces. A merciless war, after having given the last fatal blow to justice, raged over all the world, and brought it to the verge of barbarism.

This turbulent epoch left good lessons for us all. We are able now to judge calmly its men and its passions. Our opinions on international law are no longer those current fifty years ago. We see belligerent rights in another light. Even England has ceased to enforce them rigorously, and defends at this moment the immunity of her flag.[4] Of the principles of Sir W. Scott nothing is left but their historical

[4] The manuscript of this paper was dated from Kharkow, 16 January, 1862.

value. Why, then, should not we express our opinion of him honestly? I hope that his foreign critics will be heard in your Society as favourably as his English admirers. An international judge, whatever authority he may have in the eyes of his countrymen, is responsible to all countries for his principles and acts. He is bound "to render justice in mercy" to all the world. His moderation will sooner or later be appreciated by humanity; his faults will never escape a well-merited censure. Now, Sir W. Scott was undoubtedly a great jurist. For his acuteness and practical genius he may be compared with the celebrated lawyers of Rome. He excelled in casuistry, and made great discoveries in international law; but it was not permitted him to administer it according to the spirit of universal justice. I admire in him sincerely the qualities of a statesman: I find the study of his clear and logical decisions very instructive and edifying, but I cannot agree to his principles of prize-law. He was not impartial in his views on belligerent and neutral rights. I have certainly nothing to say against his personal character; but it seems to me that as a judge he was not free from the political passions of his time. I believe, also, that in our age international law may be administered better, *i.e.,* with greater moderation and liberality, than it was administered by Sir W. Scott.

I come now to his school. The number of followers of Sir W. Scott is very considerable in England. Chitty, Oke, Manning, Reddie, Wildman, and some other jurists, have treated international law according to his principles. The character of their works is as practical, if not as exclusively so, as that of the ancient English school. With the continental jurists they have principally discussed the question of belligerent and neutral rights. The best defender of British interests is Reddie. His opinions found a strong opponent in M. Ortolan, a captain in the French navy. The polemics between them possess much interest for a student of international law. Without going into the detailed criticism of both authors, I may say here that M. Ortolan stands nearer to the truth, at least in his general principles. Mr. Reddie's ideas seem to be less clear, though his learning is very great. For instance, in defining the sources of international law, he gives but confused notions of them. In his opinion, the rules followed by prize courts form a customary law of nations; treaties he considers in no other light than as exceptions to those rules. It is easy to understand the tendency of Mr. Reddie's arguments; they point to the necessity of giving to belligerents a legislative power over neutrals. There are few jurists who will support him so far; his sophistry is too evident. Independent communities are bound in their mutual relations by no other law than by treaties or usages established *tacito consensu.* Prize courts, whatever may be their authority during the war, have no power to create universal rules; their decisions are often corrected and revised by mixed commissions or in treaties of peace.

During the last seven or eight years, there have been published in England some capital works on international law. As they are perfectly known to you, I may give my opinion of them in a few words. Let me begin with the *Commentaries* of Dr. Phillimore, as they embrace the whole of international law. I know no English book on the subject that has had so many readers in the continental states of Europe as these four volumes. They contain an immense quantity of matter. The learned author has paid great attention to the practical questions of our time, and we must give him the praise of fairness, and respect for international law. The casuistical, documental, and historical parts of his commentaries are indisputably the best. I cannot speak as highly of the philosophical parts; but it seems that Dr. Phillimore did not intend to develop his general principles as largely as might have been expected.

However this may be his work is very useful. It abounds with materials and facts collected with care, and attesting long years of study. I do not agree with all the opinions of the learned author, but I appreciate highly his profound erudition, as, I am sure, many others of my profession do. He has contributed much to our present knowledge of international law, and amply earned, by his researches, the reputation of a conscientious inquirer in this branch of jurisprudence.

The recent work of Dr. Travers Twiss is not so large as that of Dr. Phillimore, but has its great and peculiar value. It is a clear, concise, well-digested, and systematical book. The philosophical part of it is the best; the historical very correct and satisfactory. I hardly know an elementary book better adapted for a student. May the second volume of it be as good as the first! I regret only to see Dr. Twiss defending the views of Mr. Reddie, on the sources of international law (treaties and usages), as they are erroneous in my opinion. But this is an important point to be discussed by jurists, and already touched on by me above.

Let me mention here also a treatise on private international law, published by my learned friend, Mr. Westlake. If not for his modesty I would speak more of his useful work, but you are aware of its value. I pass it over, as so many other treatises mid essays written in England by able and competent men. My paper is already too long, and should be concluded. I must add, however, that the present state of this branch of jurisprudence in your country appears to be more satisfactory than it was thirty or forty years ago. I wish only that the study of international law might be more diffused in England. In fact, you have in your hands great instruments for promoting its knowledge. Your foreign relations and commercial affairs are coextensive with the world; your diplomatic service is supplied with able and cultivated men; your parliamentary papers and blue books give you the best political information. In short, I find but one serious obstacle to the diffusion of international jurisprudence in your country, and that is, the general indifference of Englishmen to European affairs. But you may struggle with it if you will make an effort. You have to do with all educated and practical people. Make your countryman but understand better his position in Christendom, his human rights and interests, and he will enlarge his views. In our time we should not despair of conquering public opinion by honest exertions in favour of mankind. Let us only be constant in good works, and the general feeling of their importance will be awakened. It is to be regretted that international law has in England no special organs, nor any such periodicals as are *Les Archives Diplomatiques* in France. A review of this character would be of great use for the enlightenment of the English nation on questions of foreign policy. Public lectures on it might contribute also to this purpose. I am happy to state that the study of international jurisprudence is now revived at the University of Oxford, where a new (the Chichele) professorship has been created for it. May Cambridge follow this example given by her rival sister!

You will ask me, perhaps, why I have omitted my own country in this sketch. The fact is that I have little to say about it. International jurisprudence, as an independent branch of knowledge, was introduced into the Russian universities so late as 1885. Before that time, we had but few public interpreters of it. Our diplomatists generally received their education abroad. The present intellectual movement promises to bear fruit in Russia for all parts of human knowledge. Some good books, dissertations, and essays on international law have already been published. I do not enumerate them before you, because they are written in a language known but to few Englishmen. Unfortunately, a good elementary work on the subject has not yet appeared in our country. It is high time to prepare for the diffusion of political knowledge among our people. For my own part, I have never despaired of Russian civilisation and communion with Europe. Now, by the abolition of serfdom, is struck the last and fatal blow at our aggressive policy, as it was generally styled; and Russia has entered on a new era of peace and international law. We hope that the more advanced nations of the west will sincerely aid us in our honest efforts, and look with sympathy on this large portion of mankind, struggling with ignorance, and regenerating itself with civil liberty.

I come now to the conclusion of my paper. The subject I proposed to treat before you is nearly exhausted. But I cannot dismiss it without offering some general remarks on it. After having surveyed the principal countries of Europe, I feel it my duty to answer a last question, namely: Is our generation much advanced in their knowledge of international law?

I do not profess to belong to that class of men who idolise the nineteenth century, and revile its predecessors. Human knowledge is the fruit of long and combined labours; it grows from age to age, and is bequeathed from one nation to another as their common inheritance. Any man understanding how to use it can make himself its temporary owner, and at the same time divide its fruits with his fellow-creatures. Monopolies are not admitted in the world of ideas and good works. Human reason has no limits to its useful activity but those of nature and social life. We know, for instance, how difficult it is to begin a practical undertaking, and how easy comparatively to continue one. The same may be said of the intellectual history of mankind. Those who were the first to search for truth are the architects or constructors of knowledge; they take the foremost place in its annals; their thoughts and deeds guide their posterity for a long time. Look on Plato, or Aristotle, or Bacon: seen from a distance, they stand like giants and heroes. Having given existence to them, nature seems to be exhausted, and to repose itself for a while.

Such has been the history of international jurisprudence. Men of large creative power and all-embracing genius came first. They laid the foundation-stone, and traced the general plan of the edifice, but left the labour of its improvement and partial reconstruction to future generations: then, by successive efforts, were collected new materials for building it. Every age, in working for itself, contributed something to the common treasure. Great practical truths were discovered; great errors of the past were shaken off. The critical spirit of the eighteenth century led to new improvements of knowledge. In short, tradition has been as valuable as invention, experience as powerful as abstract reasoning, in the advancement of international law. The peculiar character of the present age is the division of labour. The jurists of the nineteenth century have lived chiefly in the detailed work; their tendencies and performances have, for the most part, had special, not general, subjects in view. There are few, if any, of them who would embrace such a problem as that of Grotius or Bynckershoek. The age of great men is over; but ordinary powers, when well employed, are not to be despised. If, on surveying the field of knowledge, we observe on it a sufficient number of able workmen, shall we despair of their ultimate success? By no means. They have a unity of action. They differ in some opinions only because they search for truth. *Du conflit des opinions jaillit la vérité,* says a French proverb. International jurists of all countries are bound to each other by invisible ties. They work for the common benefit of humanity, and are animated by a cosmopolitan spirit.

Unfortunately this world of ours is not yet free from prejudices and passions. Impartial minds are still to be sought, and should be much appreciated. In natural philosophy and mathematics man is independent in his researches of external influence. On the contrary, liberty of thought on social questions is less protected. Among political writers we find people of every description. Even in our days hired and subservient hands are the most ready for work, and, which is more to be regretted, have power with public opinion. A large number of books and pamphlets are still written by them. I hope that no honest man will give the name of international jurists to this crowd of popular flatterers and creatures of bad governments. Their place in the history of knowledge is not to be envied; they stand in the last rank of scribblers. Their *inspired* works give them sometimes money, but never a. good and lasting reputation. May society be soon delivered from its false and worthless friends!

But this occasional degradation of juridical and political ideas should not be exaggerated. Those who judge humanity by its worst examples may be accused of pessimism. Some men are easily corrupted, but others act sincerely, and resist all the temptations of power and money. To the glory of our nature, impartial minds and elevated characters appear in all ranks of society, in all countries, in every epoch of history. In jurisprudence and politics, honesty of thought and intention is as much and as often exhibited as in practical life. International law, I am happy to say, has been founded and supported chiefly by men who have left after them an unspotted name, whose tendencies and opinions, even whose faults, were derived from pure motives. Some of these men were animated by the noblest feelings of our nature. Grotius gave to all his followers a good example of heroic virtue. He suffered persecution and exile, was called visionary and even traitor by his contemporaries; but there were few scholars in his time who worked more than he for the common benefit of humanity. Among the Dutch and German jurists of the eighteenth century we find also a great number of elevated characters. And our age, as you know, can boast of many impartial inquirers after truth. The more we render them justice the better for us! Our duty is to remunerate good works, tending to the progress of knowledge, with our admiration and gratitude. What are then the general results of these honest efforts to improve international law? It is gratifying to see that the labours of human benefactors are not lost upon society. The principles of international justice are understood now, not only by a select circle of scholars, as in former times, but by all the civilised communities of the Christian world. The conscience of humanity is acknowledged to be the highest tribunal in Europe; to no practical man, whatever may be his position, is it allowed to despise it. Powerful governments and nations are obliged to submit to its dictates. Crimes against international law no longer pass unnoticed, and are seldom left unavenged. It is impossible, of course, to prevent them while human nature is subject to passions, but they become more and more dangerous to their authors. Few men dare to meet the general indignation of their fellow-creatures. Evil examples given in France by the first empire, are repudiated by the second. "The epoch of conquests is past for ever," said the nephew of the greatest of modern conquerors. Even during war, the principles of international justice are no longer forgotten, as they were fifty years ago. An act of unnecessary cruelty by an enemy is reprobated in all Europe. Military prisoners are never subjected to ignominious labour, but treated with courtesy and magnanimity. Privateering is abolished, neutral commerce better protected; but the most important fact we have to notice here is the increasing aversion to war itself, at least between Christian nations.

You see then that the influence of international jurisprudence has ever been salutary, and that its efficiency is beyond doubt. May it work and prosper for our common benefit! In feeling gratitude for what has already been obtained, we expect from it more in future. Whatever may be the faults of international jurists, they have understood the practical necessities of every epoch, and worked accordingly. When it was most important for humanity to define the privileges of diplomatic agents and to mitigate military cruelty, they found rules of universal justice for the mutual relations of governments, which, being adopted *tacito consensu,* stand now established and respected every where. This was the problem resolved by Grotius, Puffendorf, Bynckershoek, and Vattel. Their followers felt that they had another no less important duty to perform. After 1815 came a new pacific epoch of railways, steam navigation, and telegraphs. The commercial intercourse of individuals was to be secured and protected. Hence the system of private international law elaborated by Savigny, Story, Fœlix, and others; hence numerous treatises on the rights of consuls, works on copyright, on the extradition of criminals, on belligerent and neutral rights, &c. This literary movement is still continued, and probably will continue uninterrupted during many years. There are some other problems to resolve in the international law of the present time, which we have mentioned elsewhere. In fact, in this ever-living branch of jurisprudence, in which whatever is done still leaves more to do, we may reasonably expect that the good sense of every age will point out the practical questions to be resolved by jurists. Let them only mind their principal aim — the common benefit of humanity. A positive law, having been once created, should be improved continuously and patiently: it grows with the society that gave it life and power. It is like a large house, made fit for human habitation and standing on a solid basis; nothing but some general calamity makes it fall to ruins. The international law of Europe is a child of modern civilisation. It sprang into being from practical necessity, *par la force des choses.* Its growth was as natural as the growth of the Christian world, founded on justice, supported by conscience, and by the common interests of humanity; its principles are firm and invulnerable. Political storms and convulsions may reform some of its provisions, but the general edifice stands consolidated by the Christian religion, by philosophy, by the experience of ages, and by the opinions of honest men.

There are, however, still sophists and sceptics in this world, who make violent attacks on international law, and try to depreciate our knowledge of it. I revert to them once more, only to exhibit their new failure. You have heard, perhaps, of the recent work of Proudhon *(La Paix et la Guerre),* two volumes, published at Paris last year. It belongs to the class of books read by the multitude, and written in popular language. I have perused it carefully, and am able now to give here my opinion of it. Its author is the celebrated sophist of our time. He wrote some pamphlets about political economy, and combated successfully its doctrines. The revolutionary party of continental Europe proclaimed him the greatest of philosophers. After the appearance of his book on Justice (1860), with a bold epigraph, *destruam et œdificabo,* it might have been expected that he reserved his most dreadful blows for the international jurisprudence of Europe. They are struck at last, and its edifice stands unimpaired. We are out of danger; there is no harm in the sophistry of M. Proudhon. His work does not deserve to be seriously criticised. It is utterly insignificant. In his first volume, our sophist tries to prove that war is a religion of humanity, and that every effort for mitigating it is useless; in his second, that war is the result of pauperism, and will be extinguished with it.

The right of force *(droit de la force),* according to Proudhon, is established in human societies by natural law, as firmly as *the rights of love, of labour, and of intellect.* I do not know whether you understand this new classification of human rights; to me it appears senseless. In asserting that war is the universal religion, Proudhon calumniates humanity: his opinions on the right of force, as if it were the foundation of the family, are repudiated by history; nor can I agree with him that war is the result of pauperism. On the contrary, pauperism seems to be the result of war, at least in some countries. However this may be, modern nations have never grown rich by war and conquest. But the most wonderful part of Proudhon's book is its last chapter: he proclaims at the end of it, *"que l'humanité! ne veut plus la guerre."* Why, then? Because humanity has abjured its religion? The same inconsistency we find in his judgments on the works of Grotius, Vattel, and other great lawyers. In his first volume he says they are stupid; in his second, he repeats their opinions in his own manner. If those opinions have no value, why did he not give us new truths? Because he possesses none. His book does not make us wiser; paradoxes, for the most part, are good for nothing. International law, as understood by Proudhon, is worthless, like an arid field; we do not find in it mutter for our intellectual food.

I certainly do not affirm that international jurisprudence has attained in our days its utmost perfection. On the contrary, I find in it various defects. But I have strong reasons for expecting its regular development by those who are able to distinguish in it truth from error. A work of many centuries cannot be destroyed and reconstructed at once by such sophistry as that of Proudhon. Human knowledge has in itself an ever-working power of renovation: its history is an incessant battle of discordant opinions. They meet on equal terms, and have a fair trial.

An international reformer, I hope, will be better prepared to fight for his idea than was M. Proudhon, and will understand a little more of history. Even in our time, men acquainted with the new exigences of practical life, and defending the interests of civilisation, are sure to be heard. A practical truth, by whomsoever it may be discovered, finds support in human society. International law is gloudually gaining ground in Europe. Great and useful discoveries are made in it by such men as Mohl, Laurent, Hautefeuille, &c. Their example should not be lost on us. Unequal as may be our talents for the great task lying before us, we should never despair of ameliorating and reforming the international law of Christian communities. Let us only be true to our duties of men and of brethren! If we be but impartial in our inquiries and good in our intentions — if we have on our side the strong sense of justice and the feeling of humanity — our works will not perish with us. The international jurists of the nineteenth century can do nothing better than emulate each other in those honest arts by which alone our knowledge has ever been advanced. The surest way for us all is still —

Certare ingenio, contendore nobilitate,
Noctes atque dies niti præstante labore,
Ad summas emergere opes rerumque potiri.

PRIZE LAW:

PARTICULARLY WITH REFERENCE TO

THE DUTIES AND OBLIGATIONS

OF

BELLIGERENTS

AND

NEUTRALS.

BY

PROFESSOR KATCHENOVSKY,
OF THE UNIVERSITY OF KHARKOV, RUSSIA.

TRANSLATED FROM THE RUSSIAN

BY FREDERIC THOMAS PRATT, D.C.L.,
ADVOCATE, DOCTORS COMMONS.

LONDON:
STEVENS & SONS, 26, BELL YARD, LINCOLN'S INN.

1867.

LONDON:
PRINTED BY C. ROWORTH AND SONS,
BELL YARD, TEMPLE BAR.

TRANSLATOR'S PREFACE.

At the present time, when the question of Neutrality commands so much public attention, it may be useful to ascertain what are the opinions and views on that subject entertained by Publicists and Jurists of other countries. Those of the Continent generally are well known from the extended literary intercourse which has now been for some years in existence.

There is, however, one country, that of Russia, the intercourse with which is unfortunately still very limited. With the internal arrangements and proceedings of that vast empire few foreigners, not residing within its limits, possess even a general acquaintance, and that but a very imperfect one. The alterations and improvements, however, which have been of late introduced into its institutions are of such a nature, and so important, as to arrest the attention and deserve the consideration of the statesmen and people of all other countries. Within the last few years the emancipation of the serfs has been successfully carried out under the auspices of the present Emperor; trial by jury introduced; the courts of justice thrown open to the public; and causes civil and criminal fully reported in the public journals.

(iv)

With reference to international law, that empire has peculiar claims upon our notice. It was by the Empress Catherine II. that an earnest attempt was made, by the establishment of the "armed neutrality," to protect the rights of neutrals, and impose some restrictions on the cruelties of war; and whatever may have been the real motives for that work, and these still are in a certain degree involved in obscurity, it can hardly be denied that its immediate effect was to mitigate the sufferings incident to war, and that it has since on many occasions served as a model for statesmen and philanthropists who have been engaged in furthering the same praiseworthy object.

At a time when great attention has been bestowed in promoting education amongst the numerous races of this extensive empire, the important subject of international law has not been overlooked by the government, who have established in the various universities of that Kingdom professorships of this particular science.

Among these professors the name of Professor Katchenovsky, the author of the present work, stands most prominent. He is also well known in the literary circles of the Continent for the extent and accuracy of his attainments, and is the author of several learned and interesting works which well deserve the attention of our countrymen.

I have selected the present one on account of its connexion with the subject of the day. During the course of my labours I have been so fortunate as to become intimately acquainted with the learned author, who has kindly revised my translation, and supplied me with several valuable notes and additions. These are printed from his own MS.* His knowledge, indeed, of our language is so correct and extensive, that had his important duties at the University admitted of it, this work would have appeared to much more advantage in his own translation.

I think it right to add that my labours have been limited to the giving a correct and faithful translation of the author's work. With many of his opinions, it is almost unnecessary to state that I do not coincide; the author himself has, indeed, modified some of those he had entertained, and expressed them in more moderate terms. I cannot doubt but that after a more intimate acquaintance with the legal institutions of our country, he will more highly appreciate even those established by our Constitution for the administration of international law.

* The matters here referred to are the prefatory remarks, the additional notes, and postscript.

AUTHORS CITED.

(viii)

(ix)

b

(x)

CASES CITED.

INTRODUCTORY REMARKS.

An impartial observer of international practice can easily perceive what is the fundamental distinction between maritime and continental warfare. In fact, our civilization has not yet succeeded in enforcing upon the naval agents of belligerent powers the milder customs adopted by European armies under the name of "Manière de guerre." A discrimination, in the treatment of combatants and of non-combatants, is tolerably well observed on land, but almost entirely ignored at sea. Maritime war may still be described without any great exaggeration as "Bellum omnium contra omnes." Its piratical principles, since they were first established in the Middle Ages, have as yet scarcely undergone much improvement. Naval operations consist not so much in regular engagements and sieges as in depredations upon pacific traders, and generally inflict greater losses and sufferings on private individuals than on states. Contributions levied by the soldiery upon an invaded country seem to have but local or temporary effects, in comparison with the usual atrocities of maritime war, which, being conducted by belligerents with the sole object of destroying each other's commerce, entails capture and captivity upon every enemy on board, whether shipowner, master or member of the crew. From time immemorial up to the middle of the present century this system of legal piracy has been pursued with unrelenting rigour. The best instrument for it seemed to be found in privateering. This peculiar institution, as might be expected, originated at that period of history when the regular navy

(2)

was yet in its infancy, and governments had no other means of carrying on maritime war than by the active co-operation of their subjects. Hence arose the custom of employing pirates or robbers to fit out ships (armer en course), and to give chase to the enemy (courrir sûs à l'ennemi). Acting at their own risk and peril these adventurers enjoyed for a long time most extensive privileges, and disposed of their prizes without any control or supervision.

The first measures for the regulation of maritime warfare in Europe belong to the 14th and 15th centuries. In the course of this period, freebooters (Corsarii, Écumeurs de mer, Freibeuter) were converted into a sort of irregular militia, under the name of privateers (Captores, prædatores, armateurs en course, câpres, privatkaper), and subjected to the jurisdiction of Admiralty Courts. We should, however, add, that the practical results of this reform soon appeared to be insignificant; the prize law was still constructed on the same principles, and administered by belligerents with great severity. Accordingly we find in the 16th century privateering carried on to the same extent as before.

Even the establishment of a regular navy did not affect the existence of this piratical institution; on the contrary, the developement of international commerce opened more extensive fields for its exercise. The surveillance of neutral traders was entrusted chiefly to privateers, who received full authority to search every merchant ship on the open sea, to examine the papers found on board, and to seize her on the least suspicion of irregularity. They became objects of terror to the whole world. The Admiralty Courts rather approved than restrained their rapacity. In fact, how could it be otherwise? Being established by the belligerent, they were bound to obey his decrees, and were naturally inclined to interpret them favourably to his interests and to those of his agents. It must be added, that the mercantile spirit of that age was extremely jealous and intolerant. The great object of maritime warfare was to annihilate the trade of the enemy. Neutral commerce seemed to counteract this, and was accordingly considered by belligerents an illegal and dangerous traffic. In order to put a stop to its activity they had recourse to all sorts of contrivances; neutral governments, however, were not prepared tamely to surrender the rights of their subjects, but, on the contrary, determined to check by energetic measures the violence of privateers, as well as to resist the arbitrary judgments of Admiralty Courts.

At the close of the 16th century that remarkable contest commenced, on the issue of which the free intercourse of nations chiefly depended. What the principal powers, however, engaged in this struggle agreed upon was not observed for more than two centuries. Even in our time we cannot say that this result is fully attained.

A careful revision of prize law, which was projected in the year 1780, was never carried out, and may be still considered as the great problem to be solved. The importance of this subject seems to increase from day to day, and can hardly be exaggerated. Navigation and commerce have now attained such vast proportions, that connected by them the human race seems to form as it were but one body; hence anything which impedes the free intercourse of nations seems to involve every community in one common distress. When a rupture occurs between maritime powers, the place where we may see the unmistakeable signs of an impending calamity is the Exchange.

Disturbances of prices, bankruptcies, monetary panics are then matters of daily occurrence, and affect the most distant markets. It cannot be otherwise, a maritime war has by its nature no local limits, but necessarily extends over every sea. This free element puts no obstacle in the way of belligerents. By the directions they may give to their cruisers they hold in their hands the intercourse of nations.

It is true that, since the Conference of Paris, 1856, the danger of the revival of privateering has passed away, but the total abolition of capture is not a necessary result. It is still in the power of belligerents to cause great annoyance to neutral merchants by intersecting all the tracks of com-

(4)

merce, and by giving arbitrary interpretation to prize law. Is this tyranny to be endured much longer? we think not. A reform in maritime warfare is required for the security of the world. To the honour of our age it must be said that Europe feels its necessity, and acts accordingly. In 1866, the governments of Italy, Austria and Prussia took the first steps towards the abolition of legal piracy. It may be reasonably hoped that their example will be followed by all great maritime powers. But no reforms can be safely perfected before the lessons of history have been weighed with due care and impartiality, for (this being the first duty of statesmen and jurists) on its performance depends very much the improvement of human society. Unfortunately political reforms are seldom discussed without prejudice and passion. In international questions the considerations of justice rest on still more debateable ground. We scarcely know any branch of political science in which the investigation of truth is so impeded by the influence of birth, party, creed and other human distinctions. On the first glance at the history of international law, we find in it nothing but continual contests between governments, accompanied with the acrimonious polemics of lawyers. Much time and patience are required to trace these disputes to their final consequences. The common interests of nations are scarcely ever sufficiently kept in view by contending parties. In discussing their mutual grievances they seem almost to forget the principal point. At length when we come to an improvement it seems to have been effected less by the efforts of man than by the natural course of events (par la force des choses), the progress of civilization. As an instance of this we give the settlement of neutral rights; it is true that the question is delicate, but still its difficulties may gradually be overcome by fair discussion. Now, if it be asked what was the conduct of the statesmen and jurists who were most interested in this question in the 18th century, the majority of them can hardly be absolved from serious responsibility. The works published on the subject at that time abound in misstate-

(5)

ments and errors, and, what is worse, are imbued with a spirit of animosity and distrust. Of course the majority of these publications were written by parties engaged for the purpose, or dictated under the influence of party. But even men of character did not hesitate to load with acrimony and abuse their opponents, as well as foreign governments and nations. Of course this manner of treating the question rather led to the embroilment than the elucidation of the points in dispute. The present times seem to be more inclined to the calm consideration of neutral rights. Since the Congress of Vienna they have seldom been defended at the point of the bayonet, and have consequently ceased to irritate the minds of men. Some living authors have almost succeeded in infusing a pacific spirit into this part of international jurisprudence. Their example is worthy of imitation, as the subject seems far from being exhausted in practice or theory. The Declaration of Paris (1856), concerning neutral rights, is but a meagre recapitulation of the principles of 1780. Misunderstandings between belligerents and neutrals are still of frequent occurrence. The last American war gave rise to some new questions between England and the United States, which have not yet been settled. Arbitrary interpretations of prize law are even more to be feared, as little has yet been done to prevent them, or to make the proceeding in Admiralty Courts less vague. In short, the legality of captures made by belligerents upon neutrals appears, in some cases, as doubtful to us as it did to our forefathers. Besides, if it be taken into consideration, that in recent works on neutrality there still occur many divergent opinions and obscurities, a new attempt to clear up the difficulties of this subject will not be deemed altogether out of place.

The historical method seems to be preferable in these researches. The results obtained by it in other branches of jurisprudence cannot but encourage us to adopt it in that of international law. In fact, abstract theories will here hardly serve any practical purpose. Although the celebrated philosophical school of jurists established on the Continent by

Puffendorff and Wolf has ceased to exist, it has left behind numerous errors and but few truths. Its endless disputes on the validity of natural law, in the intercourse of independent states, are now buried in oblivion. Instead of falling into the mistakes of their predecessors, the present generation has adopted a different mode of thought, and resorted to the original traditions handed down to us by Grotius. The proper study of an international jurist being the general interest of mankind, it is now understood that he has no better guide in his course of study than history. The success of Grotius himself cannot be otherwise explained than by his deference to its lessons. In the introduction to the treatise "De Jure Belli ac Pacis" we find the following remarks on the advantage of consulting history:—"History supports our arguments by examples and opinions; examples furnished by the most prosperous times, and the more enlightened nations, are to be preferred. Neither ought opinions to be disregarded, especially when they are unanimous, for international law cannot otherwise be better ascertained."* In fact this truly great man never considered himself as a universal legislator or supreme judge, but rather confined himself to the modest part of interpreting the dictates of conscience or the convictions of mankind. Having himself made an extensive use of ancient history, he probably hoped that that of modern times would be as carefully investigated by his successors. Hence we have reason to rejoice that the present school of jurists, having rejected abstract theories, pursues the same course of inquiry which the founder of international law did. It is true that historical researches require much diligence and labour, but it is no less true that, when made carefully and extensively, they give us a clearer insight into the opinions and convictions of mankind of right and wrong. The very source of international law is to be found in history. All

* Historiæ duplicem habent usum qui nostri sint argumenti; nam et exempla suppeditant, et judicia. Exempla quo meliorum sunt populorum, eo plus habent auctoritatis. Nec spernenda judicia, præsertim consentientia; jus enim gentium non aliter probatur.—Grot. de Jur. B. ac P.

(7)

traditions, precedents, customs and treaties are recorded in it, and cannot be met with elsewhere. The common prejudice that the historical method leaves no room for criticising law, or recommending its improvement, hardly deserves a serious refutation. An international jurist, when standing on this firm ground, is by no means called upon to renounce his independent judgment. The study of practical questions only makes him less opinionated and less prone to chimerical tendencies, but does not pervert the original or creative powers of his mind; on the contrary, it may be reasonably expected that, after devoting his time to the study of history, he will find himself fortified by experience, and better prepared to give sober advice in the management of human affairs.

In order to contribute his humble part to the improvement of international law, the author has adopted the historical method in the present work, and accordingly he has given in it an account of the principal treaties and decrees by which the conduct of privateers and cruisers towards neutral merchants was regulated from the Middle Ages to our own days. In his opinion, without such a review, no safe conclusion could be arrived at on the question of neutrality, and on the matters of dispute still pending between the governments of Europe and America. It seemed to him of great importance to trace the origin of the rules established by prize courts in their procedure, and in their interpretation of the general rights of neutral commerce. In short, the author has embodied in this work as much information on the subject of captures as it was in his power to supply. How far he has succeeded in his efforts to lay down the principles of law, and to point out their effects on our civilisation, he leaves the public to judge. But a brief statement of the results he has obtained may not be altogether out of place. The obstacles to the reform in maritime warfare depend, for the most part, on the unsettled condition of the law of neutrality. They may, however, be removed without much difficulty, if governments are willing to follow to their ultimate consequences the principles of 1780.

The Declaration of Paris, being a recapitulation of them with an additional article on privateering, did not, of course, satisfy public expectations.

A general maritime code should now be prepared for the world at large.

It was already projected in 1780, but the statesmen of that period were prevented from completing their work by the great revolutionary war. The circumstances of our age are much more favourable for carrying out this plan. A careful revision of prize law would be a step in the right direction. England and America seem to be the powers most interested in an equitable settlement of belligerent and neutral rights. In fact, the most angry discussions between them turn principally on this point. Now, instead of appealing on such occasions to special commissions, or to arbitration, in each particular case, as has hitherto been the practice, why should not nations come to a general understanding about maritime captures? The codification of the laws relating to this subject might be entrusted to the best jurists of our time. The labour of preparing any act of international enlistment, and general instructions for Admiralty Courts, with the other component parts of the code, seems to offer no serious difficulty. The principal object is to lay down general rules in accordance with strict justice, bearing in mind the lessons of experience. A code thus prepared should, of course, be ratified by all governments and nations. If England and America take the initiative in such an enterprise, their example will surely be followed by the other powers. The benefits arising from such a code can hardly be overrated. There is no better way of putting an end to the injuries inflicted upon commerce during a time of war, than by providing one uniform prize law for all nations. But even more important results may be obtained by a code of this kind. It is high time for Europe to adopt milder customs in maritime warfare. If jurists are entrusted with full powers to

(9)

deal with this important question they may certainly arrive at a satisfactory conclusion. An indication of this concord is already visible in many publications of the last ten years; the authors of these works agree in assigning a neutral character to the enemy's subjects engaged in maritime commerce. As to the old doctrine of belligerent rights, that finds but few supporters, and their opinions seem to be dictated rather by self-interest or prejudice than by adherence to the rules of justice.

But whether the reform proposed be effected by a code or by a conference of diplomatists resembling that of Paris, the author does not despair of seeing it accomplished. In fact, he has no other ambition than to draw the attention of the European public to the subject. The circumstances under which this work originally appeared in his native country (1855) were not favourable to its success. Russia being then engaged in war had no interest in defending neutral rights. In recording the glorious traditions of 1780, the author might have been suspected of holding impracticable views, hardly compatible with the duties of a patriot. Happily belligerents did not then forget the lessons of history, but willingly gave their adherence to the principles of the armed neutrality. The Conference of Paris (1856) seemed to be still more favourable to a liberal interpretation of these principles. The opinion expressed by the author on the original publication of the work respecting privateering has been justified by its abolition. But as he advocated more advanced views on maritime law, *i. e.*, the immunity of private property from capture, and as this result is not yet attained, the same work may not be too late in making its appearance in an English dress. Twelve years, however, having already elapsed since its first publication, a short account of subsequent events is necessarily added as an appendix to the original text.

The sources of information, to which the author has had access in his researches, are the following:—

1. General collections of treaties and other diplomatic

documents. Unfortunately the decrees and instructions given by belligerents to privateers and Admiralty Courts are to be found only in the more recent work of Prof. Martens' Recueil, and have not been noticed by Dumont and Wener. In order to supply this omission the author had recourse to subsidiary works on prize legislation. The most interesting of these was published in London by Sir C. Robinson, under the title of " Collectanea Maritima."

2. Reports of Admiralty Courts. The custom of giving publicity to the legal decisions on prize matters was not simultaneously adopted in all countries. Even where we find it introduced at an earlier date, the reporting was very imperfect to the end of the 18th century. As to the more ancient decisions, they are known to us only in a few fragments, the greater part indeed are entirely lost. A detailed history of the prize jurisprudence of Europe could not therefore be given. Such a work, without speaking of its magnitude, would be embarrassing even for English and American jurists. The author had not the benefit of access to any large library before the first appearance of this book. At that time Robinson's Reports could not be met with in the south of Russia, and were to be studied only in Pritchard's Admiralty Digest. The same difficulties, of a purely local character, prevented the author from consulting voluminous reports of prize cases published in France and in the United States of America. He felt still more this deficiency of original information with reference to other countries. But the scarcity of materials did not discourage him from pursuing his researches. He thought that the careful study of legislation, as well as of the works published by foreign jurists on the subject, enabled him sufficiently to appreciate the general spirit of European prize law, and to point out its historical modifications. If he has failed in this, competent critics will correct his opinions. It must be added, that the Russian prize practice is not included in this treatise for a very simple reason,—regular Admiralty Courts never having existed in Russia. The duties of such tribunals

were discharged by temporary commissions, whose reports have not been published. The author, however, thinks that in his country prize commissions hardly enjoyed a very extensive jurisdiction; at least it appears from Russian law that, with reference to neutrals, they were bound to follow treaties, and to submit every doubtful case to the approval of the Minister of Marine.* As to the captures made upon the enemy, they were usually considered the property of the crown. To cruisers, the Russian government; according to the general rule, gave nothing but prize rewards. Another interesting fact to be noticed here relates to privateering; this institution never seems to have flourished in Russia, the very language of the country has no term corresponding to it. It is true that John the Terrible, Peter the Great, and Catherine II. distributed in some of their wars "letters of marque" to foreigners, but the Russians themselves, so far as the author knows, never took part in any expedition for the purpose of making prizes. Even in 1812, when the merchants of Odessa and Taganrog (for the most part naturalized Greeks or Italians) applied to the government for commissions to arm ships against the French, this request was formally rejected.

3. Special works or dissertations on privateering and prize laws. The most important of this description was published by Professor T. F. Martens in 1795, under the title "Essai concernant les armateurs, les prises et surtout les réprises." It is still considered as a classical work and of great authority on the subject. But with all due deference to this eminent man, we may be allowed to state that his work, being purely dogmatical, contains only an excellent arrangement of the international law of his time. As to the history of privateering, Martens has given but a brief sketch, added to which, his attention being directed principally to re-captures, the other questions of prize law are treated by him as secondary. It is evident, then, that the valuable essay of Martens has afforded

* See Minutes of the Proceedings of a Committee appointed for the preparation of a Maritime Code (1850), p. 33, and Art. 946 of the Russian Code, vol. ii.

to the author of this book less assistance than might have been expected. The same may be said of the two articles on privateering, published by Kaltenborn in "Bülau's Jahrbücher der Geschichte" (1849), and compiled chiefly from Martens.

As to Wheaton's Digest of the Law of Maritime Captures, (New York, 1815), it was known to the author only from reviews and the latter works of this American diplomatist; its contents also appear to be dogmatical. The author acknowledges himself to be more indebted for historical facts and critical suggestions to other eminent jurists of the present century. Here, namely, may be mentioned the excellent article on Maritime International Law by the late Professor Wurm (Rotteck's Staats Lexicon, 13; Zeitschrift für der gesammte Staatswissenschaft 1851-52), as well as the larger works of Reddie and Ortolan upon the same subject.

4. Treatises and pamphlets on belligerents and neutral rights. A description of all the publications of this kind would be fatiguing to the reader. A long series of them has appeared in England, France, Germany and other countries of Europe since the middle of the 18th century; they must be used, however, with great caution. There is no branch of international jurisprudence on which so much has been written, but the very abundance of such works proves little, if anything, in their favour; on the contrary, it may be alleged as an instance of their insufficiency for solving the important questions connected with the subject. In fact, the authors to whom we here allude seldom take an impartial view of the subject, and are much inclined to exaggeration; almost every one of them stands up for his favourite theory, or considers himself to be the champion of his country. Some lawyers, indeed, may be reproached with distorting historical facts. Only in our time has the question of belligerent and neutral rights been approached by a few distinguished authors with a sincere desire of arriving at the truth. At the same time, however, that the author gives them full credit for extensive researches and great erudition,

he has followed his own path of inquiry, and, as the reader will see, comes to some independent conclusions as to what international law should be.

It now only remains to add a few observations concerning the plan of the present work. It is divided into five chapters or periods. The author has adopted this division for the purpose of making it correspond to the successive modifications of the law of maritime capture with reference to neutral commerce. In fact, the conduct of privateers and prize courts towards neutrals was not so uniform as towards enemies, but greatly varied under the influence of international policy. Thus, when belligerents had the ascendancy, or were allowed without opposition to pursue their selfish views, this legal piracy tended to increase; at other times, on the contrary, it was interfered with, or held in check by the coalition of neutral powers. As long as this conflict lasted, the parties were seldom inclined to adopt a general rule (mutuo consensu), or to come to an equitable arrangement; each of them had its temporary triumphs and defeats, the effects of which prevented the natural growth of milder customs in maritime warfare. However that may be, these periodical revolutions and re-actions have afforded some kind of data for prize law; the author has tried to record them faithfully in this treatise.

In order to enable the reader to catch the distinctive features of the principal historical epochs, it will not be out of place to give a short summary of the work.

1. The first period, beginning with the Middle Ages, terminates with the 16th century. Neutral commerce had not then attained any great proportions, and was left to the mercy of belligerents by the Consolato del Mare. The more important facts to be observed relate to the origin of privateering, which first showed itself in the south of Europe at the close of the 14th century, and, although in the course of 200 years it extensively prevailed, it was, even to the end of that period, chiefly directed against the enemy.

2. The second period was replete with innovations. A

great impulse was given to them in some countries of Europe by the establishment of a regular navy, and by the decrees of belligerents abrogating or modifying the rules of the Consolato del Mare, whilst, on the other hand, neutral commerce about that time very considerably extended its operations. Under these circumstances it became necessary to devise new principles of public law, for securing the free intercourse of nations in maritime war. But all the efforts of the statesmen of the 18th century, for reconciling the interests of belligerents and neutrals, seem to have been tried in vain. In pursuing their own selfish or contradictory policy, governments were not yet prepared to concede equal rights to each other. Holland only succeeded in protecting her merchant ships from capture, by the grant of privileges from, or entering into treaty with, other powers, whilst the efforts of Sweden and Denmark for the like purposes were ineffectual. At the close of this period the principal powers of Europe adopted the immunity of enemy's cargo on board neutral ships; at least such a rule of reciprocity was established between England, Holland and France. The treaty of Utrecht contains also some few provisions against the violence of privateers and the abuses of power in prize courts.

3. The results obtained for international law in the course of the next eighty years (1713—93) were of greater importance. The principal event of that period is the celebrated coalition for the purpose of protecting universal commerce against belligerents, formed by Russia under the name of "the armed neutrality." This great league was first formed in 1780, and being supported by public opinion was effectual in mitigating the cruelty of the American war, while at the same time new principles of a general maritime code were introduced, and partially enforced. Their final adoption, however, was unfortunately frustrated by the opposition of England, and the breaking out of the French Revolution.

4. This short period (1793—1815) may be termed re-actionary, owing to the great political convulsions of Europe. During that eventful time the barbarous customs of the

Middle Ages were revived, and international law seemed to be disregarded or superseded by arbitrary power. The contest between England and France at length assumed so violent a character that they did not hesitate to destroy neutral rights, by prohibiting to all nations intercourse with the enemy. The commercial inquisition established by Napoleon, under the name of the "continental system," was maintained with unabated rigour. England opposed it with the doctrine of "paper blockade" and general reprisals. This unnatural condition of society of course could not long continue, and having brought on a general European war terminated in the fall of the French empire.

5. With the Congress of Vienna came the period of repose. It might then have been reasonably expected that the leading powers of the coalition against France would have directed the attention of the Congress to maritime international law, but this was not the case. The question of neutral rights, which had already occasioned so much violence and bloodshed in former times, was once more postponed and left to uncertain futurity. Happily, notwithstanding that omission, the principles of the armed neutrality almost spontaneously revived, for subsequent treaties, and the very decrees of belligerents, seem constantly to prove this; while, at the same time, privateering as well as the rules of the Consolato del Mare were abandoned. But the most interesting feature of this period is, its tendency to diminish the number of captures. Here we discover the indications of a most important improvement in international law, which we may hope will be completed in the course of the present or next generation.

After having given this summary of the work, the author begs to state that he has endeavoured to make the subject intelligible to the general reader. In his opinion, international questions do not belong to the exclusive domain of lawyers, but ought to be understood by society at large, whose interests consist in forming an independent judgment of their own affairs. It is true that jurisprudence has its niceties and technicalities, but it depends very much on its professors to explain their meaning by the use of clear and intelligible terms. Having done his utmost to accomplish this, the author cannot but regret that his work necessarily abounds with references. The subject being by its very nature rather intricate, it was impossible to omit the consideration of its disputed points. A detailed account, however, of all the historical facts and documents relative to neutral rights would have made the work too voluminous. The author has adopted an intermediate course, and only introduced into the text the principal results of his inquiry, inserting in the notes references to documents and matters of controversy.

Kharhov, $\frac{12}{24}$ *Nov.* 1866.

PERIOD I.

From the Twelfth to the End of the Sixteenth Century.

European society, as established under the feudal system, hardly imposed any restraint upon the violence of individuals. Every free man at that time claimed the right to redress his own wrongs, the law never interfering between contending parties. Governments, imperfectly established, were too weak to repress internal feuds, and seemed ready to dissolve into general anarchy. Nothing but the moral influence of the Church, and the feelings inspired by chivalry, checked the rapacity of the upper classes and alleviated the sufferings of the lower. Whilst political communities were in such a chaotic state, international relations were very limited. Even in the time of peace the condition of a stranger in a foreign land was very precarious: he was almost unprotected in his person and property. Every individual assumed the right, on the merest pretext of injury, "currere super malefactorem, donec plenarie fuerit emendatum." In these troublous ages, however, continued peace was a rare phenomenon, and war scarcely ever ceased. In the absence of a standing army, recourse was had to mercenary troops, feudal militia and untrained masses. Disregarding discipline, insensible of the advantages of union by the appointment of a commander-in-chief, belligerents gave full freedom to every individual to fall on the enemy (courir sûs aux ennemis) and to plunder him without mercy.

Several centuries elapsed before governments, by the repression of anarchy, became independent political bodies. The gradual decline of the feudal system introduced a new order of things into Western Europe: supreme power obtained the ascendancy over private individuals; militia and condottieri were superseded by standing armies, and international relations assumed a more regular shape.

Governments, having established their power on land, met with more difficulty in repressing anarchy and in maintaining the authority of law at sea. During the prevalence of feudal disorders, piracy was carried on by companies, and increased to a great extent. Finding that society cast no reproach upon this occupation, but considered it honourable, the members of these associations were prepared rather to die than relinquish their pursuit. The bold piratical chiefs spread terror on the coasts and in the adjacent towns. Powerful sovereigns dared not attempt to extirpate them, and were satisfied if they could only repel their fierce attacks. The energetic protests of the Catholic Church, the coalitions of the Italian republics and of the Hanseatic Towns were equally unsuccessful against piracy (*a*). Governments, having no efficient navy of their own, could not afford protection to the navigation and commerce of their subjects, and the greatest violence pervaded every sea. Each individual was his own legislator and judge in all questions relating to prize law, levying war or remaining at peace as best suited his purposes.

As long as this state of things continued, merchants dared not singly undertake distant voyages, but generally formed societies for mutual protection, and, selecting a commander, bestowed upon him full power to decide any disputes which might arise among themselves (*b*). They soon naturally

(*a*) In Italy, although temporary coalitions against pirates occur very often, yet commercial rivalry and continual wars between republics were so favourable to piratical societies, that in the very middle of the 13th century they established themselves even in the immediate vicinity of Venice, on the shores of Dalmatia. *Dumont*, i. 1, 209; *Raumer*, Hohenst. v. 406 (1 Ausg.). The attempts of the Hanse to suppress pirates in the Baltic and German seas were repeated with greater energy. See *Sartorius*, Urkundliche Geschichte des Ursprungs der Hansa, herausg. von Lappenberg, 1830, ii. 174, 186, 238, 247, 329, 330, 359, 375, 480. However, neither the Italian republics nor the Hanse towns succeeded in obtaining their object.

(*b*) These voyages were called in the Middle Ages *safety voyages* (Voyages de conserve); we meet with mention of them in the 6th century. *Pardessus*,

ceased to confine themselves to defensive measures, and became aggressors; they undertook, also, expeditions for the special purpose of repressing piracy (*c*). The desire of plunder, and the passion for adventure, induced many enterprising men to devote their lives to this exciting pursuit; but traversing every sea without the restraint of law, they in their turn, as if by a sort of infection, acquired habits of plunder, became dangerous to the public peace, and turned their arms even against their own countrymen.

Such was the insecurity of navigation during the time of peace. In maritime war, according to the custom of the Middle Ages, as we have said, every individual might fit out ships against the enemy (faire la course), capture prizes and dispose of them at his pleasure. Governments not only did not prevent, but encouraged these practices, because, in the absence of a regular navy, they were obliged at the commencement of war to provide themselves with ships, either bought or hired of private individuals. These *corsairs* or freebooters, being the chief instruments of war and totally independent of the maritime authorities, could scarcely be distinguished from piratical bands (*d*). The annals of the

Collection des Lois Maritimes, ii. cxxii. Beginning with the 11th and 12th centuries, they came into general use, as is seen in maritime laws. See *Pardessus*, Collection, i. 141, 222; ii. 98; iii. 21, 192, 304.

(*c*) In "*Saxo Grammaticus*" we meet with a curious account of one of these companies, founded in the 12th century at Roskilde, for the purpose of carrying on war with pirates. Eo tempore propter incursus, qui a maritimis crebri prædonibus edebantur, apud Roskildiam, Wethemanno auctore, piratica cœpit, cujus hæc disciplina, hi mores fuere. Navigia piratæ magis idonea sibi visa absque possessoris permissu assumendi potestatem habebant, octavâ acquisitorum parte naulum daturi . . . . Crebrum iis cum hoste certamen, sed ubique facilis ac pæne incruenta victoria fuit. Prædam ex equo partiebantur, nec major gubernatoribus portio, quam privati remigis erat . . . . . Stipendiis defecti, impensas a civibus contrahebant, præmii loco prædæ dimidium recepturis. Hic piraticæ cultus, ut dixi, Roskildiæ cœptus ab urbis gremio etiam ad agrestes manavit, ab omni fere Scandinaviæ parte subsidia mutuatus. Enim vero angustus primum et tenuis magna brevi incrementa contraxit. Sed neque ante redditam terris pacem ulla ex parte remissior fuit. Sax. Gram. Hist. ed. Muller, 1839, ii. 687.

(*d*) The treaties and laws of the Middle Ages called them by the same name by which they designated sea-robbers: "Piratæ, prædones, corsarii, qui

12th and 13th centuries abound with accounts of the daring deeds in war of these enterprising men. They undertook expeditions, and made descents on the coasts, setting fire to the towns. It was not to be expected that corsairs would observe treaties or pay regard to allies; they attacked the first ship they met with, threw the crew overboard, and carried off the cargo (*e*). The belligerents, impelled by a desire to prohibit all commerce with the enemy, sanctioned these proceedings (*f*). In the Consolato del Mare, a collection of maritime customs compiled during the Middle Ages, we see reflected the anarchical mode of carrying on warfare. The corsairs were released from all responsibility; the right of plunder was left to the discretion of their commander. Having fallen in with an enemy's ship, every one knew what to do with it; hence, in such a case, it was useless to prescribe laws. But being less able to restrain the cruelty of the belligerents, the Consolato endeavoured at least to save neutral property from corsairs, and for this purpose laid down the following rules:—

1. If a captured ship belonged to friends, but the cargo was the property of the enemy, the merchant was bound to deliver up to the commander the enemy's goods, or forward them according to his order to a place of safety. The commander, however, paid him the freight, according to the register, the evidence of the crew, or the market price.

2. If the owners of the ship asserted that the goods were

piraticam exercent, &c." *Robinson*, Collectanea Maritima (Lond. 1801), p. 22, not.; *Ducange*, Glossarium Latinitatis, voce corsarius, pirata.

(*e*) *Matth. Par.* a. 1242, 1254, 1264. In illo tempore non erat rex, neque lex nautis posita, sed quod quisque rapere vel ferre valebat, hoc suum esse dicebat. *Pardessus*, Coll. 4, 195. Almost all the nations of Western Europe made use of corsairs in the time of naval wars, as is seen in the annals of the Middle Ages. *Pardessus*, Coll. ii. xlv, xlix, cxx; iii. lxxxi, 12; v. 393; *Sartorius*, Urk. Gesch. i. 274, note 1.

(*f*) *Reddie*, Historical and Critical Researches (Lond. 1844-5), i. 167. Thus at the time of the war between England and Spain, 1294, the Portuguese were forbidden to lade Spanish goods on board their ships. *Rymer*, ii. 632. See also *Robinson*, 159. Generally speaking, very few treaties permit neutral trade.

(21)

their own property, the commander had to refer to the register, and, in the absence of any register, to the testimony of the crew on oath, and, if satisfied, to restore the cargo.

3. If the whole or greater part of the cargo belonged to the enemy, and the person in command of the captured ship refused to convey it to a place of safety, the commander of the corsair might sink the ship, being only bound to save the crew. The law in this case wholly disregarded the complaints of the party whose property had been seized.

4. If a captured ship belonged to an enemy, but the cargo to neutrals, the latter could ransom the ship from the corsair, but failing to do so, the corsair not only was empowered to seize his lawful prize, but was also entitled to freight for the conveyance of the goods, and was freed from all responsibility to the neutrals for any damage their goods might sustain, as this was owing to their unwillingness to enter into an arrangement and pay the sum demanded by the corsair (*g*).

In this manner did this celebrated compilation define the mutual rights of belligerents and neutrals. If the above cited principles be carefully and impartially analyzed, it cannot be denied that the Consolato makes a vigorous effort to establish order at sea, and that the idea of neutrality is more clearly expressed in it, than in any other legislative document of that period; but, on the other hand, it is difficult to concur in opinion with the English jurists, who find in these laws immutable principles of neutrality. The Consolato, as we see, subjects neutrals to the authority of the commander of the corsairs, and, while admonishing him not to behave towards them in a proud or arrogant manner, at the same time releases him from surveillance of any kind. We search here in vain for any traces of regular prize jurisprudence. The corsair is considered as an irresponsible organ of the belligerent party, and the final acquisition of property in captures depends only on his bringing in the ship safely to some port of his own country. To speak more accurately, according to the rules

(*g*) *Consolato del Mare*, ch. 158—9, 231 (*Pardessus*), iv. 208, 303. See *Wheaton*, Histoire, i. 72—78. (2me Ed. Leipz. 1846.)

of the Consolato, the chief commander of the corsairs, or the admiral, was the prize judge. He decided the fate of the ship, and from his decision there was no appeal. Nay, further, when a ship was sent out armed, the authorities of the coast did not interfere in the expedition (*h*). It is evident, therefore, that the Consolato del Mare gives to the commander of the corsairs a decided advantage over the neutral merchant, and leaves international commerce very inadequately protected. The inefficiency of these rules of the Consolato is attested by historical facts; that compilation, as Pardessus proves (*i*), being the product of the autonomy or self-legislation of the Middle Ages, but not of political authority. It served only as a guide for settling disputes amongst merchants, and principally contains the customs of private commercial confederacies. With respect to the few provisions which touch upon international relations, they were only applicable so long as maritime wars retained their savage and irregular character, whilst neutrals were ignorant of their respective rights and unable to defend themselves against belligerents.

Society continued in this disordered state for many ages. Constituted authority, being insufficient to repress the anarchy at once, proceeded with caution, indirectly but continuously. First of all it was necessary to put an end to *private feuds*, as they caused considerable disturbance to international tranquillity; therefore, in the 13th century, governments found it necessary, when entering upon treaties of peace, to appoint from each contracting party special mediators (conservatores pacis), to whom they referred mutual complaints and the decision of their differences. The injured party was only entitled

(*h*) *Consolato*, ch. 245 (*Pardessus*, ii. 340-1). The so-called *bons homens* (prud' hommes), to whom the Consolato advises application to be made *in order not to sin before God and man*, cannot be considered as prize courts in our sense of the word; they serve only as mediators between seamen and determine the rewards to be paid for the rescue of ships from the hands of the enemy. *Pardessus*, ii. 339.

(*i*) See the introduction to the 2nd volume of the Collection of Maritime Laws.

(23)

to redress his own wrongs, when justice was denied him, or when the other state rejected the decision of the arbitrators. In these cases private persons obtained special patents (lettres de marque ou de représailles), which were granted in the 14th century by local authority, and in the 15th century by the supreme government (*k*). Having enforced the observance of treaties of peace, governments began to exert themselves for the establishment of order, even during war. Corsairs, however, taking advantage of their independence, were unwilling to submit to these regulations; they did not always distinguish between friends and foes, and became more and more dangerous to the peace of the world. Incessant complaints were made against them, not only by neutral merchants, but by their own fellow citizens. To satisfy the injured and to pursue the guilty was a matter of difficulty, as long as each subject might with impunity arm vessels and make prizes (*l*). This was the reason why governments found it necessary to put a restraint upon the independence of corsairs, and to subject them to supervision. In fact, by the end of the Middle Ages the authority of the royal admiral was extended over every vessel, and in maritime towns prize courts were established. This remarkable improvement in the customs of maritime warfare was made in some states earlier, in others later. We consider it necessary to trace it in the history of Europe (*m*), and will endeavour to do so as far as our materials will admit. Unfortunately the origin of privateering is still obscure; the documents relating to it are dispersed in the archives of different states.

(*k*) For the details see *Martens*, Essai, sect. 4; *Kaltenborn*, Geschichte der Kaperei (Bülau, Jahrbücher, 1849, s. 104); *Pütter*, Beitrage, 151; *Wheaton*, Histoire, i. 82, 83. In England, as appears from acts of parliament, even in the year 1353, letters of marque were granted by the king; on the contrary, in France this reform was not entirely completed before the year 1485.

(*l*) *Dumont*, i. ii, 63, 95; *Pardessus*, Coll. v. 468, note.

(*m*) The origin of privateering has been generally little investigated. *Martens* expounds it very briefly, Essai, § 5, 6; *Kaltenborn* adds nothing to the researches made by *Martens*. Taking advantage of the documents which a e published by *Raumer*, *Robinson*, and *Sartorius*, we have endeavoured to clear up the question to a certain extent.

(24)

The first instances of privateering are observable in the countries bordering on the Mediterranean. We see that in the year 1288, the king Alphonso III. directed the maritime cities to take security from the corsairs, that they would not plunder their fellow countrymen, and that they would not attack the enemy during the time of truce, or in a neutral port. It was also imposed as a duty upon every privateer to bring his prizes to the port from which he had sailed. If it appeared that the ship or cargo were captured illegally, the court was bound to restore them to the former owners. The king forbade any functionary to take part in the armament of ships, or in the expeditions of privateers (*n*). In the 14th century, as is evident from documents still in existence, privateering had already attained in Arragon and Catalonia extensive proportions, and become the business of special companies. The government frequently supplied corsairs with ships, provisions, &c., and granted them various privileges, in return for which they were to bring into the treasury a certain per-centage of the prizes they made (*o*). On the other hand, the corsairs, who fitted out ships on their own account, were left in full possession of their captures (*p*), and were not

(*n*) The statute of Alphonso III. is the oldest legal enactment respecting privateers; it is printed in *Pardessus* (Coll. v. 349). *Capmany* quotes also one document, from which it is evident that corsairs were bound to deliver to the king part of their booty, leaving them entirely independent in other respects. *Pardessus*, v. 395, n. 4.

(*o*) Some regulations of a similar kind are mentioned by *Capmany* and *Pardessus*. Amongst them are some remarkable privileges granted by Alphonso III. to a privateering company, established upon occasion of a war with the Genoese. The king granted to them ships, and only required that the privateers should not break the truce nor disturb neutral merchants. Retinemus tamen et inhibemus expresse firmiterque præcipimus ne personis, terris aut bonis quibuscunque aut quorumcunque, qui in pace vel in treugâ nobiscum fuerint . . . aliquod damnum, offensa &c. quomodo libet inferantur. *Pardessus*, v. 303.

(*p*) The compilation of customs, according to which prizes were divided, has reached us as a supplement to the Consolato, and contains thirty-seven chapters. According to the opinion of *Pardessus* it was made in the beginning of the 14th century. Before his time it was considered to be an integral part of the Consolato, but *Pardessus* has proved that it was inserted here

subjected to the interference of government until the year 1356 (*q*).

About the same time privateers appear in the Italian cities, first at Pisa in the year 1298, then at Genoa 1316, and at last at Sassari in the year 1319 (*r*). The government placed them under the control of the municipal authorities. However in the kingdom of the Two Sicilies, privateers formed a separate corporation with a president at their head (1399). They deposited with him as security, "de non offendendo fideles, truegatos et amicos," a certain sum of money, and were bound to give him a per-centage upon their captures. Prize causes were directed to be decided under the supreme authority of the admiral in a special court formed of a vice-admiral, assessors and notaries (*s*).

In the course of the 14th century almost all the states of Southern Europe endeavoured to suppress anarchy in maritime warfare, and for that purpose deprived corsairs of their former independence; the same improvements were gradually introduced on the coasts of the North and Baltic seas, notwithstanding the anarchy which prevailed there, and the obstinacy with which corsairs, availing themselves of the dissensions between neighbouring countries, defended that independence. The first attempt to check them is noticed in Flanders, at the beginning of the war with the Frisians (1327—1347). Each privateer was required to have a commission and to acknowledge the authority of the admiral; to

by accident, and has not any direct connection with this remarkable document of maritime jurisprudence. *Pardessus*, v. 396—432.

(*q*) This is evident from the decrees of Peter III., king of Arragon (*Pardessus*, v. 465—472), according to which all privateers were bound to give security and to pledge themselves by oath to observe the law.

(*r*) The ordinances on privateers issued by these cities are almost exactly alike (see them in *Pardessus*, iv. 440, 586; v. 282). The decree of Pisa for the first time requires patents or charters (breve curiæ maris).

(*s*) *Pardessus*, v. 257. The law does not say by what rules they ought to be guided. Probably about the same time were published in Venice the first ordinances about privateering and prize jurisdiction, but I have not had an opportunity of meeting with them in any collection of maritime laws accessible to me.

whom neutral merchants might address their complaints (t). But it is probable that these laws were for a time without much effect.

Nowhere did private maritime war prevail to such an extent as between England and France. The perpetual rivalry of these nations, and the feudal dissensions of the time, afforded the corsairs full scope for their operations. They dispersed themselves along all the neighbouring coasts, and, regardless of truces, carried on unceasing depredation. The commerce of the Hanse Towns suffered particularly at their hands. As long as each vassal of note had his fleet, his "custodes maritimos," the government could not put a stop to violence at sea and protect merchants. It was only in the year 1373 that the French king, Charles V., created an admiral for the whole kingdom, and reserved for his decision all prize cases. The admiral was bound to grant to the privateers letters of marque, and to administer to them an oath for the observance of the law. Besides this, they were forbidden to dispose at their own pleasure of their captures, but it was enjoined on them to bring in untouched (avant que nulle chose se descende) every prize, in order that an investigation might be made whether it was really taken from the enemy (*u*). Severe punishments were ordained for concealment of a prize, and for plundering or ill-treating a neutral crew. In case of unjust seizure compensation was awarded.

(*t*) The documents referring to the history of privateering in Flanders are met with in the collection of *Schwartzenberg*, Groot Placcat and Charter Bœk Van Vriesland, Leenwarden, 1769, pp. 180, 203, 261—9, 318, 351. See also *Wurm* on "Maritime Prizes" in the Staatslexicon, xiii. 139 (2 Ausg. Altona, 1843).

(*u*) Et par bonne et meure deliberation il regardera par la conscience ou contention les depositions d'iceux preneurs ainsi faite en secret, ou par la veue des dites prinses, s'il y a vraie apparence qu'elles fuissent de nos ennemis. At all events the admiral was bound to deliver the prize to the privateers after the inventory was made, in case of the appearance to the suit of the neutral merchant; this ordonnance was by mistake formerly referred to the year 1400, that is, to the time of the reign of Charles VI. (*Robinson*, Coll. Mar. p. 75; *Martens*, Essai, p. 33), but *Pardessus* has undoubtedly proved that it was issued by Charles V. Coll. iv. 224.

But before the 15th century there was hardly any active surveillance over privateers, except that of the "conservatores pacis" (*v*). In the year 1426, Henry VI. transferred to the privy council, the chancellor and admiral, or his lieutenant, the prize jurisdiction (*x*).

The Hanse Towns did not so soon succeed in putting an end to the independence of corsairs, although in the middle of the 14th century (1362—64), by the recesses or ordonnances of the confederation, it was ordained, that, in consequence of a war with Denmark, letters patent should be delivered to each privateer, and a sum of money required from him as security or bail, yet these arrangements did not effect their purpose (*y*). In the year 1377, there appeared in the Baltic sea a piratical company of a formidable description, to the great detriment of commerce. Instead of directing all their forces against these freebooters, Rostok and Wismar, having taken part in the war between Margaret

(*v*) See for example the truce between England and Brittany in the year 1413, and the acts of parliament in the year 1414. *Dumont*, ii. 234; *Martens*, Essai, p. 33, 34.

(*x*) *Robinson*, Coll. Mar. 95, not. However, in the opinion of some English jurists (see *Pritchard's* Admiralty Digest, pref. vi, vii, Lond. 1847), there existed in the time of Edward III. an admiralty court for the determination of maritime causes. *Pardessus* refers its foundation to the time of Edward I. (Coll. iv. 195). It cannot, indeed, be historically proved that this court had jurisdiction over privateers. The royal admiral, as is seen from the old collection of English customs (the Black Book of the Admiralty), divided the prizes only among ships of war.

(*y*) Recesses of the Hanse Towns, 1362-63-64, are inserted in *Sartorius* (Urk. Gesch. des Urspr. der Hansa, ii. 503, 533, 542), of which the last is particularly remarkable. "Item concordatum est, quod quicunque voluerit velificare *sub eventu proprio* ad invadendum hostiliter regnum Daciæ, ille si habuerit tanta bona immobilia in civitate, ex cujus portu velificare voluerit, dicere debet hoc coram consilio hujusmodi civitatis, quod amicis non debet inferre nocumenta, sed solum inimicis; extunc dabuntur sibi *literæ apertæ* illius civitatis, quod fecerit hujusmodi certificationem bonis suis et quod promoveatur et non impediatur in quemcunque etiam portum cujuscunque civitatis ipsum contingat pervenire; si autem non habuerit bona tanti valoris, ponet fidejussores, quod si dampna per eum alicui mercatori amico inferrentur, quod refundi debent per eundem, vel fidejussores, aut bona sua." Besides this, privateers were forbidden to supply the enemy with arms and provisions.

and Albert of Mecklenburgh, pretender to the Swedish throne, opened their ports to them, gave them commissions (Raubbriefe, Stehlbriefe), and employed them against Denmark and Norway. Afterwards, when Margaret besieged Stockholm, the pirates were enjoined to furnish her army with provisions; hence they received the appellation of Vitalien (Victualien) Brüder. These plunderers made no distinction between friends and foes, but attacked indiscriminately every merchant ship, and declared war against all the commercial world (*z*). The Hanse Towns soon saw their mistake, but it was too late to rectify it. The number of the piratical ships increased every year, and the whole of the squadrons were directed against the inhabitants of the sea coasts of Lapland, Esthonia, Prussia, and Pomerania. Their place of rendezvous was Gothland, where they brought their captures. Neutral merchants, after sustaining great losses, sought satisfaction, but their demands and complaints were disregarded. The Hanse Towns themselves were obliged to discontinue their foreign trade. At last, in the year 1395, the governments on the coast of the Baltic concluded peace, and agreed to act with united forces against the pirates. Unhappily the dissensions and rivalry of the confederation soon checked their progress. The pirates, escaping from one place to another, at the first news of war hastened to offer their services to either of the belligerent parties. In order entirely to get rid of these corsairs, the Grand Master of the German order of chivalry even undertook an expedition against Gothland (1397). The greater part of the pirates escaped from him, and retired to the coast of the German ocean. From that time Eastern Friesland became their haunt, that same territory which, at the end of the 14th and beginning of the 15th century, was the theatre of cruel wars between the owners of the coast. In the year 1416, the Vitalien Brüder re-appeared in the Baltic, and took part in the war between the Duke of Schleswig and the Danish king

(*z*) They also called themselves the friends of God and enemies of all the world; "Gottes Freunde und aller Welt Feinde."

Eric VII. In 1426, they received commissions from the Hanse Towns themselves, which up to this time had endeavoured to suppress them; and only seven years later (1433), after an obstinate struggle with almost all the states of the Baltic coast, they disappeared altogether (*a*).

At a much later period decrees respecting privateers were published in the Netherlands. Here, apparently, the corsairs retained their independence up to the time of Maximilian, who in 1487 established an admiralty, and forbade that any ships should be fitted out by individuals without the sanction of government. This statute was confirmed by Charles V., with some additional articles (*b*).

In this way, at the close of the 15th century, maritime wars gradually assumed in Europe a different phase. Instead of independent corsairs, we find privateers established under the authority of government, and controlled by prize courts appointed for that purpose. In order to give the last blow to anarchy, governments introduced into treaties of peace and commerce the following rules:—1st. That every armed ship, prior to sailing, should deposit, as security for good behaviour, a certain sum of money. 2nd. That privateers should be bound always to bring their prizes into the port whence they had sailed. 3rd. That no one should deal with a capture or treat it as a legal prize, until it had been declared to be such by a judicial sentence (*c*). Since that time all prize causes have been regularly adjudged in the admiralty court, now the "forum competens" for neutrals. Independent nations, however, did not submit unconditionally to this jurisdiction of the

(*a*) A curious account of this savage horde may be found in the historical almanack of *Raumer* (1841, s. 1—159). Their internal organization is little known to us; we only know that the Vitalien Brüder divided their prizes into equal shares, whence their name *Liekendeler* (Gleichtheiler) is derived.

(*b*) *Pardessus*, p. 18; *Pardessus*, Coll. iv. 13, 14; *Wheaton's* Histoire, i. 77. In the decrees of Charles V., 1549, privateers were for the first time forbidden to take commissions from both belligerent powers: for later regulations see *Martens*, Essai, s. 14.

(*c*) See *Dumont's* Coll. vols. 3 & 4. All these treaties agree in fundamental principles, and are directed to the putting an end to plunder and the checking of violent conduct at sea.

(30)

belligerent parties. Already, at the end of the 15th century, we find clauses in treaties, in which neutral governments adopt measures for the protection of their subjects against partiality in prize judges, and make provision against procrastination in the conduct of the suit (*d*). The behaviour of privateers with regard to neutrals was also more strictly regulated and the definition of war contraband was more clearly laid down. Instead of the arbitrary search of the ship, a statement on oath of the master and crew, or a verbal declaration of the ownership of the cargo, was received; for this, from the 16th century, was substituted an inspection of the ship's papers (*e*). The Hanse Towns demanded still greater privileges for their commerce from belligerents; they were the zealous defenders of the freedom of the neutral flag and cargo, and during the height of their power succeeded in securing it by supplying their merchants with convoys (*f*). But in the year 1497, when their power declined, these privileges were set aside. The belligerents continued to follow the principles of the Consolato del Mare with regard to enemy's cargo on board neutral ships; some even declared as legal prize neutral goods on board enemy ships.

(*d*) As far as we know, France and England directed their attention to this subject before any other nation of Europe. The treaty concluded between Charles VIII. and Henry the VI. (*Dumont*, iii. 2, 376; *Robinson*, Coll. 83) requires prize courts to decide cases within the term of one year, "tam super damnis et spoliationibus, quam interesse partium." The injured party was entitled to appeal to the Privy Council (ad supremum concilium Principis), which also revised the case in the course of six months. Before appeal a certain sum should be deposited on both sides as security for costs. These rules (salubria statuta) were confirmed in the treaties between England and France in the years 1498, 1515 and 1518, which prescribe in general the manner of conducting prize cases "summarie et sine strepitu et figurà judicii" (*Dumont*, iii. 2, 401; iv. 1, 204, 280). In *Dumont* is also inserted a privilege of the same kind granted by Charles VIII. in 1489 to the Hause Towns (iii. 2, 240).

(*e*) *Wheaton*, Hist. i. 87—89; *Robinson*, Coll. Marit. 1—29.

(*f*) At the time, however, of their own wars the Hanseatic league by no means followed this liberal policy, but on the contrary endeavoured to throw impediments in the way of neutral commerce and to extend the catalogue of war contraband. *Sartorius*, Gesch. des Hanseatischer Bundes, ii. 661—663; iii. 507—510.

(31)

Up to the end of the 16th century, these measures generally adopted in Europe against piracy appeared sufficient for its suppression in time of war. The idea of neutrality was but imperfectly understood and hardly recognised in public opinion. Neutral commerce had not, as yet, excited such general interest, or given occasion to such disputes amongst nations, as it has done since; with the exception of the Hanseatic towns it was nowhere very extensive. Privateers, being the chief if not the only organs of war, directed their efforts principally against the enemy.

PERIOD II.

From the End of the Sixteenth Century to the Peace of Utrecht (1713).

Towards the close of the 16th and beginning of the 17th century a gradual change took place in maritime warfare. With the establishment of fleets on an extended scale privateers no longer served as necessary auxiliaries in naval operations. They would, indeed, have lost their former importance, had not a new and fertile source of gain opened before them; in short, they began to direct their attacks against neutral commerce, which had now attained larger proportions.

Under the influence of mercantile jealousy, governments encouraged by every means in their power expeditions against foreign merchants, and promised, as a reward to the privateer, not only all the property of the enemy he could seize, but in many instances even neutral ships and goods. Hence in almost all the countries of Europe, a more or less intricate system of prize procedure prevailed, and maritime warfare, in which belligerents alone were formerly concerned, produced consequences injurious to the commerce of the world at large. Privateers penetrated into the most distant seas, and everywhere interrupted navigation, whilst Admiralty Courts condemned ships and cargoes, under pretext of the most trifling breach of the decrees of the belligerents. In order to protect themselves from such violent and arbitrary attacks, neutral states were forced into a struggle with the maritime powers, which was the more difficult for them owing to their weakness and want of union. However, at the end of this period, they succeeded in modifying some of the severities of the prize procedure, and in introducing into it new principles. The freedom of the neutral flag was thus acknowledged in almost all the treaties of the 17th century, and confirmed by the principal European powers in those of Utrecht.

The celebrated contest beween the Netherlands and Spain opens a new period in the history of privateering. This contest deserves our attention for the following reasons: 1. From this time the belligerents renounced the observance of the Consolato del Mare, and began to issue arbitrary decrees against neutrals. 2. The number of privateers sensibly increased to the detriment of general commerce.

As soon as the rupture between Philip II. and the rebellious provinces commenced, there appeared in Holland a band of privateers known by the name of "Gueux de la mer," who, under the influence of patriotic motives, armed small vessels on their own account, and fitted out expeditions against the Spaniards. As the people of the Low Countries had scarcely any regular navy, and had to struggle with a power well supplied in that respect, William of Orange availed himself of the services of these men, and in 1562 gave them commissions to act as privateers. In fact they inflicted considerable injury upon the enemy, and captured many of his ships. This patriotic enthusiasm of the privateers, however, quickly evaporated and gave place to less generous motives. Having destroyed the Spanish trade, they began to attack, without distinction, every one they met with, and consequently soon degenerated into pirates (*a*). Instead of adopting any energetic measures to meet this system of plunder, Holland by her severe decrees augmented the difficulties of European commerce. Thus by a proclamation of the 27th July, 1584, the States General forbade all nations to hold intercourse with Spain (*b*), and directed their Admiralty

(*a*) See Annals of *Hugo Grotius*, i. 2, An. 1571. William of Orange, however, had only a nominal authority over these men; their real commander was Count William de la Mark, a man, according to Grotius, of a savage character and totally devoid of merit.

(*b*) This proclamation is quoted by *Lamberty*, in his Memoirs (ix. 247), "que personne de quelque nation, qualité ou condition qu'il soit, conduise ou trans-

(34)

courts to condemn as lawful prize, not only the property of the enemy, but also neutral ships laden with Spanish goods. In vain England and the Hanseatic Towns protested against these arbitrary measures. Holland refused to make compensation (*c*) to the injured merchants, and had not the power to restrain the "Gueux," who continued their course of plunder almost to the end of the war, in spite of the hostilities which threatened them on all sides. The other belligerent powers issued decrees of equal severity. Thus England, as an ally of Holland, seized vessels bound to the enemy's port, laden with corn and provisions (*d*). Spain also declared it to be criminal to carry on commerce with her mutinous provinces. Hence the only means left to neutrals of protecting their subjects was to have recourse to reprisals.

From this time privateering became a regular institution in Western Europe, and having attained gigantic proportions was much favoured by the severe decrees against neutral commerce, which were generally issued at the breaking out of a maritime war. Thus we shall in vain look in these decrees for a just and accurate definition of the principles of neutrality, their object being to encourage privateers at the expense of neutral nations. Relying upon their physical strength, regardless of principle, and influenced by mere mercenary motives, belligerents considered only their own individual

porte à l'avenir de ce pays ou de l'Espagne *ou bien aussi des autres Royaumes et Etats*, soit directement vers l'ennemi, les villes, ports et places des Pays-Bas de sa domination, aucuns vivres, munitions de guerre ou *aucunes autres marchandises* et effets, de quelque sorte ou qualité qu'elles puissent être, sans exceptions ni reserve quelconque. *Robinson*, Collectanea, p. 160.

(*c*) Grotius himself declared in the Assembly of the States General, that the government was not bound to compensate neutrals for the violent conduct of privateers, which opinion was unanimously adopted.

(*d*) Order of Council, 1589 (*Robinson*, Collectanea Maritima, p. 136). In this same year about sixty vessels, laden with corn and belonging to the Hanseatic Towns, were seized. The diplomatic papers relating to this subject may be found in *Robinson*, see "Responsum Hamburgensibus datum," Collectanea Maritima (127—144). Queen Elizabeth afforded powerful protection to privateers. The well-known English commanders, Sir Francis Drake, Frobisher, and others, received from her, not only ships, but also subsidies in money. *Martens*, Essai, p. 63, note, § 16.

interest (*e*). Since the peace of Westphalia, the commercial policy of Holland afforded the only exception to this state of things. In order to prove this conclusively we will examine the prize practice of the principal European states.

1. *England.* The treaties relating to privateers and prize procedure which had been concluded between England and France at the end of the 15th century remained in force until the time of Elizabeth; and in addition to these, both sides, in questions relating to neutrality, referred to the Consolato del Mare. But already, at the end of the 16th century, as we have seen from the Order in Council of 1589 (note (*d*), p. 34), the English laws were directed to the extension of war contraband. Still more is this tendency to be noticed in the decrees of Charles I., 1625—6, whereby neutral ships with forbidden goods were considered lawful prize, not only when captured "flagrante delicto," but even on their return voyage from the enemy's port (*f*). Arbitrary rules about war contraband continued to be in force during the Commonwealth and after the Restoration (*g*). The procedure of the prize courts of Great Britain, however, until the end of the 17th century, presents no instances of such systematic malpractices as those which occurred after the peace of Utrecht. In the times of Charles II. and James II. there presided an admiralty judge, far in advance of the age in which he lived, *Sir Leoline Jenkins,* whose judgments were models of moderation and firmness, particularly as compared with those of some of his successors, for although his decisions have not come down to us in their original form, we can collect from his reports and letters to the king and the lords of the Admi-

(*e*) *Martens*, speaking of this period, makes the following just remark, "plus les besoins de la guerre étaient multipliés, plus le commerce fut étendu,—plus il semblait important d'empêcher, que celui des nations amies ne pût sous l'ombre de la neutralité servir à renforcer l'ennemi, ni même acquérir durant le cours de la guerre une prépondérance capable de l'emporter encore après le rétablissement de la paix." Essai sur les Armateurs, § 6, p. 37.

(*f*) *Robinson*, pp. 54—58.

(*g*) *Wildman*, Institutes of International Law, ii. 213. London, 1850.

ralty, that, in the solutions of questions between privateers and neutrals, he was guided not only by the laws of his country, but by the general principles of justice (*h*). He also, in his construction of treaties, strictly adhered to their literal meaning, while in the absence of treaties he followed custom, and in balancing evidence did not show any leaning towards privateers, but considered it his duty not to condemn any one in his absence, as "No man ought to be condemned unheard."

With respect to the neutral flag he followed the doctrine of the Consolato del Mare. The principal sources of English prize law at this time were "lex mercatoria," or maritime and commercial customs, their deficiencies being supplied by treaties and orders in council. From the foregoing materials Charles I. had contemplated the drawing up of a prize code, but this intention was never carried into effect (*i*). To the end of this period the judges adhered to custom, or to precedents. The prize act of Queen Anne, 1708, did not alter the former course of procedure; it related only to the distribution of prizes and to the rewards to be allowed to cruisers and privateers (*k*).

2. *Denmark,* like England, also published severe decrees on the subject of war contraband. In this respect the ordonnance of 1659, issued on occasion of the war with Sweden, is particularly worthy of attention: it prescribes to neutral

(*h*) The letters and reports of Jenkins were collected by Wynne in his Life of Sir Leoline Jenkins, vol. ii. 628—780. See *Reddie*, Researches, i. 170—176.

(*i*) See in *Robinson's* Coll. Marit. (pp. 64—74), the curious instructions of Charles I. 1626, to Carleton, Coke, Julius Cæsar and others, members of the prize court, "to consider of, inquire, discover and finde out all such doubtful causes as have or may happen about reprisals at sea," also to compare the laws of other nations, and to draw up rules for the prize court. The learned author, however, adds that he had been unable to find any report which had been made in compliance with the king's wishes.

(*k*) *Robinson*, Coll. 188—211. The details of English prize practice at this time contain little that is interesting with respect to international law, and are given in the works of Godolphin, Exton and Molloy. The Scotch practice was similar to that of England. *Reddie*, Researches, i. 178, 180.

(37)

nations the very form of the ship's papers, and not only forbids to supply the enemy with provisions, but declares as lawful prize goods intended for Swedish ports, as well as Swedish merchandise found on board neutral ships (*l*). At the time of the great Northern war, Denmark did not modify her arbitrary rules, but considered, as contraband of war, provisions, ship timber, &c., and ordered enemy cargo on board neutral ships to be captured (*m*).

3. *Holland* and *Spain*. When in the year 1621 the war was renewed between these two countries, harsh decrees against neutral merchants were again promulgated by both governments, and, as an instance of this, the edict of the States General, 1630, may be cited. This edict extended the definition of blockade, and increased the severity of the prize courts to such a degree that many European powers were obliged to put an end to their commercial intercourse with Belgium (*n*); but at the end of the war a change took place in the policy of the Low Countries. They became very zealous defenders of the liberal principles of neutrality; the former laws were abrogated, and, by the edict of 1652, privateers were ordered to deal with neutrals in conformity with existing treaties (*o*). Spain on the contrary retained her harsh ordinances respecting prize jurisdiction to the end of the 17th century.

4. The practice of the *Italian States*, according to Casaregis, was founded on the Consolato del Mare; enemy's property, on board a neutral ship, was reputed prize, but the

(*l*) *Robinson*, Coll. Marit. 176—187.

(*m*) *Martens*, Merkw. Fälle, ii. 168.

(*n*) *Robinson*, Coll. Marit. 158, 166. This edict was published on the occasion of the blockade of the ports of Flanders; it subjects to condemnation not only those ships which break the blockade, but also those whose destination was to a blockaded port, "quand même on ne les aurait rencontrez que bien loin encore de là, de sorte qu'ils pourraient encore changer de route et d'intention. Ceci étant fondé sur ce qu'ils ont déjà tenté quelque chose d'illicite et mis en œuvre.... Egress is also considered a breach of blockade, and subjects the vessels engaged in it to condemnation. English jurists generally cite this decree in justification of the harsh practices of their own country.

(*o*) *Dumont*, vi. 2—36.

(38)

capture was not subject to condemnation until it had been taken into a port of safety, and had been in the hands of the captors for the space of twenty-four hours, while goods on board an enemy's ship were reputed to be enemy's property until the contrary was proved (*o*).

5. *France,* from the middle of the 16th century has introduced principles of the most harsh and oppressive character. The Consolato del Mare, with all its severity, at least permitted neutrals to carry enemy's goods, and even allowed them freight. On the contrary the French ordonnances of 1543 and 1584 follow the rule, " La robe de l'ennemi confisque celle d'ami," and condemn both neutral ships with enemy cargo, as well as neutral cargo on board enemy's ships (*p*). In short, the very transport of the goods of an enemy was considered illegal. The object of France in publishing these decrees was a desire to encourage privateers and to punish neutrals for duplicity towards belligerents (*q*); but

(*o*) See *Casaregis,* Discursus legales de Commercio, 1737; *Reddie,* Researches, i. 224.

(*p*) Voulons et ordonnons, que si les navires des nos dits subjets sont en temps de guerre prises par mer d'aucuns navires appartenant à autres nos subjets ou à nos alliez, confederez ou amis, esquels y ait biens, marchandises ou gens de nos ennemis, ou bien aussi navires de nos dits ennemis, esquelles y ait personnes, marchandises, ou autres biens de nos dits subjets, confederez et alliez, *que le tout soit declaré de bonne prise,* et des à present comme pour lors avons ainsi declaré et declarons par ces presentes, *comme si le tout* appartenait *à nos dits ennemis. Pardessus,* Coll. iv. 295—324; *Robinson,* Coll. 105—126. With respect to neutral ships laden with contraband of war, in the edict of 1581, it is said: – Nous avons permis et permettons à nos dits subjets les prendre et emmener en nos ports et havres, et les dites munitions retenir selon l'estimation raisonnable, qui en sera faite par notre dit admiral. From these words Grotius (De Jure B. ac P. iii. 1, § 5, n. 6) concludes, that contraband of war was subjected not to condemnation, but to the right of pre-emption by the captor; but the French law was hardly so indulgent; it ordains that in case of dispute respecting munitions, between the royal admiral and the privateer, they should belong to the latter, but may be purchased by the government at a moderate price. Hence, it is evident that the right of pre-emption ("droit de pré-emption") here belongs to the government with reference to its own privateers, and not to privateers with reference to neutrals.

(*q*) Et pour ce que par cy-devant soubs couleur des pratiques et intelligences que ont aucuns de nos alliez et confederez avec nos ennemis, lorsqu'il y avait aucune prise faite sur mer par nos subjets, plusieurs procès se suscitoyent par

they provoked against her such remonstrances on the part of other nations, that in 1650 she was forced to abrogate them (*r*), and hence the prize practice became a little more lenient, retaining this character until 1681.

From this brief sketch of prize practice it appears that the belligerents by their regulations subjected neutral commerce to very various and arbitrary restraints, and even sometimes would not tolerate it at all. However, some jurists (Reddie, Robinson, &c.), desirous to give to the prize law historical importance and international authority, have endeavoured to prove that, throughout Europe, it had one common origin, the Consolato del Mare. Their opinion, however, can hardly be admitted to be correct, for in the Consolato, as we have seen, there is no trace of prize jurisdiction; it leaves to the cruiser himself the separation of the property of friends and foes, and does not at all relate to the questions of contraband of war and blockade. Consequently, the regulations of the 17th century could only have borrowed from it the rules concerning neutral flag and cargo; but these rules, as far as we can judge from edicts, were not fully acknowledged or strictly observed in all parts of Europe. Even England (*s*),

nos dits alliez, voulant dire que les biens, prins en guerre, leur appartiennent, soubs ombre de quelque part et portion qu'ils avaient avec nos dits ennemis, dont se sont ensuyes grosses condemnations à l'encontre; au moyen de quoi, iceux nos subjets ont depuis craint esquipper navires en guerre: nous pour remedier à telles fraudes, et afin que nos dits subjets reprennent leur courage, ordonnons, &c.

(*r*) Jenkins asserts that on the publication of the French ordonnances, many statesmen and jurists protested against them. Life of *Jenkins*, vol. ii. 720. In fact from the journals of Edward VI., published by Burnet in his History of the Reformation, it appears that England declined to acknowledge these unjust principles of neutrality. (*Robinson*, Coll. 105—107, note.) Holland even had recourse to reprisals, and compelled France to abandon these regulations and restore to the merchants their property. See the convention upon the subject between France and Holland. (*Dumont*, iv. 3, 3, 3.) Although, in one decision of the Parliament of Paris in 1592, it is said that the rule, "la robe de l'ennemi confisque celle d'ami," had not been applied in the case of any neutrals for the space of forty-nine years, yet both ordonnances were not formally annulled before the year 1650. *Robinson*, Coll. p. 119—121.

(*s*) Even in the 15th century England, particularly in her relations with smaller

the most zealous defender of this celebrated compilation, sometimes modified them by treaty; other belligerent powers also admitted with great reluctance the freedom of neutral goods on board an enemy's ship, which the Consolato insists upon. Even in cases in which this rule was strictly followed, the Admiralty courts showed a great leaning towards privateers; they eagerly sought after the cargo of an enemy, and seldom released that of friends. Lastly, the customs of the Middle Ages relating to prize had for neutrals this manifest inconvenience, that, upon the least suspicion, the privateer had a right to seize these ships, and to put a stop to their commerce. This is the reason why, with the extension of navigation and trade, these rules were modified by the mutual consent of belligerents and neutrals.

In fact, the 17th century abounds with treaties relating to privateers and Admiralty courts. The principal attention of the neutrals was, at this time, directed to the admission of the immunity of the flag by the introduction of the rule, "Le pavillon couvre la cargaison." In order to induce the belligerents to concede this point the neutrals gave up in return, as lawful prize to privateers, their own goods on board an enemy's ship ("le pavillon confisque la cargaison"). In this manner the old system of the Consolato lost its authority (*t*). It was very inconvenient and burdensome to commerce, and hampered the prize jurisdiction, whilst the new rule had a directly opposite effect. It got rid of innumerable difficulties arising in the courts about the property of the cargo, and

states, demanded a change in the principles of the Consolato, and adopted the rule that the flag does not protect the cargo but serves to condemn it.

(*t*) There are very few treaties which retain the system of the Consolato del Mare; to this class may be referred, chiefly, alliances and some commercial treaties, namely, that of Denmark with Spain, 1641 (*Dumont*, vi. 1, 209), and with England, 1670 (*Schmauss*, i. 952), those of Sweden with England, 1654—6 and 1670 (*Dumont*, vi. 2, 80, 125); the rest maintained the rule "le pavillon couvre la cargaison et la confisque." *Hautefeuille*, iii. 223, 230, &c. On the other hand, the full immunity of the neutral flag and cargo was admitted from the year 1604 in all capitulations with Turkey and her dependencies. See also the remarkable treaty of France with the Hanseatic Towns, 1655 (*Dumont*, vi. 2, 103).

(41)

directed the judge to inquire only about the nationality of the ship. Holland, being the principal commercial power, appeared as the most ardent defender of these liberal principles. Immediately on the termination of the war with Spain, she made it the main object of her policy to secure the immunity of the neutral flag; and, in the middle of the 17th century, succeeded in establishing it by treaty. It was, however, extremely difficult to induce France to acknowledge the rights of neutrality. Of all these powers, she was the last to concede these immunities, until at length Holland induced her to abrogate her decrees, and she then concluded some treaties in favour of the freedom of neutral commerce; yet these concessions must be looked upon as merely temporary (*u*). Taking advantage of his superiority on the continent and his naval forces, Louis XIV. in his ordonnance of 1681 again resorted to the rule " la robe de l'ennemi confisque celle d'ami." It is evident that hence a struggle between France and the neutral governments was inevitable; but, before we touch upon its results, we consider it necessary to examine here the principal features of this celebrated code, which contains some curious regulations concerning privateers and prize procedure (*x*).

In the ordonnance of Louis XIV. the duties of privateers are defined according to the former French laws. Every privateer is required to deposit with government, as a security, the sum of 15,000 livres, and bring his prize to a port of his native country. No one can dispose of a capture until it had been adjudged as lawful prize by a competent tribunal (*y*). However, in extreme cases, the ordonnance does

(*u*) How unwillingly France acknowledged the right of the neutral flag is evident from the report of the Dutch ambassadors. *Reddie*, Researches, i. 197.

(*x*) The laws respecting prize are included in the third book of the French code (Titre ix.) *Pardessus*, Coll. iv. 325—418; *Reddie*, Researches, 146—157.

(*y*) The code, however, of Louis XIV. permitted privateers, in conformity with the former ordonnances of the 16th century, to seize part of the goods on board a captured ship, which was called "le pillage." In the Middle Ages privateers, in conformity with this custom, robbed the crew of articles of dress and jewels,

not forbid to take ransom from an enemy's ship, and only requires that the papers and two of the officers of the liberated ship should be brought before the proper authorities (*z*). The code declares the possession of a prize for twenty-four hours sufficient to acquire the right of property in it. With respect to prize procedure, the ordonnance is founded upon former edicts, and particularly on that of 1584, which in many respects is the most favourable to privateers (*a*), and considers lawful prize ships laden with the goods of an enemy, as well as goods found on board an enemy's ship, without any exception. In vain courts of justice endeavoured to mitigate the severity of the code. By the edict of 1692, the king most positively commanded that it should be enforced, in all its severity, against neutrals. At the time of the war of the "Spanish succession," Louis XIV. published some additional decrees against neutral commerce. Thus, in 1704, the produce of an enemy's country, and manufactures of an enemy, were declared lawful prize in whatever ship they were found. In 1705, it was ordered that, however little ground

and divided them amongst themselves. Agreeably to the ordonnances of 1543 and 1584 pillage to the amount of 10 écus was allowed. A similar custom existed in England, but in 1661 it was subjected to limitations by act of parliament, and was entirely abolished at the end of the 17th century. *Robinson*, Coll. 192—3, not., and *Masse*, Cours du Droit commercial, Paris, 1844, i. 365.

(*z*) In the Middle Ages, as is evident from the Consolato del Mare, contracts of ransom of an enemy's ship were very common, and were permitted by law (*Pardessus*, ch. 158 - 9, 245, p. 208, 338); but afterwards, when governments forbade the arbitrary disposal of captures, ransom probably disappeared. *Martens'* Essai, 23, not. The ordonnance of Louis XIV. restored this practice, but in the 18th century it was altogether put an end to. *Martens*, loc. cit.

(*a*) The details of French prize practice may be found in *Valin's* Commentary on the Code, and in his Dissertation on Prizes. But the works of this author are not of much importance with respect to international jurisprudence, and chiefly relate to his country's laws. He considers the rule, "la robe de l'ennemi confisque celle d'ami," as an established principle of neutrality. In his opinion neutrals, who receive on board their ships the property of an enemy, or freight an enemy's ship with their own merchandise, act in opposition to treaties, and aid one belligerent power to the injury of the other. *Büsch*, Ueber das Bestreben der Völker einander in ihrem Seehandelrecht wehe zu thun. Hamb. 1800, p. 68.

(43)

the privateers had to arrest the ship, the neutral should be condemned to pay the costs of suit.

The tendency of the French regulations must have rendered the reign of Louis XIV. the golden age for legal piracy. Constant wars between naval powers afforded privateers rich booty. The king, on his part, liberally bestowed upon them rewards and privileges. Hence, from the middle of the 17th century to the peace of Utrecht, they abounded not only upon the shores of France, but extended even to the New World. Here, amongst the West India Islands, adventurers of different countries, under the name of Filibusters or Buccaneers, formed an independent society, which, between 1660—85, became an object of terror to every one engaged in the pursuits of navigation and commerce, and particularly to the Spaniards. The governors of the French colonies, instead of destroying this dangerous band, rather encouraged their system of plundering, and even granted them letters of marque without subjecting them to the usual restraints. The consequences of this policy were very serious, for the Filibusters turned their arms against the French themselves, and acquired sufficient power to be able to compete with the regular navy of France. The European governments at last determined to put down these pirates, and in 1712 finally destroyed them (*b*).

We will now return to the treaties. The more dangerous privateers were to neutral commerce, the more civilized nations exerted themselves to establish the immunity of the flag. Subsequently, Louis XIV. modified his harsh decrees, and, after having conceded some privileges to the principal maritime powers, sanctioned in the treaties of Utrecht, 1713, the rule " le pavillon couvre la cargaison et la confisque," at least with reference to England and the States General (*c*).

Thus was the question about flag and cargo settled, by

(*b*) To introduce here a detailed history of the Filibusters would exceed the limits of this work. For the particulars of their history see the important work of *Oxmelin*, Lond 1741.

(*c*) See treaties of Utrecht, in *Dumont*, viii. 1, 345, 409.

receding from the system of the Consolato del Mare, and abrogating the rule " la robe de l'ennemi confisque celle d'ami." The neutral nations, however, were far from having put a stop to all the malpractices of the belligerents. The abuses of the privateers always met with support and encouragement in the prize courts. In order, therefore, to secure the safety of the neutral merchant, it was necessary to reform entirely the prize procedure by putting an end to unnecessary delays, and reducing the legal expenses, &c. It was not, however, easy to carry out these improvements. The belligerents considered themselves quite independent, with reference to everything relating to the constitution of their own Admiralty Courts. In the 17th century, however, there ap-appeared a systematic tendency to lay down in treaties some rules for the determination of prize causes. The first attempts of this kind were made by England and France; for which purpose, in the year 1602, the two governments appointed special commissioners, who agreed that prize causes should be terminated in the course of six months; that the legal expenses should be reduced; that punishment should be inflicted on the privateers for cruelty; that they should be required to give bail and security; that the neutral merchant should be compensated for his goods pre-empted by one of the belligerents; and, generally, that compensation should be awarded to him in the shape of damages. But the French government, considering these measures insufficient, required changes to be made in the rules of evidence; England, however, would not agree to alter her practice, and thus, after long discussion, the conference was broken off, and in the treaties of 1606 no mention was made of prize procedure (*d*). It remained, therefore, unsettled until the year 1632, when both governments agreed that some improvement should be made in the practice of the Admiralty Courts; as, for instance, that the privateer, within twenty-four hours after bringing his prize into port, should furnish the court with the papers found on board; and, further, it was forbidden to treat neutral subjects

(*d*) For a full explanation of this matter see *Robinson*, Coll. Mar. 35—53.

(45)

as prisoners during the progress of the suit. The treaty of 1632, moreover, required security from the privateers in 10,000 livres, and that they should make compensation for injuries unjustly inflicted on neutral merchants (*e*), all which regulations were afterwards definitively adopted by the maritime powers, at the treaty of Utrecht (*f*).

Still the treaties of the 17th century pay little attention to the formalities of prize practice, and do not touch upon the subject of evidence, whence many serious abuses arose. About this time there were laid down in the prize courts many arbitrary rules, very harassing to neutrals. Leaving the belligerents to vary their own forms of trial, treaties only required them to give just and impartial sentences, while, at the same time, they granted to the ambassadors of friendly powers the right of interfering in behalf of their fellow countrymen, and of bringing their cases before a court of appeal (*g*). Generally, the neutral states considered the ships of their subjects as lawful prize only in the following cases (*h*): (a) If it were discovered that the master had not a legal passport, or sailed with a double set of papers, or threw his papers

(*e*) If the sum thus received should prove insufficient for the payment of damages, then a claim might be made on the person who fitted out the privateer. See the treaty in *Dumont*, vi. 1, 33. With regard to the amount of money to be deposited as security and which varied in different governments, see *Martens*' Essai, § 15.

(*f*) See treaty of Holland with France, 1646, *Dumont*, vi. 342, and with England, 1674, *Dumont*, vii. 1, 283. The first requires from the privateers bail in the sum of 12,000 livres, the second in that of 2,000*l.* to 5,000*l.* sterling according to the discretion of the judge.

(*g*) Thus in the treaty between Holland and Sweden, 1667 (*Dumont*, vii. 1, 37) it is said "ut judicibus Admiralitatis ordinariis alii extra ordinem judices periti, quique in partibus non sint, adjungantur;" see also the treaties of Holland and England, 1668, 1674, *Dumont*, vii. 1, 74. The last of these requires "ut jus super prædis captis administretur secundum justitiæ et equitatis normam a judicibus omni suspicione majoribus." The neutral is also entitled to more favourable consideration with respect to appeal. These rules were confirmed by the treaties of Nimeguen and Utrecht. *Dumont*, vii. 1, 327—9, 357—62, 438—42; viii. 1, 345, 409.

(*h*) See generally the treaties of the 17th century respecting neutral commerce.

(46)

overboard. (b) If they conveyed soldiers of the enemy, or attempted to enter into blockaded ports; but a neutral ship, laden with contraband of war, was considered free, the forbidden articles only being subject to seizure. The greater part of the treaties, and amongst them those of Utrecht, even permitted the neutral, after having given up the contraband, to continue his voyage without molestation (*i*). Besides these regulations, all the treaties of the 17th century forbid neutrals, under pain of confiscation of ship and cargo, to resist visitation ("visite"). On the other hand, in order that visitation might not be made an occasion of oppression on the part of the belligerent, it was defined with greater accuracy. The privateer, having fallen in with a neutral ship, was bound to announce his intention to proceed to visitation ("semonce"), and, remaining at gunshot distance, to send two or three men in the ship's boat with his commission ("lettre de marque"). These men were to verify the ship's papers, and not to touch the cargo (*k*); being only entitled to seize her when the documents were insufficient or suspicious.

But, however much European governments might attempt to mitigate them, the inconveniences of visitation still continued very harassing to neutral commerce. From the historical documents of the 17th century (*l*) we learn, that privateers very often were guilty of great cruelty ("multa atrocia et barbariem spirantia"), for not confining themselves to an examination of documents, but, desiring to find out whether contraband goods were not concealed on board, they searched the ship, interrogated the crew, and sometimes even had recourse to torture. We must also add that privateers, relying on the connivance of the prize court, arrested neutral ships at their own discretion, and it was not difficult for them then to prove the legality of the capture. If the

(*i*) Respecting contraband see *Dumont*, i. 1, 209, 571; ii. 103, 264; vii, 30, 31, 283—4, 317, 386—392; viii. 1, 32.

(*k*) Very few treaties permit search. See for example the treaty between England and Sweden, 1661; that between England and Holland, 1667; and between England and Dantzic, 1706. Suppl. au Recueil de *Martens*, i. 45.

(*l*) See treaty between England and Holland, 1674, *Dumont*, vii. 1, 282—5.

(47)

judges found anything incorrect in the form of the papers, they commonly pronounced in favour of the privateers (*m*). It is not, therefore, astonishing that the neutral states should endeavour to free their subjects from visitation. Thus, in the year 1599, the French king, Henry IV., complained to Queen Elizabeth of the wanton conduct of the English privateers, and the queen, in token of her special confidence in and favour for him, declared French ships free from visitation, under the condition that they should not convey into Spain corn and ammunition. This privilege, however, did not remain long in force, and, notwithstanding the efforts made by the French diplomatists to secure it by treaty, was abrogated by the English (*n*). In order to protect themselves from violence and inquisitorial search, the neutral governments were obliged to have recourse to convoys. In 1653 the Swedish Queen Christina, on the occasion of a war between England and Holland, published a declaration, according to which her fleet was ordered to accompany Swedish merchant vessels, and in no case to permit visitation. The commanders of the convoy received instructions to take care (a) that the neutrals did not violate their duty, and did not carry contraband; (b) to behave in a courteous manner to English and Dutch ships of war, and in case of necessity to show them the queen's certificate. In 1654, on the occasion of peace being concluded between England and Holland, this declaration ceased to be applicable (*o*).

(*m*) In order to check the malpractices of the privateers, some treaties prescribe to the neutrals a form of passport; but this, it appears, was of little benefit, as the privateers and prize courts besides the passports demanded other papers, and the question, whether they were sufficient as proof of the nationality of the ship, as well as of the property of the goods, was left to the decision of the belligerents.

(*n*) *Robinson*, Coll. Mar. 47—50.

(*o*) The declaration of Christina is printed in the English language in Thurloe's Collection of State Papers (*Thurloe*, i. 424—6, London, 1742) and in *Robinson* (Coll. 145—157). The reason of its publication is clearly explained in its introduction. The queen resorts to " convoys on account of the malpractices of privateers, and the abuses of Admiralty Courts, seeing that on the one hand the ships and effects of our good subjects are attacked, plundered and

(48)

The example of Sweden was followed by the States General. In 1656, when Cromwell began the war with Spain, they resolved to dispatch their ships with strong convoys under the command of Ruyter. In fact this eminent admiral conducted a number of merchant ships from Cadiz to Zealand, and would not permit the English to visit them; but Cromwell, on his side, detached a strong squadron to look out for the Dutch and made them surrender (*p*). In vain they tried, at the conclusion of the peace, to induce the English to exempt from visitation ships under convoy, Sweden alone adhered to the new principle (1675) (*q*).

In looking over the treaties of the 17th century, it is easy to observe amongst them a considerable similarity. The acknowledgment of the immunity of the flag, the limiting of blockade and the accurate definition of contraband of war show that the minds of statesmen and public opinion were sufficiently prepared to understand the true principles of neutrality; but, on the other hand, it cannot be denied that these principles were admitted only as privileges for a few favoured nations, and not as immutable laws acknowledged by all in time of war. Neutral commerce was thus rather left in a precarious and subordinate position, because great naval powers, with the exception of Holland, were generally found amongst the belligerents, who not only had no motive to support the principles of neutrality, but whose interests were strongly opposed to them. No less injurious to the interest of commerce was the want of unanimity which prevailed amongst the neutrals. The belligerents stood in no fear of a strong and united opposition, and therefore did not pay much deference to their wishes.

robbed by pirates and privateers, acting under sundry commissions, nay often by entirely unknown ships, in the open seas; on the other, that one or other imputations are laid to their charge against all reason, under which colour and pretence they are stopped, detained, and injured."

(*p*) See *Thurloe*, State Papers, iv. 461, 698, 713, 729, 730, 740, v. 696.

(*q*) *Thurloe*, State Papers, iii. 32, v. 663, 682; *Dumont*, vii. 1, 317. See also *Wheaton*, Histoire, i. 193—7. In the Danish ordonnance of 1688, ships under convoy were declared exempt from visitation. *Wheaton*, i. 192.

(49)

The first attempt to unite in defence of neutral commerce was made at the time of the maritime war, 1689—97 (*r*). At that period England and Holland, under the influence of a strong animosity against Louis XIV., not only refused to be bound by treaties which they had entered into with other nations, but forbade them to hold any intercourse with France. These strong measures provoked resistance on the part of Denmark and Sweden; who for a long time confined themselves to representations, but perceiving that their demands and protests produced no effect, they determined to enter into an alliance, and to arm a fleet for the protection of their commerce (1693). These coalitions soon attained the object they had in view; the belligerents finding it more prudent to abandon their arbitrary proceedings and to pay due observance to their former treaties in conformity with the law of nations (*s*). But this moderation was not of long continu-

(*r*) See Convention between England and Holland, 12th August, 1689. (*Dumont*, vii. 2, 238.) It declared every vessel going to or coming from France to be lawful prize. Even Reddie, the learned defender of the English principles, admits that this convention is contrary to the rights of neutrality, but throws all the blame upon Holland. "For on this occasion Great Britain was so far misled by Holland as to commit one of the few departures from the common law of nations with which she can be justly charged, by concurring with the States General in a sweeping declaration of blockade against the ports of France or a general interdiction of commerce with France by sea" (Researches, i. 202). This charge, however, against the Dutch is hardly just. From the despatches of Nicholas Vitzen, the Dutch ambassador at that time at the court of St. James,' it is evident that the Dutch for a long time would not agree to conclude a treaty on the conditions proposed by England. *Büsch*, Ueber das Bestreben der Völker einander in ihrem Seehandel recht wehe zu thun. Hamb. 1800, S. 229—234; *Totze*, La Liberté de la Navigation neutre (Londres et Amsterdam, 1780), p. 163.

(*s*) The Convention of 1793 is inserted in *Dumont*, vii. 2, 325. Sweden and Denmark on this occasion met with the sympathy of many jurists. In the year 1695, there appeared at Rostock a work by *Grœning*, "Tractatus de Navigatione liberà," in which the author defends the immunity of the neutral flag against the violence of privateers. The rights of belligerents and neutrals ought in his opinion to be determined by treaty, and not by the decree of any one power. He considers neutral property free, with the exception of contraband (*Reddie*, Researches, i. 134—9). In general *Grœning* in his ideas differs very decidedly from contemporary authors, and, which is more important, is the first person who insists upon the necessity of an armed neutrality (cap. vi., ix.): "licere sere-

E*

(50)

ance; at the beginning of the 18th century, when the war spread over almost all Europe, abuses revived, treaties were forgotten and their place supplied by harsh decrees, neutral commerce found no supporters, and suffered hopelessly from the violence of privateers and the malpractices of prize courts. Such a wretched state of things was put an end to by the treaties of Utrecht, 1713, when the principles of neutrality, which had been proclaimed in the 17th century, but disavowed during the war of the "Spanish Succession," were sanctioned at least by the principal maritime powers of Europe. It remained to invite other states to adopt these principles, and to enforce their strict observance upon belligerents.

nissimis Svecorum et Danorum regibus propter damnum subditis a piratis illatum, repressaliis uti et negatum *jus commercii armis asserere*."

PERIOD III.

From the Peace of Utrecht (1713) to the Year 1793.

We have just said that, at the Congress of Utrecht, the maritime powers of Europe came to an arrangement about the fundamental rights of neutral commerce, but, unfortunately, they did not propose to other nations to adopt them as a general law, and consequently, at the breaking out of the first maritime war, privateers and prize courts reverted to their former irregularities. Under different pretexts the belligerents again endeavoured to extend the authority of their decrees, and, by suspending the operation of existing treaties, to curtail the commercial intercourse of nations. Arbitrary search was substituted for visitation, and the limits of contraband as well as of blockade became indefinite and uncertain. The most dangerous opponent of neutral commerce was England. Having attained great preponderance, and aspiring to the sovereignty of the sea, she strove to impose her maritime law on the rest of Europe. In order to check her violent and arbitrary proceedings, the Continental Powers formed a coalition for the purpose of compelling belligerents to adopt liberal principles of neutral commerce. This great problem being the work of the Empress Catherine II. (whose reign commencing in 1762, terminated in 1796), we can readily understand why this period is of such great importance with respect to international law. In reviewing the events of this time, we perceive that during the American war the above-mentioned coalition was greatly favoured by circumstances, and had a very beneficial influence. We will now direct our attention to this important event, and endeavour to show how it originated, and with what success it was carried out.

(52)

The commercial treaties of Utrecht only remained in force until the peace of Western Europe was disturbed. Thus, in the maritime war of 1739 between England and Spain, France and Holland also took part, and, consequently, the position of the neutrals again became precarious. As a belligerent power, Spain was particularly inclined to act with violence. We might cite as instances of this, her decrees of 1718 and 1740, by which she established the rule "la robe de l'ennemi confisque celle d'ami," and considered as war contraband all enemy's goods and manufactures ("marchandise du crû ou de fabrique de l'ennemi") (*a*); exceptions were made only in favour of the French and Dutch. No less oppressive to neutrals were the regulations of Sweden, published at the time of the great northern war (*b*). France, though mitigating the ordonnance de la marine in 1744, still sanctioned the capture of the property of an enemy on board neutral ships (*c*). But

(*a*) The details about Spanish prize legislation and jurisprudence in the middle of the 18th century may be found in the work of *D'Abreu,* Trattado sobre las Presas maritimas (Cadiz, 1746), which was afterwards translated into French by Bornemann (1802); we should add, however, that this work is of little interest with reference to the general principles of international law. D'Abreu, like Valin, occupied himself only with the decrees and prize laws of his own country, and contented himself with protesting occasionally against the irregularities of prize procedure.

(*b*) By the ordonnance of 1715 (Robinson, Coll. 167—175) Charles XII. subjected to condemnation enemy's goods on board neutral vessels, as well as neutral goods on board enemy's ships ("le pavillon ne couvre pas la cargaison et la confisque"), and extended blockade to all the ports of the Baltic occupied by the Russians, or adjacent to Russian territory; on the contrary, Peter the Great declared neutral commerce free, and limited the right of capture to ships having contraband on board. *Declaration,* 17th April and 28th June, 1719. Polnoe Sobronic, N. 3398, or Russian Statutes at Large, and *Mors. Sbornik,* 1854, N. 6, p. 195, &c.

(*c*) It is true that the French decrees of 1744 are more moderate than those of Louis XIV. (*Reddie,* Researches, i. 247—251); but still they adopt the edict of 1704 respecting "marchandise du crû ou de fabrique de l'ennemi," and authorize the privateer to arrest a neutral ship, when there is the slightest reason to suspect that enemy's property is on board; therefore we may say that the prize practice of France in the middle of the 18th century was by no means liberal. In her relations with weaker powers she even endeavoured to introduce the principle "le pavillon ne couvre pas la cargaison et la confisque." See her treaties with the Hanseatic Towns, 1716; with Hamburg,

(53)

the Continental Powers occasionally made an exception in favour of some friendly states, admitted the rule of reciprocity, and were generally inclined to acknowledge the immunity of the flag (*d*). The conduct of Great Britain, however, towards neutral commerce was entirely different, for having, at the peace of Utrecht, attained maritime supremacy, she uniformly adopted in all her wars measures for encouraging her privateers at the expense of other nations. In order to prevent neutrals from obtaining commercial advantages while she was engaged in war, England obstinately adhered to the old system of the Consolato del Mare, and tried to impose it upon all nations without exception. With respect to the new principles of neutrality, which had been introduced into the treaties of Europe from the 17th century, the cabinet of St. James,' considering them dangerous innovations, contravening the general purposes of war, persisted in refusing to modify their prize regulations. War contraband and blockade were not strictly defined in the British Prize Courts, but varied from time to time according to circumstances. In the place of regular visitation the right of search was established as a rule, and the Court itself was more favourably inclined to privateers than neutrals.

The difference of views concerning neutral rights between England and Continental governments became more evident after the peace of Utrecht, when there appeared a general inclination, on the part of the latter, to adopt the new principle of the immunity of the flag. England, at first, seemed disposed to coincide in that movement, but after the war of the "Spanish Succession" she decidedly separated from the rest of Europe, and, as a preponderating power, found it more ad-

1769; with Mecklenburg, 1779; *Dumont*, viii. 1—468; *Martens*, Rec. i. 640, ii. 709.

(*d*) On examining the treaties of this time we find the immunity of the flag admitted by Holland, Sweden, Denmark, France, the German Empire, and even Spain. At the breaking out of the war, 1744, the king of France formally prescribed to his Admiral not to apply the French decree to Sweden, Denmark, and Spain (*Valin*, Traité des Prises, i. 63, 75). Spain on her part also respected the neutral privileges of the Dutch and French (*D'Abreu*, i. ix. § 7).

vantageous to adhere to the prize practice of the Middle Ages. The war of 1739—48 afforded the first occasion for a collision. As soon as hostilities broke out between Great Britain, Spain, and France, the King of Prussia addressed himself to the English ministry for an explanation of the principles of neutral commerce upon which England was disposed to act. Lord Carteret answered verbally, that the Prussian flag should enjoy the same privileges as the flag of other states which had no special treaties with England, and that nothing but arms and ammunition should be considered as war contraband. In fact, until 1745, the English privateers did not interfere with Prussian commerce, but as soon as Prussian merchants began to trade in French goods, some of their ships were seized and declared lawful prize. In consequence of the numerous complaints of his subjects, Frederic II. protested against the seizure, but as England disregarded his remonstrances, he appointed a special commission for the investigation of the facts, and resolved to give compensation to his merchants out of the Silesian loan, the interest of which he was bound by treaty to pay to the English. Hence arose a serious controversy between Prussia and Great Britain, which is to us particularly interesting, as both governments on this occasion set forth their respective views of prize jurisdiction (*e*).

The Prussian commissioners expressed their opinions respecting neutral commerce to the following effect:—1. That the belligerent power had the right of visitation of neutral ships, and of seizing contraband. 2. The immunity of neutral flags ought to be allowed. Such, in their opinion, was the meaning of treaties. Although the Prussian government had not entered into any specific convention on this subject with that of England, they were entitled to the benefit of these general principles, the rights of neutrality being one and the same for all nations. Hence the commissioners

(*e*) The diplomatic documents relating to this case may be found in *Baron K. Martens'* Causes Célèbres du Droit des Gens. ii. 1—88. *Wheaton* also gives a summary of it. Histoire, i. 260—271. Leipz. 1846.

(55)

came to the conclusion, that the interrogatories the English Courts of Admiralty had proposed to the Prussian merchants: "To whom do the goods belong?" "Are they not dispatched on commission on account of the enemy?" "At whose risk are they sent?" were contrary to international law. 3. Timber, planks, corn, salt, and other articles with which the Prussian ships were laden were not to be considered contraband, even according to the words of Lord Carteret himself; and, speaking generally, the laws of war contraband should not be applied to neutrals when on their return voyage to their own ports. 4. Belligerents have not the right to enforce their decrees on neutral merchants, since their respective rights and duties can only be determined by the mutual consent of governments, and accordingly the judgments of the English Admiralty Court are not "ipso jure" binding on the King of Prussia; but, on the contrary, he is entitled to claim damages on behalf of his subjects from the belligerents, and failing to obtain them to have recourse to reprisals.

For the purpose of defining the principles of prize law, and in order to put an end to this dispute, the English government also appointed a commission, consisting of four members. Their report, presented to the king, states:—1st. The general principles of law. 2nd. The facts of the case. 3rd. The application of the law to the facts. 4th. Remarks on the opinions of the Prussian commissioners.

1. *With reference to what is international law in time of war*, the commissioners set forth that, in their opinion, a belligerent is fully entitled to capture not only war contraband, but also all the property of his enemy; neutral cargo only being considered free. To insure the due application of the principles of this law regular courts were established, whose duty it was to examine the proceedings of the privateers and decide all questions relating to prize. These courts, in accordance with immemorial custom, were established by the belligerents in their own territory, and were guided in their decisions by treaties and international law. All cap-

tures are to be brought to the country of the privateer, and are not to be considered lawful prize until so adjudged. Ship's papers, together with the testimony of the master and crew, who were on board at the time of the capture, furnish the evidence in these cases. It is the duty of the prize judge to examine the case impartially, and to release a captured vessel in the event of its being proved not to belong to an enemy. In doubtful cases further proof is to be admitted. A privateer, who has arrested a neutral vessel without sufficient grounds, is not only to be deprived of his prize, but condemned in damages and costs. On the contrary, if the papers of the captured ship should prove to be false, or equivocal, or if any have been thrown overboard; if the testimony of the crew be vacillating, confused, or inconsistent with the papers, in all such cases, although the prize may be declared illegal, international law subjects the neutral to payment of costs and damages, wholly or in part, at the discretion of the judge. Even in cases of restitution the neutral is liable to be condemned in costs and damages, if his conduct is open to suspicion. The same principles are applicable to cases when neither from the papers nor from the evidence it can be ascertained, without further proof, that the property belongs to a neutral. Disputes respecting prize causes may, according to custom, be carried to the court of appeal, which is composed of the chief officers of state. In the absence of any appeal, it is to be presumed that the parties acquiesce in the judgment, and the process is at an end. Such a course the English commissioners considered to be both just and regular, since it had been sanctioned by treaties and the general concurrence of the nations of Europe. They were also well convinced that in Great Britain, Admiralty Courts were thoroughly independent in the exercise of their jurisdiction, and acted impartially. The commissioners, however, did not deny that some governments furnished exceptions to the rules before alluded to—viz., by following a more lenient course in visitation and recognising the immunity of the flag,—but they asserted that these arrangements depended upon treaties,

(57)

and merely applied to those governments which had entered into them, without in any manner affecting third parties.

2. Having laid down the fundamental principles of prize jurisprudence the English commissioners entered upon *the facts* in detail, and contended that the British Prize Courts had not been guilty of any injustice towards the Prussians, but, on the contrary, had acted towards them with great leniency, by releasing some ships which had been seized with contraband on board. Hence Prussian subjects were, in their opinion, in no case entitled to damages, as their cases had been legally adjudicated upon; moreover, many of them, not having appealed, must be taken to have acquiesced in the judgment.

3. *After having thus applied the law to the facts,* the English commissioners came to the conclusion that all the Prussian subjects, before presenting their petitions to their king, should have had recourse to the court of appeal, but not having done so, their complaints were inadmissible.

4. *Having thus disposed of the principles laid down on the part of Prussia,* the English jurists expressed their opinion that the practices of neutral commerce, upon which the Prussian commissioners relied, were privileges having their origin only in treaties, and that the general rules of international law were to be found in the Consolato del Mare, whose authority, based on international customs, and supported by such publicists as Grotius, Loccenius, &c., could scarcely be doubted; and Prussia, having no special treaty on the subject with England, was bound to conform to the regular course of prize jurisdiction. They also added that the claims of the Prussian subjects were groundless; as at one time they contended for the freedom of the ship on account of the cargo, and at another for the freedom of the cargo on account of the ship, while the English Prize Courts acted in these cases in conformity with international law, and without reference to the principles of that of their own country.

These arguments, however, did not shake the opinion of the Prussian commissioners, who presented to the king another report, wherein, amongst other things, they stated as follows:—1. The belligerent powers acted unjustly in arresting neutral vessels, laden with the goods of an enemy; a neutral vessel being as inviolable as neutral territory. To submit to such an arrest would be to surrender to the mercy of the enemy the right of international commerce. 2. The immunity of the flag is the rule and not the exception, being the right of all neutral states, and the more so, because it does not interfere with the belligerent seizing contraband, and maintaining blockade. 3. The rule "free ship, free goods," generally involves another, which is that neutral cargo on board an enemy's ship is lawful prize. 4. England at the time of the last war did not uniformly adhere to any particular system, neither to the Consolato del Mare, nor to the more moderate rule of "free ship, free goods," whence privateers derived great profits, at the expense of neutral commerce. 5. Prussian subjects were therefore fully justified in complaining of the oppression of the English, and seeking protection from their own king.

This remarkable controversy was terminated in the year 1756 by the Declaration of Westminster, according to which England made compensation to the Prussian subjects, and Frederic II. removed the sequestration from the Silesian loan. England, however, after this concession, did not make any general modification of her prize practice, but during the time of the seven years' war continued to molest neutral commerce. Holland had more reason than any other power to complain of the conduct of the English privateers. In vain she relied for protection, first, on the observance of strict neutrality, and secondly, upon the treaty of 1674, whereby the immunity of her flag and other advantages had been guaranteed to her by Great Britain; but the cabinet of St. James,' applying to her to act as an ally in that war, and receiving an evasive answer, English privateers were directed to deal with Dutch vessels according to the principles of the Consolato del Mare (*f*).

(*f*) *Wheaton*, Histoire, i. 256; *Totze*, La Liberté de la Navigation, p. 198—205.

(59)

These causes of discord were soon supplemented by others, which originated as follows:—Immediately on the breaking out of hostilities, the French government determined to change their colonial policy, and to permit Dutch subjects to trade with their colonies, upon condition of obtaining a special certificate or licence for that purpose, whereupon the Dutch, considering that all the ports and coasts of the belligerents were open to them, readily availed themselves of these new markets, but suffered severely in consequence of their mistake. The English cruisers and privateers having seized their ships, they were condemned by the Admiralty Court on the ground that a ship provided with a passport from an enemy lost its neutral character. The French government, in order to protect the Dutch merchants, then opened to them free trade with their colonies, and dispensed with licences; but even this had no effect on England, whose privateers persisted in their former practices, and the Admiralty Court declared the captures to be lawful prizes, alleging in support of their judgment the following reasons: 1. Neutrals have no right to carry on in time of war a commerce which is not permitted them in time of peace. 2. A ship, trading on account of the enemy, has forfeited the immunity of its flag, and cannot be considered neutral (*g*). Thus originated the new rule of

(*g*) On that occasion the English jurist, Dr. Marriott, published a pamphlet (The Case of the Dutch Ships considered, Lond. 1759), in which he openly defended the views of the Admiralty Courts about international law and prize jurisdiction (*Reddie*, Researches, i. 311—313): "The authority of publicists, as well as the practice of European states or governments," says Marriott, "concur that during war a belligerent is entitled to seize the property of his enemy wherever he may find it; therefore two maritime powers cannot enter into hostile relations, without injury to the commerce of other nations. Neutrality is necessarily attended with some inconvenience." In reply to the question, what are the inconveniences of neutrality? Dr. Marriott answers, "that every ship directing its course to the port of an enemy, or sailing thence, is exposed to the strong presumption of being the property of an enemy. In order to obviate this suspicion, the merchant is bound to submit to visitation." After having in this manner admitted the necessity of arrest, Marriott proceeds still further; "neutral cargo," he says, "may be condemned for its illegal destination according to circumstances,—for instance, if destined to places under blockade; the ship also is liable to confiscation in case of the practice of any

1756, its result was to give to the English privateers many rich prizes. The Dutch stood not alone in their complaints on that occasion. Denmark had also suffered from English privateers and prize courts, and in order to protect her subjects against further violence, she sent to London a special diplomatic agent (*h*) to confer with the British government on the subject, but unfortunately to no purpose.

The northern powers, finding that other nations were suffering in common with themselves, from the oppression of the belligerents, in the year 1759 entered into a convention for the defence of their neutrality, and the Baltic was consequently closed to privateers (*i*). This convention was the significant indication of the approaching struggle for the rights of neutral commerce, and the first step to the celebrated coalition of 1780. France also entered into this convention, which remained in force to the end of the seven years' war.

deceit on the part of the master on account of a contraband cargo, or for carrying on trade under the flag of an enemy." From this Marriott comes to the strange conclusion, that Dutch ships and goods, destined to French colonies, were lawful prizes according to international law, and for a breach of the laws of neutrality. An impartial reader may hence perceive in what light the Consolato del Mare was considered in the English Admiralty Court.

(*h*) The agent in this commission was Hübner, the celebrated defender of neutral commerce. In 1759 he published his work, "De la saisie des Bâtiments neutres," in which, protesting against the violence of the belligerents, he endeavoured to establish the rights of neutrality on the principles of common sense and justice. We can here only refer to his views on prize jurisdiction. Being himself well acquainted with the irregularities of Admiralty Courts, he considers them incompetent to decide prize causes, and adduces the following reasons in support of his opinions. 1st. No one ought to be a judge in his own cause. 2nd. Neutral merchants are not *de jure* subjects of the belligerent. In all such cases the Danish publicist requires that they should be decided not by the decrees of one or the other belligerent, but in conformity with international law. The whole burden of the proof concerning the legality of the capture, and the violation of neutrality, he contends, should fall on the privateer alone, and thinks that neutrals would find the best security during maritime war in mixed prize courts, where members from both sides should be appointed, for no other courts could be expected to be impartial in such matters.

(*i*) This convention between Russia, Sweden, and Denmark, may be found in *Martens'* Suppl. au Recueil, iii. 36. Two years before its conclusion, France having favourably received the representations of the neutral powers, slightly modified her prize practice.

(61)

On the re-establishment of the peace of Europe by the treaties of Paris and Hubertsberg, 1763, the treaties of Utrecht were renewed (*j*).

In the year 1776 commenced the memorable struggle between England and the United States of America. Experience proves that civil wars are particularly cruel, and are seldom conducted on any principle of justice or international law. Consequently, in order to remove all pretexts on the part of the belligerents for the oppression of commerce, the neutral powers hastened to publish decrees in the same spirit, enjoining their subjects under fear of punishment to observe strict impartiality in that war (*k*). But these measures were to no purpose, as, amongst the belligerents, France alone made any perceptible modification in her former practice about neutral trade (*l*), whilst Spain openly avowed her inten-

(*j*) *Martens*, Rec. iii. 16—100; *Wheaton*, Hist. i. 257.

(*k*) We may observe that these decrees generally forbid a neutral subject to apply for letters of marque, and to act as a belligerent privateer. In the preceding century every maritime war afforded a pretext for plunder; amateur privateers sprung up on every side, and aggravated the sufferings of the neutral merchants, but in the 18th century we observe the first measures on the part of governments to check the piratical habits of their subjects. See treaties between France and Holland, 1739, and also between Sweden and Naples, 1742. *Martens*, Essai, § 13.

(*l*) The decrees of the belligerent powers may be found in Martens' Recueil, iii. 101—157. The French decree of 1778 is more worthy of attention, on account of the novelty of the principles of neutrality therein set forth. It considers as lawful prize, 1st. Neutral ships whose papers have been thrown overboard. 2nd. War contraband. If, however, the contraband does not exceed one quarter of the cargo, the ship is to be released. Even this rule the French government was afterwards prepared to modify according to circumstances. 3rd. Ships purchased from the enemy by neutral subjects, when there is no bill of sale on board, or sentence of condemnation by an Admiralty Court. 4th. Neutral ships, the master, supercargo or agent of which are enemy's subjects. 5th. A ship on board which the muster roll (rôle d'équipage) has not been authenticated by a neutral authority. According to this decree, only the papers found on board at the time of capture are admissible as evidence of neutral property. A passport is considered to be in force for one year only, and is invalid if granted to an enemy's subject not naturalized in the neutral country, or when the ship is not actually in port. Unfortunately, however, this decree, which forms an era in the history of French prize jurisdiction, was considered to be a mere temporary measure, the effect of which depended on circumstances, and might be abrogated at the will of the government.

(62)

tion of acting towards the neutrals in the same way as they allowed the English to treat them. Great Britain returned to her former system, and, taking advantage of the internecine character of the war, endeavoured wholly to suppress neutral commerce. Regarding her enemies as rebels, and their allies as abettors of civil war, she forbade all nations to have any connection with her former colonies. The English privateers, taking advantage of this feeling on the part of their government, and in the hope of all their captures being condemned as prizes, attacked every suspicious looking vessel they encountered. It must be added that the list of contraband goods was considerably enlarged, and the definition of blockade rendered still more vague at that time (*m*). Marriott, then judge of the Admiralty Court, laid down the following principles of maritime war as immutable :—1. The belligerent has a right to seize on board neutral ships everything which might be made use of by the enemy for his defence. 2. Great Britain, lying between the German Sea and the Atlantic Ocean, forms, by its very position, a natural blockade to all the ports of France and Spain. 3. The rights of neutral nations depend on the customs or practice of the belligerents; treaties are but temporary privileges, valid only as long as the Admiralty Court finds it convenient to make use of them (*n*).

(*m*) The facts relating to the arbitrary proceedings of the English privateers at this time are collected by *Martens*, Merkw. Fälle, ii. 59—128; *Totze*, La Liberté de la Navigation, p. 206, &c.; *Schlosser*, Gesch. der 18-ten Jahrh. iv. 353—8.

(*n*) The judgments of Marriott were collected and published under the title of "Decisions in the High Court of Admiralty during the Time of Sir J. Hay and of Sir J. Marriott." The analysis of the most important may be found in the work of *Büsch*, "Über das Bestreben der Völker einander in ihrem Seehandel recht wehe zu thun," S. 117—187. It is a matter of surprise to us, that such a judge should find favour with jurists of the present time. "It is true," *Reddie* says, "that Marriott was in many respects inferior to his successor Sir William Scott, but his faults and mistakes proceeded not so much from prejudice against neutrals as from patriotism; moreover, they could be easily rectified by means of appeal." Researches, i. 56. But from whatever motives Marriott acted, it is evident from documents of that time, that the higher court seldom reversed his decisions. Neutral merchants did not even dare to appeal, as they were convinced that it would be fruitless, and only increase the legal expenses of the suit,.

(63)

The effect of this prize practice threatened ruin to neutral commerce, since it was evident that England would allow no maritime law but her own to be enforced. Happily, however, international justice at that time found powerful supporters in other parts of Europe; for, from the year 1780, Russia formed with seven other powers a strong coalition, which checked the violence of privateers, and secured the rights of neutrality (*o*).

There was no difficulty in the allies agreeing upon fundamental principles: they resolved—

1. Only to permit the seizure of neutral vessels where the duties of neutrality had been unquestionably violated.

2. To require from the belligerents that judicial proceedings against neutrals should be commenced without delay, and in accordance with an uniform, clear, and legal system.

3. In case of neutrals having unjustly suffered, to compel the belligerents not only to pay damages, but also to make compensation for the insult offered to the neutral flag, otherwise to have recourse to reprisals.

4. To adopt these rules as the principle of a future maritime code (Code Maritime Universel).

The armed neutrality soon succeeded in its object, and put an end to the irregularities of the Admiralty Courts. France, Spain, Holland and the United States revoked their former decrees, and published new ones in conformity with the declaration of the Empress Catherine (*p*). Great Britain

and hence the mistakes of Marriott were not so easily remedied as Reddie thinks. See *Büsch*, S. 148—156.

(*o*) *Martens*, Recueil, iii. 158. See Additional Note at end of this Period, p. 70.

(*p*) The French government had already in the year 1780 directed their admiral and privateers not to molest neutrals, even though apparently destined to enemy's ports, and in no case to capture them, unless they had a cargo of war contraband, or were engaged in the transport of English troops, or harboured Englishmen under a neutral flag. *Code des Prises*, ii. 866—868, 875, 886. *Martens*, Recueil, iii. 163. The Dutch decree of 1781 also adopts the principles of the armed neutrality. (*Martens*, Merkwürdige Fälle, ii. 313, Art. 42.) The same may be said of Spain and of the United States of America, whose decrees are to be found in *Martens*, Recueil, iii. 161; *Wheaton*, Histoire, i. 367.

herself was at last obliged to yield to the influence of this powerful coalition, and mitigated, though not avowedly, the severity of her prize laws (*q*). One of the best results of the coalition was the diminution of privateers, according to the testimony of a contemporary, who says, "At the end of the war privateering had almost disappeared, and neutral commerce flourished almost as much as in a time of profound peace" (*r*).

At the conference of Versailles, the commercial treaty of Utrecht was again renewed by England, France, and Spain; but knowing by experience that such renewals were of little practical utility, and fearing that the belligerents would return to their former malpractices, the members of the "armed neutrality" resolved to proceed with the work which had been so successfully commenced. Accordingly the principles of 1780 were more fully developed, and having been introduced nearly by all the nations of Europe into their commercial treaties and alliances, found support even in America. In the course of the next ten years, namely, from the peace of Versailles to the year 1793, measures were taken and rules laid down in order to reform the prize law of the belligerents, and to secure the independence of neutrals at sea. Reviewing the treaties of that time (*s*) we find in them some im-

(*q*) In the years 1781—2, secret instructions were given to the English privateers, to the effect that they should carefully abstain from collision with neutrals. With respect to Russian ships, England showed no intention to enforce visitation, as we may conclude from the letter of Lord Malmesbury to Count Panin. See *Lord Malmesbury's* Diary and Correspondence, London, 1845, i. 232, 319, 410. The cabinet of St. James,' however, never formally recognized the armed neutrality, but made every effort in its power to dissolve the coalition. Of the English statesmen Fox alone did not agree with his fellow-countrymen, and even intended afterwards to conclude with Holland, through the mediation of Russia, a treaty of peace on the principles of 1780. *Lord Malmesbury*, iv. 25, 26, 42, 53; *Wheaton*, Histoire, i. 367, 368.

(*r*) See *Dohm*, Denkwürdigkeiten meiner Zeit, Lemgo, 1815, S. 153. See also *Büsch*, 284.

The treaties of 1783—1793, in which are developed and explained the principles of the "armed neutrality," are to be found in the 3rd and 4th vols. of the collection of *Martens*.

portant clauses concerning the right of visitation (visite), evidence in prize courts, and the legal forms of proceeding.

1. *Visitation.* The declaration of 1780 made no mention of the right of search, and as long as the "armed neutrality" remained a powerful coalition, privateers did not venture upon a search or any other irregular proceedings. In order to prevent at a future time a repetition of such abuses, the treaties (1783—1793) generally assume that visitation ought to be confined to the verification of the papers; while search, breaking open coffers, interrogating the crew, &c., are all strictly forbidden to privateers. However, if on board the ship there are not found any papers, the privateer may, with the concurrence or at least in the presence of the owner or master, put a seal upon the cargo, make an inventory of it, and bring the ship into a port of his own country. Search then can only be made in the presence of an officer of the Admiralty Court, and immediately before the commencement of the suit. A neutral subject, on board of whose ship are found contraband goods, may deliver them up to the privateer, and is entitled to continue his voyage with the rest of the cargo without molestation (*t*). The declaration of 1780 is also silent on the question, whether a ship sailing under neutral convoy is free from visitation, but shortly after the establishment of the "armed neutrality," England and Sweden entered into an angry discussion on that subject, whereupon the Swedish government addressed a note to that of Russia, to ask its opinion upon the point, and received for answer, that the subjecting of ships under convoy to visitation would be insulting to the national flag; and that cruisers or privateers of the belligerents ought to be satisfied concerning the neutral character of the ship and cargo, with the verbal information of the officer in command. This opinion of the Russian court met with general approbation, and being considered as one

(*t*) With respect to the treaties of the United States with Holland (1782), and of Russia with Denmark (1782) and Austria (1785), see *Martens*, iii. 427, 468, iv. 72, &c. The same principles are adopted in a treaty between France and England (1786). *Martens*, iv. 155.

of the principles of the "armed neutrality" was inserted in almost all the treaties of that time from the year 1782 (*u*).

2. The *evidence* in prize cases is, according to treaties, the ship's papers (*x*), namely, passport, and documents about the nature and destination of the cargo. As to the ownership of the cargo the neutral is not bound to have documents relating to that, because the property, even of an enemy, is considered free under a neutral flag ("frei Schiff, frei Gut"). The passport, which is not usually given for more than two years, and should be renewed on the return of the ship to its own country, ought to contain the name of the ship and of its owner, as well as the domicile of the master, which is to be duly particularized. Prize courts formerly condemned all ships built in the country of the enemy, and purchased by neutrals in the time of war, without admitting any excuse in justification. The "armed neutrality" endeavoured to put an end to this practice, though the different governments did not come to an agreement, without a long discussion as to the alterations which should be introduced into the maritime law on this subject. The points in dispute, however, were at last settled, by empowering the neutral to order ships to be built in the country of an enemy on his own account, or to purchase those already built, and the belligerent was bound to admit, as conclusive proof, the bill of sale. To this was added that the subject of an enemy who had been naturalized, or who was employed in the service of a neutral power, should enjoy the rights of a neutral (*y*).

(*u*) *Martens*, Merkw. Fälle, ii. 35—8. Here also we may refer to the treaties of Russia with Denmark, and of the United States with Holland (1782), of Russia with Austria (1785), also with France, the kingdom of both the Sicilies and Portugal (1787), and of Prussia with the United States of America. *Martens*, Rec. iv. 72, 196, 229, 315.

(*x*) See particularly treaties of United States with Holland (1782), with Prussia (1785), and of England with France (1786).

(*y*) See treaties mentioned in notes, pp. 64, 65. In the treaty between England and France (1786) we find the following rules relating to Prize Courts. "Si quelque navire marchand se trouvait dépourvu de ses lettres de mer ou de certificat, il pourra être examiné par le juge compétent, de façon cependant que par d'autres indices et documens il se trouve qu'il appartienne véritablement

(67)

3. With respect to the manner of conducting legal proceedings in prize cases, the treaties of 1783—93 contained but few rules; they only require that cases between privateers and neutrals should be settled impartially, without delay, and in conformity with international justice. Should the judgment be considered unjust or oppressive, diplomatic agents are entitled to intervene in behalf of their fellow-countrymen, and to bring the case before the Court of Appeal (*z*). A privateer, having captured a neutral ship without sufficient grounds, is held liable to damages to the injured party; but unfortunately the amount of compensation is nowhere determined in treaties; Holland and the United States alone have laid down carefully defined rules on the subject, namely, that the privateers shall repay all the legal expenses, and a per-centage for "lucrum cessans" to the owner, and all persons who may suffer from the illegal capture (*a*). All the above-mentioned treaties are imbued, so to say, with one and the same spirit, having a tendency to lessen the cruelties of maritime war, to put an end to the illegal plunder of neutrals by privateers, and to mitigate the harsh decrees of prize courts. It is remarkable that the authors of the "armed neutrality," even

aux sujets de l'un des dits souverains, et qu'il ne contienne aucune marchandise destinée pour l'ennemi, il ne devra point être confisqué mais sera relâché avec sa charge."

(*z*) In addition to the treaties already cited, reference may be made to that between Denmark and Genoa (1789), in which the influence of the "armed neutrality" is apparent. *Martens*, Rec. iv. 438. Denmark and Genoa imposed upon their consuls the duty of defending neutrals in the prize court, and appointed advocates for the same purpose; it was also agreed, when the evidence of neutrals and captors was conflicting, to give the preference to the former, "parceque l'intérêt du capteur doit toujours rendre ses accusations suspectes." This remarkable rule, however, does not occur in other treaties.

(*a*) By the clauses of this treaty the rights of neutral merchants in the prize courts are fully secured. *Martens* is perfectly right in observing, that neutral merchants cannot be considered as compensated by the mere payment for the cargo plundered and injured, but are also fully entitled to an indemnity for what might have been gained, if the vessel had in due course reached its place of destination ("lucrum cessans"). Essai, s. 30, p. 95. Other treaties abrogate some unreasonable contributions imposed on neutrals, as, for example, fees or other duties. *Martens* also gives a full account of the conventions relating to prize jurisdiction of that time, and of the decrees on that subject.

(68)

when belligerents, adhered to their principles. As an instance, we may cite the ordonnance of the Empress Catherine on privateers (1787), issued on the occasion of the war with Turkey, which, being in perfect conformity with the declaration of the Empress in 1780, is, according to the opinion of Hautefeuille, one of the most liberal decrees ever published by a belligerent. The Empress prescribed to privateers the courtesy due to neutrals, and greatly restricted the right of visitation, confining it to particular seas (*b*). Sweden in the decree of 1788 also sanctioned the principles of the "armed neutrality," and conformed her prize jurisprudence thereto (*c*). The declaration, however, of the court of St. Petersburgh, published at the end of the war with Sweden (May 6, 1789), was much more extraordinary, for therein the Empress promised the protection and the assistance of the Russian fleet to the merchants of all neutral nations (*d*). Thus the freedom of neutral commerce became every year more prevalent in Europe, and naval wars were greatly mitigated. Some states found it even advantageous to put an end to privateering. The first attempt to that effect was made by the United States of America in a treaty with Prussia, in which also the right of seizure of war contraband was modified into that of preemption ("droit de préemption") (*e*). The question of the abolition

(*b*) *Martens*, Rec. 336. However it is to be observed that in that war the Greeks, and not native subjects of Russia, received letters of marque from the Empress. In the first war with Turkey (1767—74) Russia had not recourse to privateering. *Martens*, Rec. ii. 32, 33; Essai, p. 46, s. 9.

(*c*) *Martens*, Rec. iv. 394—410. In this decree Sweden admitted the immunity of the neutral flag, and exempted from visitation ships proceeding under neutral convoy. Only in the definition of war contraband does the decree not altogether correspond with the declaration of 1780; for instance, it includes in the list of prohibited goods, besides arms and ammunition, money, but the Swedish king, in consequence of a protest from several powers, subsequently revoked this decree, and returned to the principles of the "armed neutrality."

(*d*) *Martens*, Rec. iv. 428.

(*e*) The treaty of 1785 was concluded by Franklin, the well-known opponent of privateering. In his opinion, this institution ought to be put an end to for the good of mankind and the maintenance of peace. The custom of plundering merchant ships is a remnant of piracy, it produces no benefit at all. At the

(69)

of privateering was subsequently taken up by France (*f*). Unfortunately these humane projects were not destined to be carried into effect, for in 1793 there commenced in Europe a long revolutionary war, which threw all international relations into confusion, almost annihilated the political institutions of Europe, and shook to its foundation the very idea of neutrality.

commencement of a war, indeed, some rich ships may fall into the hands of the captors and be taken by surprise, but the enemy soon becomes more careful and protects the commerce of his subjects by strong convoys. Consequently in the course of war, as the number of privateers increases so does the value of the captures diminish.

(*f*) In 1792, the French diplomatic agents were instructed to ascertain how far foreign nations were inclined to abolish privateering. Unfortunately the political circumstances of that time prevented any sympathy or confidence being placed in the intentions of France. With the exception of the Hanseatic Towns (which made no use of privateers) not a single state of Europe responded to the question proposed. See *Büsch*, 290, 3; *Ortolan*, Diplomatie de la Mer, ii. 56; *Cauchy*, Du respect de la propriété privée sur Mer, annexes, N. 1—4. As to the United States, they answered the French communication favourably, though rather in a vague manner.

ADDITIONAL NOTE BY THE AUTHOR.

Page 63.

In a juridical work like the present, the "armed neutrality" is chiefly considered in its effects upon treaties and international customs; as to the political events which led to its foundation they are recorded by some contemporaries of Catherine II. It would be long, and even useless, to enumerate here all the books and pamphlets which give or pretend to give information on the origin of this celebrated league. As the chief authorities upon the subject may be cited the memoirs of M. *Dohm* (Denkwürdigkeiten meiner Zeit, Hannover, 1814-15-18); Count de *Goertz* (Mémoires sur la Neutralité armée, Bâsle, 1801, Paris, 1804), and Sir *James Harris'* (Lord Malmesbury) Diary, London, 1845.

These diplomatists, though differing from each other in some details, look upon the whole affair nearly in the same light. According to their opinion, the declaration of 1780 arose out of a court intrigue, aimed at the influence of Prince Potemkin, the great favourite of the Empress, and had no other object than to ruin his political power. Catherine herself seemed to have been almost an involuntary agent in the hands of Count Panin, the minister of foreign affairs, with whom the scheme originated. The defence of neutral rights furnished this statesman with a good pretext for overthrowing his rival. By giving full credit to this testimony, and deriving all our information from the same source, it might be supposed that the authors of the "armed neutrality" hardly knew what they were about, and that they only became fully aware of the importance of their acts from subsequent events, and when almost the whole of Europe had acceded to the principles of 1780. Now all this story seems to us, if not a pure invention, at least a great misrepresentation of the facts. The truth is that the success of the Russian policy having excited great envy, the open and secret enemies of the "armed neutrality" had recourse to every kind of obloquy and literary abuse, in order to discredit it in the eyes of the world. Consequently the most absurd rumours, about the authors of the coalition as well as their motives, were circulated abroad, and have been repeated up to the present time. However difficult it would be to refute these calumnies without access to the state archives, where the whole correspondence relating to the subject is deposited, we humbly submit to our readers the following considerations, which are founded upon documentary evidence, or derived from Russian historians.

The first circumstance to be noticed is, that the contention between Prince Potemkin and Count Panin had no such signification, with reference to the "armed neutrality," as foreign diplomatists seemed to imagine. The principal question in dispute was the English alliance; in fact, the first of these statesmen strongly recommended his sovereign to take part in the American war; the second, on the other hand, advised her to stand aloof from the great conflict,

(71)

wherein she would be no gainer, and might lose the advantage of being appealed to as an impartial mediator. As long as the Empress hesitated to avow her decision on the best course to be pursued, the opportunity for a neutral league was necessarily delayed. It may be also easily understood why the cabinet of St. Petersburg kept all these proceedings a secret from the English minister, whose connections with Potemkin were probably as well known to Catherine as to the minister for foreign affairs. It must not be supposed, however, that the declaration of 1780 burst forth as the feat of a skilful courtier, devised to injure a rival. We have every reason to believe that this act had been long in preparation, before the Empress found a favourable opportunity for offering it to Europe, as the most efficient measure against the violence of belligerents. Some diplomatic papers of that time, published from the state archives of St. Petersburg a few years ago (see the *Maritime Magazine*, or the *Morskoi Sbornik* for 1859, Nos. 9—12), prove that the seizure of Russian merchandise near Cadiz by Spanish cruisers was only the last of many grievances reported to Catherine by her ministry. From the very beginning of the war the atrocities of privateers induced the Russian government to take serious measures for the protection of commerce. Thus in 1778, when American cruisers made their first appearance in the northern seas, the Empress gave orders that a squadron should be stationed near Archangel to convoy English traders. Soon afterwards Catherine represented to Denmark and Sweden the urgent necessity of common action against cruisers in the Baltic (Lettres du *Comte Panin* à *M. Sacken*, Chargé d'Affaires à Copenhague, 16 Août, 1778, et note du *Comte Bernstorf*, 28th Sept. 1778). It is remarkable, however, that Count Panin, by recommending the Empress to declare in London and Paris her firm intention to close the entrance of the northern sea to all cruisers, prevented at that time all further proceedings against belligerents, and this declaration appeared to him quite sufficient for the purpose. In the confidential report addressed by the Count to Catherine, and approved by her on the 22nd Dec. 1778, we observe that his intentions were then not so hostile to England as Sir James Harris expected. The dangers of a breach with Great Britain are therein set forth without reserve. The Russian minister submits to his sovereign the future line of conduct to be adopted towards belligerents. In his opinion the question of neutral rights, being very intricate, great moderation and circumspection were requisite to be used in dealing with it. He strongly recommends that Russia should attend to her own interests, and avoid a close alliance with her Baltic neighbours upon that question. Thus a co-operation with Sweden appears to Count Panin not desirable for many reasons. "The Swedish policy of defending neutral rights," says he, "may cause us great difficulties, and involve our government in a disastrous war with the greatest maritime power of Europe." Accordingly, when the cabinet of Stockholm in 1779 made the first proposals for a treaty to that effect, they were declined by Catherine. In short the documents we have cited here give us no indication whatever that Count Panin was the real author of the "armed neutrality." On the contrary, the spirit of the declaration of 1780 seems not to be in accordance with his former views as well as with his general conduct as minister for foreign affairs. We are more inclined to think that the new scheme of neutral policy was originally devised by the Empress herself. The first precedent for it she might have found in the convention of 1759 mentioned before. It must be added that her various reading and intercourse with foreign diplomatists made her better prepared to conduct the foreign affairs of Russia, according to her own enlightened views, than, like some other sovereigns, to follow the advice of her council. In fact, the political talents and literary accomplishments of Catherine are so well known, that they afford sufficient grounds for our adhering to that opinion. Many important state papers were the production of her mind and pen. The authenticity of her correspondence with Voltaire is undoubted, and was never disputed. The same may be said of the "General Instruction for the Government of the Empire." This monument of the legislative wisdom of the Empress, having been transalated into foreign languages, is as well known in Western Europe as in Russia. But the most improbable part of the story about the origin of the "armed neutrality" is that Catherine when signing the declaration did not understand its meaning. Whatever her faults might have been, she was perfectly able to appreciate the consequences of her political acts. It must not be forgotten that Sir James Harris puts into the mouth of one of his confidants the following remarks upon this new plan for the defence of neutral rights: "the declaration is the child of the Empress' own brain." The five articles were sent in the rough draft to Count Panin, who made no addition to the original; see *Lord Malmesbury's* Diary, vol. i. 266. The Count himself, who very soon fell into disgrace, is reported to have abjured all participation in devising the principles of 1780. When questioned upon this point he once said, "they who think that anybody suggested to the Empress the idea of a neutral league, or has now power enough to put it out of her head, are greatly mistaken." *La Cour de Russie, il y a cent ans*, Berlin, 1858, p. 253. All these facts seem rather to corroborate our views than otherwise. However it may be, we sincerely hope that the absurd fables about a court intrigue will fall to the ground, as soon as the historical truth, contained in the diplomatic documents, shall be fully brought to light. May this be done by future inquirers. Nothing but a careful study of the whole reign of Catherine can lead impartial men to safe conclusions upon the "armed neutrality." It will then be easily admitted that its origin is due as much to the natural course of events as to the liberal tendencies of the Russian Empress, and the philosophical spirit of her time.

(73)

PERIOD IV.

FROM 1793 TO 1815.

THE continental governments having, as we have seen, agreed on the fundamental principles of prize jurisprudence, had entertained the idea of drawing up a code of neutrality; but these intentions, originating in the declaration of 1780, were frustrated by the breaking out of the French Revolution. The political events which occurred in France, and afterwards in other countries, not only prevented the further extension of the "armed neutrality," but afforded a pretext to the belligerents for resuming their former harsh proceedings. Consequently international treaties having been rescinded in the midst of the general commotion of Western Europe, Admiralty Courts began to oppress neutral merchants under the authority of the severe instructions of the belligerents, and privateers not only refused to acknowledge the immunity of the flag, but even disavowed the doctrine of the Consolato del Mare. In vain the northern powers endeavoured to form a permanent coalition for the protection of their commerce. The league they entered into (1800) only continued a few months, and failed of attaining the success which attended the first armed neutrality at the time of the American war. By the treaty of St. Petersburgh (1801) the allies even made some concession to England, and considerably modified the principles of Catherine II. In general, during the French revolutionary wars, the power of the neutral governments diminished, and England returned to the system of the Middle Ages without opposition. At the end of the 18th century the decisions of Sir Wm. Scott (afterwards Lord Stowell), supported by the British navy, were enforced on neutrals. The English government, however, failed in attaining an absolute supremacy at sea. When Napoleon established the Continental system (1806) Sir Wm. Scott was obliged to give up the rules of English practice, which he had invariably followed before. In the course of time the belligerents, attacking one another with retaliatory measures, proceeded to the last extremities, and declared neutral commerce unlawful, and even criminal in their eyes. In this manner, the very idea of neutrality was, so to say, repudiated, and privateers as well as prize courts were converted into instruments of commercial inquisition. Such are the final results of this destructive period. In order to define them more accurately, we propose to direct our attention to facts (*a*) and to lay before the reader: 1. The successive modifications of the principles of 1780; 2. The prize law of England and France under Sir Wm. Scott and Portalis; 3. The irregular character of privateering and prize proceedings at the period of the Continental system.

The decree of the year 1792, according to which France renounced privateering, was not carried out. Having declared war against Great Britain the National Convention issued letters of marque, and accordingly many small vessels were dispatched for the purpose of plundering ships engaged in commerce. The former laws, however, respecting maritime prizes, and consequently the ordonnance of the year 1778, were confirmed, and privateers received instructions to respect the immunity of the flag (*b*). In the meantime, England not only refused to adopt the principles of the "armed neutrality," but skilfully took advantage of circumstances, in order to add to the severity of maritime warfare. Observing that the enemy suffered for want of provisions, she adopted what might be called a system of famine (système de famine), namely, entered into conventions (*c*) with the principal powers of Europe in order to forbid the importation of corn and food

(*a*) Compare generally *Comte de Garden*, Histoire de Traités, vi. 301—381; *Wheaton*, Hist. du Droit des Gens, ii. 13—106.

(*b*) See the French ordonnances respecting privateers and prizes which were published at this time, *Martens*, Rec. v. 376—400, vi. 752—776; *Lebeau*, Nouveau Code des Prises, iv. (Paris, an IX.)

(*c*) *Martens*, Recueil, v. 439, 473, 483, 487.

into the French ports, and the carrying on of any intercourse with France. To counteract these measures the National Convention had recourse to retaliation, and by the decree of May 9th, 1793, enjoined cruisers and privateers to seize neutral vessels destined for England, laden with corn or provisions, or freighted with English merchandise. By this decree English property was declared lawful prize, and even neutral cargo, subject to the right of preemption (droit de préemption) on the part of the French government. These arbitrary rules were to remain in force until the interested powers obtained from England a strict observance of the rights of neutrality. A few exceptions were made in favour of Denmark, Sweden, the United States of America, and other governments with which France had treaties of commerce (*d*).

For the purpose of meeting this ordonnance of the Convention, England extended still further the right of preemption, had recourse to a stricter system of blockade, and gave to privateers such instructions against neutrals as authorized them to stop with impunity all merchant vessels (*e*).

The Danish commerce suffered particularly at this time. Up to the 19th August, 1793, 189 Danish vessels had been seized, and the compensation promised them for provisions was only very reluctantly paid, and after much delay. In vain Count Bernstorf attempted, in his celebrated memorial, to show to the cabinet of St. James, that the neutral powers had nothing to do with the peculiar character of the war, and that, according to the principles of independence, they ought to enjoy undisturbed the advantages of commerce, in the midst of the conflict. To this the English government

(*d*) See *Hautefeuille*, iii. 276, &c.

(*e*) *Martens*, Rec. v. 596—605. Besides the Orders in Council of the 8th June and 6th Nov. 1793, according to which England extended the right of preemption to all neutrals, and made lawful prize the produce of French colonies, privateers received also secret instructions very oppressive to general commerce. See *Comte de Garden*, vi 324, 330.

replied that France had placed herself out of the pale of civilization; that no power could be considered neutral with reference to her; and that all nations were bound to take part against her (*e*).

Having exhausted in conference all power of persuasion, Denmark proceeded to arm her fleet, and concluded with Sweden an alliance for the protection of commerce (1794) (*f*). About the same time the conduct of England provoked the resentment of the United States of America. Jefferson, the then secretary for foreign affairs, resisted energetically the violence of the privateers, and protested that the sale of agricultural produce was always considered free; that the belligerents were not entitled to extend the catalogue of contraband on their own authority, and added that the submission to that authority would amount to the surrendering into the hands of one nation the commerce of the world. Yielding to these remonstrances England consented to the appointment of a mixed commission, to examine the claims of American subjects to compensation; as to the exertions of the United States in favour of the immunity of the neutral flag, they remained unsuccessful. By the treaty of 1794 both powers reverted to the principles of the Consolato del Mare, and extended the catalogue of contraband to some articles "ambigui usus" (*g*).

Having made such concessions to the cabinet of St. James, the United States had no right to expect that any greater regard should be shown to their flag by the other belligerents; in fact, even before the conclusion of the treaty to which we have alluded, France had complained that the Americans permitted the English to seize and condemn as lawful prize the merchandise of their own subjects; but when the news that the treaty of 1794 was signed reached Paris, the French government im-

(*e*) See the diplomatic papers on this subject in *Martens'* Causes Célèbres, ii. 333—63; Rec. v. 569, 593.

(*f*) *Martens*, Rec. v. 606.

(*g*) *Martens*, Rec. v. 640; *Wheaton*, Hist. ii. 39—47.

(77)

mediately had recourse to reprisals, and adopted on their side towards the Americans the principles of the Consolato del Mare (Decree, March 2, 1796). In justification of which measures the Directory alleged the following reasons:— 1. According to the treaty of 1778, between France and the United States, it was laid down that all privileges granted by one of the contracting parties in favour of a third power should belong to the other party. 2. That it would be unreasonable to expect them to observe the immunity of the flag with respect to those nations who renounce it of their own accord. After this decree the cabinet of Washington lost no time in breaking off commercial relations with France (*h*).

Thus the example of one belligerent acted upon the other, and the old system of the Consolato del Mare took the place of more liberal principles of neutral commerce. The obstinacy of the belligerents increased every year, and to all the terrors of unbridled privateering was added oppressive procedure in the prize courts. While Marriott, in England, was inclined to support all the abuses of belligerents (*i*), the French government referred cases, relating to maritime prizes, to the ordinary courts of law; and even conferred a prize jurisdiction on their consuls in neutral ports. The partiality of these new judges reached its greatest height at the end of the 18th century; they called upon neutral ships to produce all papers required by the French regulations, without paying any attention to the difference of European laws in that respect, and considered every ship, which had once belonged to the enemy,

(*h*) *Wheaton*, Hist. ii. 50, 51; *Martens*, Rec. vii. 376. Friendly intercourse between France and the United States was re-established by the *Morfontaine* Treaty in the year 1800. *Martens*, Rec. vii. 484. By this convention both parties reverted to the former liberal principles of neutrality, and the immunity of the neutral flag was again acknowledged.

(*i*) This judge was the great opponent of neutral commerce; he did not consider the old English customs sufficiently severe in checking it, and laid down in the year 1794 an extraordinary rule, according to which neutral nations were only permitted to carry their own produce, and not that of other countries. *Jacobsen*, Seerecht, i. preface. Marriott defended this arbitrary limitation of trade with the enemy, on the principles of the Navigation Act, which was then adopted by many states in imitation of England.

(78)

lawful prize, though she had afterwards been transferred to a neutral by a regular bill of sale (*k*).

In the year 1798 the Directory published two new decrees, unprecedented in history; one of them shortened prize proceedings to such a degree that there was not time enough for neutrals to bring forward their evidence; the other introduced a rule, whereby the character of the ship was to be determined by the cargo, that is, it declared lawful prize all neutral ships in which were found any article of English manufacture (*l*). By the introduction of these decrees, international trade ceased to have free course; visitation degenerated into abusive search, and privateers became pirates. In answer to the question of neutral merchants, what was to be considered war contraband? the French privateers replied, "all that is worth seizing" (tout ce qui vaut la peine d'être pris).

It appears, then, that the principles of the "armed neutrality" were abandoned during these revolutionary wars. In fact, the United States of America, on the conclusion of a new treaty with Prussia in the year 1799, even proposed to abolish the immunity of the flag; or, at least, to postpone

(*k*) Several French jurists then, and afterwards some members of the Directory itself, protested against this unusual change introduced into prize practice (*Lebeau*, iv. 345, 403—415). Portalis justly says, "C'était une grande erreur d'avoir attribué la connaissance des prises aux tribunaux ordinaires. Quand il s'agit de la justice des nations entre elles; quand il s'agit des droits de la guerre et de leur exécution; quand il faut peser les traités, décider si une nation est amie ou neutre, on est étonné sans doute de voir intervenir une autre autorité que celle du gouvernement." According to the custom of all governments prize jurisdiction belongs to special courts, established for the purpose. *Pritchard*, Digest, iii. 163, 412; *Wildman*, Institutes, ii. 163, 361. The appointment of prize judges in neutral ports was also an anomaly contrary to international law; besides, the consuls, to whom the Directory gave jurisdiction in these cases, were, according to *Büsch*, often part owners of the privateering vessels, and were consequently interested in the condemnation of the neutral merchant. *Büsch*, Das Bestreben der Völker, S. 393.

(*l*) See *Comte de Garden*, vi. 335—337; *Robinson*, vi. Coll. 33, not.; *Büsch*, 332—336, 394—411; *Jacobsen*, Seerecht, 69; *Martens*, Rec. vi. 398. In a very short time after the publication of these decrees there were confiscated more than 300 neutral vessels, so that merchants did not dare to undertake a voyage, excepting under the protection of convoy.

its acknowledgment to a more favourable time (*m*). Only Denmark and Sweden adhered to the traditions of their policy, and, in order to protect their commerce, resumed the practice of making use of convoy. This proceeding was resisted on the part of Great Britain, and, in a short time, produced a violent collision (*n*). Both the neutral powers were already on the point of yielding to the English government, when they found an energetic supporter in the Emperor Paul I. Having been disgusted with the violent conduct of the belligerents, he published, August 16, 1800, a declaration for the purpose of re-establishing an armed neutrality; and, finding Denmark, Sweden and Prussia favourable to his views, signed, in conjunction with them, on the $\frac{4}{16}$ Dec., 1800, the memorable convention, in which, in addition to the principles of the Empress Catherine II., there were laid down the following rules, as being in conformity with international law.

1. Blockade is only reputed to be broken by neutrals when, disregarding the warning of the belligerent, they enter the blockaded port by force or fraud. 2. Neutrals under convoy are free from visitation; the declaration of the officer in command of the convoy to be considered sufficient (*o*).

Unfortunately the second armed neutrality was not so successful as might have been expected. The northern coalition did not last long, and was put an end to by the bombardment of Copenhagen and the death of the Emperor Paul (*p*).

On the succession of Alexander I. to the throne of Russia

(*m*) *Wheaton*, Hist. ii. 55—76; *Martens*, Suppl. ii. 227. However the right of preemption of war contraband was confirmed in the new treaty. It includes, also, some liberal interpretations of prize law. See art. 14, 16, 21, 23.

(*n*) *Martens*, Erzähl. i. 299, 302, ii. 39—58; *Wheaton*, Hist. ii. 76—83.

(*o*) For the acts relating to the second armed neutrality, see *Martens*, Suppl. ii. 344—486; and *Baron Carl Martens*, Nouv. Caus. célèb. Leipz. 1843, ii. 176—272; see also *Miloutine*, Hist. of War of 1799, a work of the present Russian secretary at war at St. Petersburgh, published in the Russian language. He also enters into the history of the second armed neutrality.

(*p*) Of treaties concluded under the second armed neutrality we can only refer to that between Russia and Sweden, 1st March, 1801. *Martens*, Suppl. ii. 307.

new prospects of peace opened to the world. He proposed to the cabinet of St. James to hold a conference, which should lay down the fundamental principles of neutral commerce; he also promised to invite the Danish and Swedish governments to accede to them, and, in fact, on the $\frac{5}{17}$ June, 1801, there was signed between Russia and England a new convention, in which both parties made some important mutual concessions; the greater part however of the regulations of the armed neutrality, such as the definition of war contraband and the free access of neutral merchants to the ports of the belligerent, remained unaltered. With respect to colonial trade, European merchants were placed on an equal footing with the subjects of the United States of America, that is, obtained the right to import from the enemy's colonies goods for their own use. But the change in the definition of blockade, though dependent on one word (*or* instead of *and*), seemed to be more important (*q*). Ships under convoy were only exempted from the visitation of privateers. The principle that the flag covers the cargo (le pavillon couvre la cargaison) was also rescinded on the condition that enemy produce and manufactures (marchandises du crû ou de fabrique de l'ennemi), purchased by neutral subjects and laden as their own property, should be free. As additional articles to the convention some clauses relating to irregularities and defects in prize practice were introduced. 1. The contracting parties gave diplomatic agents the right of protesting against unjust decisions, and of bringing the case before the highest Court of Appeal. 2. Without the consent of the Admiralty judge it was forbidden to unlade and sell the property in dispute prior to its being adjudged lawful prize. 3. If a ship were arrested without sufficient cause it was stipulated that for every day's delay compensation should be paid by the privateer (*r*).

(*q*) Lord Grenville himself says in his speech that in the armed neutrality it was required that blockading ships should be in sufficient number, "*and* stand near the port;" on the contrary, in the convention of 1801 this *and* was changed into *or*. Lord Grenville seems to attach much importance to this alteration, and to the manner in which the treaty was drawn up. V. Subst. of Speech, Nov. 12, 1801, p. 82—3, Lond. 1802.

(*r*) The convention of 1801 is inserted in *Martens*.

(81)

In the following year the St. Petersburg convention was after some hesitation accepted by Sweden and Denmark, but they gained little advantage by this vacillating policy, as Great Britain paid no attention to the observance of the provisoes she had entered into, and finding the convention too unfavourable to her interests used every effort to interpret it according to her own views (*s*). Sweden soon afterwards, yielding to the demands of the cabinet of St. James, signed a new convention with England in 1803, wherein the catalogue of war contraband was considerably enlarged (*t*).

From this rapid sketch it may be inferred that the period of the French revolution was altogether unfavourable to the principles of the "armed neutrality," for by changing the character of international relations, this prolonged contest, which extended all over Europe, gave a preponderance to the power of the belligerents, and destroyed the coalitions of neutrals. The reforms in the prize law, which, as we observed, began in the year 1783, having been interrupted, were now again

(*s*) See a curious pamphlet by *Jacobsen*, "Versuch eines Commentars zu den Russischen Beschwerden über die Beeinträchtigung des Russischen Handels durch England." Altona, 1808. In illustration of the manner in which England interpreted the convention of 1801, we quote from this work the following facts. When the members of the opposition, Lords Grenville and Howick, observed in parliament that the convention abandoned the colonial and coasting trade to neutrals, the minister, Lord Sidmouth, answered, that this was not evident from the words of the treaty, and that the contracting parties might enter into a new arrangement about it. As little foundation was there for the statement of the English ministry, that the neutral powers had shown their confidence in the impartiality of the British Admiralty Court, by declining to insist upon any conditions in favour of their own subjects; this is indeed refuted by the supplementary articles of the treaty. Sir William Scott also asserted that the convention was only applicable to Russian ships, and not to Russian produce found on board neutral ships. In that case he followed the precedents of English practice; according to this interpretation, hemp, masts and some other articles, which according to the treaty were not reputed to be contraband, were pronounced by the English judge to be lawful prize, and that even in those cases in which the legality of the neutral commerce did not admit of doubt. Complaints were also made of delay in the proceedings, and that cases which might have been disposed of in six months were protracted by the court for two or three years.

(*t*) *Martens*, Suppl. iii. 525.

inevitably postponed. In the silence or inefficiency of treaties, neutral nations were bound to submit to the rules of the Admiralty Court. This circumstance imposes upon us the duty of carefully ascertaining what was the state at that time of the prize practice of England and France, the principal belligerent powers, and to show what principles of neutrality were acknowledged in the courts of these two countries.

We have had occasion to remark on the character of Marriott, and also on the unsatisfactory state of the French prize courts. It must be added that the irregular decrees of the Directory were subsequently abrogated in France, and the rules of the Admiralty Court in England acquired solidity and a more systematic character. These improvements were due to two eminent jurists and statesmen. One of these was Sir William Scott, afterwards Lord Stowell, who succeeded Marriott in the High Court of Admiralty in England in 1798; the other was Portalis, who was at the head of the French prize court (Conseil des Prises) (*u*) reconstituted by Napoleon in 1800. They were prepared to treat questions of international law logically, and to remedy its defects by the expression of their opinion on new and intricate points.

(*u*) The materials for information about English prize practice are as follows: 1. Reports of *Robinson*, with the continuation of *Edwards* and *Dodson*, published at London, in eight volumes, under the title of "Reports of Cases argued and determined in the High Court of Admiralty, commencing with the Judgments of Sir William Scott" (1800); 2. Decisions of judges of appeal by *Acton*. "Reports of Cases argued and determined before the Lords Commissioners of Appeals in Prize Causes, London" (1811). These large collections were not accessible to me in Russia, and I was obliged to content myself with consulting *Pritchard's* Admiralty Digest, published in the form of an analytical Lexicon. "Analytical Digest of all the reported Cases determined by the High Court of Admiralty, &c., London" (1847). In addition to this work I consulted the treatises of the English jurists, *Chitty*, *Oke Manning*, *Wildman*, who consider the decisions of their favourite judge to form a complete system of international law, and quote them very largely. The more important of these works is that of *Wildman*, "Institutes of International Law, London," 1849—50, 2 vols.

As to the judgments of *Portalis*, they are only published in the large collection of *Sirey*, of access to which I was also unfortunately deprived. To supply these deficiencies I had recourse to the works of *Martens* (Merkw. Fälle), *Wheaton*, *Massé* (Le Droit Commercial, Par. 1844, i. 313—403), and *Jacobsen* (Das praktische Seerecht der Englander und Franzosen, ii. v.).

(83)

Our particular attention is due to the decisions of *Sir William Scott.* In them we find the summary of the English system of prize law, as opposed to the principles of the "armed neutrality." As to *Portalis,* he certainly did not enjoy such independent power as his eminent contemporary, but, on the other hand, he was more liberal and impartial in his views, and enjoyed more of the respect and favour of other nations. We intend to give here a comparative review of the opinions of both of these judges to the best of our power. The principal points for our consideration are those which relate to questions about neutral rights, such as:— 1. The general doctrine of jurisprudence. 2. The evidence of neutral property in ship and cargo. 3. Questions concerning war contraband and blockade. 4. Costs of suit and damages. 5. Appeals.

Nature and extent of Prize Jurisdiction (*v*). This, according to Sir William Scott, depends on international customs. Admiralty Courts act "jure belli," and therefore can be established by the belligerent powers only in their own territories, or in the ports of an ally, but not in the territory of a neutral power. Hence Sir William Scott decided that condemnations pronounced by a French consul in Norway (then neutral) were illegal (*x*). On the contrary, the authority of a competent court is admitted everywhere by the "jus gentium," its decisions cannot in any manner be altered or annulled. However, if a privateer violate the territorial right of a neutral power; for example, if he make an attack out of its port, or seize a vessel on a sea subject to its sovereignty, then the offended power may inflict upon him punishment within his territories and deprive him of his prize.

Sir William Scott refused also to a belligerent the right to decide a case concerning captures which had been carried

(*v*) *Pritchard,* Adm. Dig. 311, 315, 316; *Wheaton,* Elements, ii. 45—6, 87—9, 93—95. (French edition, Leipzig, 1844.)

(*x*) However, the English themselves during the war with the United States of America established prize courts at Leghorn. *Blackstone,* iii. 5, § 8.

(84)

into a neutral country, but this opinion was overruled by the Lords Commissioners.

The subjection of the neutral to the belligerent begins from the moment of the capture. The preliminary measures in prize cases, as laid down by the English and French legislation, are as follows: immediately on his arrival at a port in his country, the privateer is bound by his oath to deliver up to the Admiralty authorities all papers found on board the captured ship. After some days, devoted to the examination of the prize, an official is sent who administers interrogatories to the master and crew of the captured vessel. When this formality is completed, the judge names a time, in the course of which the owner of the ship and cargo should consult some professional man to prepare his case in legal form, and enter a protest against the privateer (*y*).

Hence it is evident that the Prize Court considers neutrals as plaintiffs, and privateers as defendants. This view seems to be supported by the theory of evidence laid down in the decisions of Sir William Scott and Portalis, who threw all the burden of proof on the neutrals, the privateer having only to defend himself.

The ship's papers are considered the principal evidence in the Admiralty Court. It is only by a reference to these that the neutral subject can satisfy the belligerent of his nationality, and justify his conduct during the war. But in the opinion of Sir William Scott and Portalis, these documents are not sufficient for the discovery of the truth. "The ship's papers," the English judge says, "are a dead letter; they ought to be confirmed by personal evidence" (*z*). Therefore, it is necessary

(*y*) For details on this subject, see *Wildman*, International Law, ii. 335—356, 365—378, 389, &c.; and *Ortolan*, Diplom. de la Mer, ii. 354—388 (appendice). The French law requires a separate act (called a procès verbal), explanatory of the cause of arrest, but Sir William Scott dispensed with this formality. In the opinion of the English judge every privateer captures a vessel at his own risk, and under his own personal responsibility.

(*z*) *Pritchard*, 151; *Jacobsen*, Seerecht, 1815, 434—7. "Certainly," Sir William Scott says in another place, "the ship's papers, when found in order, are almost a decisive argument; but when from circumstances it is evident they

to examine the captured crew; if they are deserving of credit and are not detected in contradictory statements, or in the perversion of truth, the court decides the case in favour of the neutral; but, we must add, the English practice gives preference to the evidence brought forward by the privateer, and only looks without suspicion upon the neutral, when the testimony in his favour perfectly coincides with the papers (*a*).

In the case of witnesses contradicting the written documents, further proof is required. To this rule the English judge admits many exceptions, and inclines, sometimes, in favour of the verbal evidence; at others, gives the preference to the documents. He states that the papers often appear suspicious, and the personal testimony clear, frank, and worthy of credit; on the other hand, cases occur when the witnesses speak with such disregard to truth, that the judge decides the case on the written documents (*b*).

New or further proof Sir Wm. Scott admits only in favour of those neutrals who have not been detected in any breach of duty or fraud (*c*). Therefore the case is considered by him as lost, (a) when there is discovered a false destination of the ship, or general want of good faith; (b) when the neutral

are false, it would be extraordinary to expect the Admiralty Court to pay any regard to them. Sometimes, a single paper undermines confidence in the neutral; sometimes all the papers are in order, but the case is decided in favour of the privateer." *Jacobsen*, ibid. 444.

(*a*) In order to justify his system, Sir William Scott says, "International law has more confidence in the evidence of a neutral subject, and only condemns his property according to the testimony of the crew, or other reliable facts;" but at the same time he required on the part of neutrals such a perfect harmony between personal and documentary evidence, as it is almost impossible for them to attain, thereby rendering it difficult for them to free themselves from suspicion.

(*b*) Generally, the doctrine of Sir William Scott concerning judicial evidence is very intricate and uncertain, as far as we can judge by the majority of cases. He very seldom preferred ship's papers to personal evidence, and, accusing the neutrals of being guilty of malpractices and fraud, gave credit only to those papers which were prepared and delivered to the ship before there was any apprehension of war. *Wildman*, ii. 368.

(*c*) Further proof is the privilege of honest ignorance, or honest negligence to neutrals, who have not violated the law of neutrality. *Pritchard*, 173—6.

(86)

intentionally mixes his goods with those of the enemy, for example, first claims all the cargo, and afterwards only part of it; (c) when the papers are concealed from the privateer, or two different copies have been discovered.

As to Portalis, his doctrine on evidence is in some respects more favourable towards neutrals, although it differs but little in substance from the English system. The most correct documents, says the French judge, sometimes protect enemies' property; on the other hand, the neutral character of the ship may appear notwithstanding irregularity in the form of the papers. All questions of neutrality are matters of conscience; to solve them, correctly, you should not pay much attention to form, but penetrate the depths of the subject, and turn to the depositions of the parties, as they may elucidate the obscure points in the case, and supply whatever is wanting in the written documents (*d*).

The number and character of the ship's papers are not uniformly defined by the rules of the prize court. Although the French ordonnances contained a list of documents to be required from neutral merchants, Portalis did not strictly adhere to these conditions. According to his opinion, it would be wrong in a judge to condemn the vessel as prize merely on account of the insufficiency or inaccuracy of some document, but he ought to weigh the matter, and distinguish irregular papers from those which are false; the first do not deprive the neutral of the right of bringing in further proofs in defence of his nationality; the last can only be injurious if a fraud is detected, which infallibly leads to new suspicions, and shakes the confidence in the whole case (*e*). Accordingly the demands of Portalis are very moderate for the recognition of neutral property in a ship; he considers one written docu-

(*d*) *Martens*, Merk. Fälle, ii. 216—218. The doctrine of Portalis about evidence is explained fully by *Jacobsen*, Das prakt. Seerecht, ii. 248, 254—406, 464—484, 512—521.

(*e*) La fraude qui paraît, fait suspecter celle qui ne paraît pas : de là tout est ébranlé, dès que la simulation se manifeste quelque part, car la foi des hommes est indivisible. *Massé*, i. 318.

(87)

ment sufficient, although the rest might be found irregular (*f*); and directs his attention particularly to the passport of the captured ship. "The passport, he says, is a special document, certifying the belligerent power that the ship does not belong to the enemy; that her flag is true, and that the master sails under the protection of the laws of his own country;" consequently the absence of a passport inevitably leads to condemnation, as the ship is bereft of the protection of a neutral flag (*g*). But, as soon as the nationality of the vessel is once admitted, no other evidence from the privateer that the neutrals have destroyed their papers is received (*h*). Sir William Scott was less favourable to the neutral; he admitted, in such cases, without distinction, the allegation of a privateer against that of the master and crew.

Besides the rules we have stated, the English courts followed some special ones in cases relating to the nationality of persons, and the property of ships or cargo (*i*). For the solution of cases relating to the first of these questions, the nationality of persons, i. e. of the master, owner and crew of the captured ship, Sir William Scott was not satisfied with personal evidence, and that of papers, but took into consideration other circumstances. In the present state of commercial affairs very often it happens that the subjects of one state continually live and carry on traffic in another: it may

(*f*) Il ne s'agit pas de justifier la propriété neutre par le concours simultané de toutes les pièces énumérées dans les règlemens. Il suffit, selon les circonstances, que l'une d'elles constate cette propriété, si elle n'est contredite ou combattue par des circonstances plus décisives. *Massé*, ib.

(*g*) *Jacobsen*, Seerecht, i. 95; *Massé*, 325—329. But irregularity in the form of the passport does not afford grounds for condemnation, if the nationality of the ship is proved by other papers; as, however, there are some treaties in which the number of the documents is specified, Portalis required from the contracting parties the strict performance of those clauses.

(*h*) Portalis says, "quand la neutralité est prouvée on ne peut admettre le reproche de simulation sans preuves. Des soupçons arbitraires ne peuvent détruire les actes authentiques." *Martens*, Merkw. Fälle, ii. 130. For the French ordonnance on this subject, see *Massé*, i. 332—336. With respect to Sir William Scott, *Pritchard* only quotes two cases in which neutral ships suspected of having destroyed papers were released, 321, 322.

(*i*) *Pritchard*, 233—247.

(88)

be asked, are we to consider them with reference to their origin or their place of domicile? Certainly, if a neutral subject formally becomes an enemy's subject, his property is considered lawful prize; but Sir William Scott did not confine himself to this alone: according to his opinion, temporary residence in an enemy's country might serve as sufficient ground for condemnation. The learned judge explains this in the following manner:—"It is true," he says, "that belligerent powers have no right to forbid neutrals all intercourse with the enemy, and merchants are quite free to enter into all foreign ports; still, if a person establishes himself permanently, or for a long time, in an enemy's country, he cannot be considered a neutral citizen; the usual plea of merchants, that they go to the enemy's country for their own affairs, serves but little in their favour. There are matters which may detain a man in a foreign country all his life; he, who went for a time before the actual commencement of the war, easily finds an opportunity to return to his native country, and we may with confidence assume that he who does not leave the enemy's territory during all the war has no right to appeal to his neutrality; otherwise foreign merchants might appropriate all the trade of the enemy, and escape condemnation." On these grounds Sir William Scott thought himself entitled to demand from a neutral subject, who had lived for a long time in an enemy's country, a satisfactory explanation. The English judge is generally inclined to suppose in such cases the existence of an *animus manendi*. But as all individuals are not to be placed in the same category, and treated as equally guilty, the circumstances of each particular case should be taken into consideration (*k*). Some branches of trade are certainly incompatible with a neutral character; for example, if the enemy's government give foreign merchants such privileges or monopolies as its own subjects do not enjoy, here it is evident that the neutral affords active

(*k*) Cases of domicile do not depend on residence alone, but on a consideration of all the circumstances of the case. *Wildman*, ii. 36—40; *Wheaton*, Elem. i. 310, 325—7.

assistance to the enemy, and his property is liable to condemnation (*l*). The goods of a company or mercantile firm, settled in the territory of an enemy, are also considered lawful prize, although part of their capital should belong to neutrals.

According to the logic of Sir William Scott it might be expected that the English judge, following the same reasoning, would admit that the property of an enemy subject living in neutral territory should be free. Without expressly repudiating this conclusion he sought different pretexts for evading it, and declared amongst other things that an enemy in no case had " personam standi in judicio" (*m*). Sir William Scott, however, did not follow strictly his rules with regard to North Americans coming to Europe, and Europeans domiciled in the East. It would be hard, he says, to molest the first, as their distance from home is so great; and the second, not mixing with the natives, are considered the subjects of the government under whose protection they carry on their trade.

The property in the ship, according to the opinion of Sir William Scott, is determined by the domicile of the owner; consequently a ship, the owner of which resides in an enemy's country, is to be considered lawful prize, although provided with neutral documents. However, the English practice does not forbid neutral subjects to buy ships of an enemy, and only requires that the enemy's title should be absolutely and completely divested. In order to prove his property in these cases the neutral is bound to produce his deed of purchase. According to law, the sale is liable to be impugned if the ship should still continue to sail under the command of an enemy master, under an enemy flag, or with an enemy passport (*n*). To obviate the plea of pretended neutrality, Sir William Scott required that the transfer of the

(*l*) This is the reason why the English do not admit the legality of the colonial and coasting trade with the enemy.

(*m*) As far as I have been able to ascertain Sir William Scott never released the property of an enemy subject settled in a neutral state.

(*n*) *Pritchard*, 454—5; *Wildman*, ii. 89, seq. Portalis followed in these cases the French ordonnance. *Massé*, 323.

enemy ship should not take place before its arrival at its destination; a sale "in transitu" the English judge considered illegal. A ship chartered for a time is liable to confiscation.

Still more severely does the English judge act against neutrals in questions respecting the ownership of the cargo; for the principles of the "Consolato del Mare" seeming to him to be too lenient, he lays down in these cases the following new rules:

1. Goods sent from an enemy port are to be considered the property of the enemy, unless the contrary be proved.

2. The produce of an enemy country, although belonging to a neutral, is declared to be lawful prize (*o*).

3. The enemy has no right to sell his goods "in transitu," otherwise a cargo liable to confiscation might escape capture (*p*).

4. Goods sent from a neutral port consigned to an enemy are subject to confiscation as enemy property, even before reaching the place of their destination (*q*).

Considering all these rules it is not difficult to understand how little opportunity Sir William Scott gave neutrals of trading with the enemy, and what encouragement he afforded to privateering at the expense of other nations. The examination of the doctrine of Sir William Scott respecting war contraband and blockade leads us to the same conclusion.

(*o*) *Wildman*, ii. 144.

(*p*) From this rule Sir William Scott admitted no exception, although the "bona fides" of the neutrals should be proved. "After the numberless cases in which this question has been decided it is not now an arguable point." The transfer of an enemy's property "in transitu" in the opinion of Sir William Scott is always made "cum animo fraudandi."

(*q*) *Wildman*, Inst. ii. 98—114. In order to justify his view Sir William Scott says, "In time of peace the property in the cargo and the mutual relations of consignee and consignor are determined by custom and contract; but when war breaks out, these questions should not be disposed of by individuals to the detriment of the right of capture, otherwise the property of the enemy will be free from condemnation; the neutral consignor has but to declare in his papers that he takes the risk upon himself, and the enemy cargo will be free and enjoy the protection of neutrality;" and thus, according to the opinion of the eminent English judge, war gives the privateer full power to arrest goods sent to the enemy.

(91)

Here we think his partiality in favour of the belligerents, his suspicion and distrust of the neutrals, are more evident; for without adhering to the "Consolato del Mare" he appeals only to the law of necessity, and extends the right of capture to the utmost limit.

The English prize courts in former times held very indefinite and arbitrary views respecting *contraband of war* (*r*). When Marriott presided, these views were still further extended, and particularly from the year 1793, to the end of the eighteenth century. Scarcely any object of neutral commerce was left free from condemnation, or not liable to the right of preemption at that time. Sir William Scott also followed these precedents, and his list of prohibited articles was consequently enlarged or reduced according to the circumstances and the exigencies of war. He considers as war contraband, ships of war, ammunition and everything that can strengthen the enemy, as, for instance, food, provisions, raw materials, ship timber, &c. Without condemning in all cases, he limits the absolute prohibition to arms, ammunition and ships of war supplied to the enemy, treats with more indulgence articles "ancipitis usus," and does not consider provisions, rosin, hemp, &c., as war contraband—1. When they are transferred in native ships; 2. When they are destined for civil use and not for purposes of war (*s*); 3. When they are in a raw state (*t*). In the last three cases the right of preemption (*u*) is exercised, and though the privateer is

(*r*) *Pritchard*, 103—113.

(*s*) Upon these grounds the Admiralty judge commonly considered as lawful prize all provisions destined for military ports of an enemy, as, for example, cheese of an inferior kind, herrings, butter, &c. *Jacobsen*, Seerecht, 651. In order to determine the use to which the articles of the cargo were applicable, the judge referred them to experts. *Jacobsen*, ibid., 645, 654; *Wildman*, ii. 215. But afterwards Sir William Scott changed his opinion, and introduced more largely condemnation. *Wheaton*, Elements, ii. 150.

(*t*) Sir William Scott on this account condemned rope, masts, ship timber, sugar. On the contrary, hemp, common wood, corn, &c., he considered less suspicious articles.

(*u*) The right of preemption, according to the opinion of Sir William Scott, belongs to the belligerents "ipso jure," although Sweden was the only

considered free from responsibility for damage, the neutral receives compensation for his cargo (*x*). As to articles reported to be undoubted contraband, the English practice punished their importation with severe penalties. Former Admiralty judges, as, for example, Marriott, generally condemned as lawful prize, not only the ship, but the rest of the cargo. Sir William Scott admitted many exceptions to this rule; according to his opinion general condemnation is a just punishment for violation of international law, but if, in case of war contraband, ship and cargo belong to different persons, then it is necessary as far as possible to distinguish the innocent from the guilty (*y*).

The penalty for the importation of war contraband in the Prize Courts falls on the neutral only when he is taken in flagrante delicto, *i. e.*, at any place between that of departure and destination (*z*). Sir William Scott, however, was not contented with this extensive interpretation, but went further, and considered as lawful prize even ships on their return voyage, if they had before carried contraband under false papers.

Still more severely did the Admiralty Courts act against neutral subjects engaged in conveying enemy officers and soldiers; in such cases they could not expect the least indulgence. The plea of the master that he was compelled by

power which has admitted it in her treaties; on the contrary we seldom meet with the "droit de préemption" in the judgments of Portalis. *Jacobsen*, Das pr. Seerecht, ii. 118.

(*x*) Respecting the amount of compensation the English judge says, "the purchaser is not bound to pay the neutral as much as he would have received from an enemy in distress" (a famine price). *Wildman*, ii. 219, 221, 222.

(*y*) Where the owner of the cargo has any interest in the ship, the whole of his property will be involved in the same sentence of condemnation; for where a man is concerned in an illegal transaction, all his property embarked in that transaction is liable to confiscation. To escape the contagion of contraband, the article must be the property of a different owner. On the contrary, Portalis, following the French regulations, considered the ship liable to condemnation only when the contraband formed more than three quarters of the whole cargo. *Martens*, Merkw. Fälle, ii. 221; *Jacobsen*, pr. Seerecht, ii. 80—93.

(*z*) In cases of contraband the offence is generally deposited with the cargo, and the penalty does not attach to the return voyage.

force to receive them on board was in no case admitted. Sir William Scott relieved from condemnation neutral ships only when the officers travelled on their own account, paid as common passengers, and their true character was not known. As to carrying despatches to the enemy, whether relating to military or civil matters (*a*), the ship was in that case considered as lawful prize, although the character of the papers thus conveyed might be unknown to the owner or master, and they might relate to very trifling matters. An insignificant paper may prove to be important at a subsequent time, and have an influence on military operations by conveying news about the enemy. If the Prize Court be only satisfied of the "mens rea et corpus delicti" of the neutral he cannot escape condemnation. Certainly justice requires that the owner of the cargo should not be responsible for the faults of the master if he does not participate in them. With respect to the conveyance of private papers, although despatched by men holding office under Government, this is not necessarily attended with condemnation, nor is the ship confiscated for the conveyance of despatches from enemy's territory to neutral countries; for example, to consuls, diplomatic agents, &c.; but in all such cases the belligerent has full right to peruse the papers addressed to his adversary. On these grounds Sir William Scott permitted privateers to seize all suspected ships, and even reimbursed them on a liberal scale their expenses and damages at the cost of the neutral.

This doctrine of Sir William Scott respecting contraband, oppressive enough as it was towards neutrals, appears to us very indulgent, when compared with the rules laid down by him relating to blockade (*b*). Here Sir William Scott exceeds the limits of moderation, and at every step refines too much.

(*a*) *Wildman*, ii. 234—244; *Wheaton*, ii. 161—4.

(*b*) The principal decisions of Sir William Scott regarding blockade are collected in *Pritchard*, 36—49, and *Wildman*, ii. 184. In the Tübingen Journal of Political Science for 1852, we find a very interesting, critical analysis of these. See article by *Wurm*, Denkwürdigkeiten des Völkerrechts, p. 477, &c.

(94)

It is notorious that a blockade, like a siege on land, is an operation of war directed chiefly against the enemy ; the English judge, however, endeavours to turn it principally against neutrals. In vain we search in his judgments for any solid definition or strict logical deductions. His arrière-pensée appears to be to give as much liberty as possible to privateers. But we will not anticipate, let the reader judge for himself. Sir William Scott divided blockade into "de facto" (or actual blockade), and legal blockade established by notification (per notificationem). International jurists find the last form of blockade very uncertain or fictitious. Sir William Scott, himself, admits that it is reputed to exist until the belligerent has notified its cessation to the neutrals. Not less ambiguous is his expression "actual blockade." To establish the validity of a blockade according to the English judge, the presence of some cruisers stationed at no great distance from the port or shore is quite sufficient. He does not consider it their duty closely to besiege the port, but chiefly to exercise surveillance over neutrals ; and it is by no means forbidden to them to leave their station for the purpose of pursuing suspected vessels.

There are two modes of notification of blockade, one by information given to the neutral governments (constructive notice), the other by that given to the merchants themselves (actual notice). In the first case the judge supposes that the existence of the blockade is known from the circulation of news, and consequently pays no attention to any merchant who pleads ignorance as an excuse. The second form of notification (actual notice) is made use of in case of "de facto" blockade. As to vessels coming out of the besieged port, notice is not required, for it must be presumed they are necessarily acquainted with the state of the case. In general, the English were not in the habit of giving notice of blockade to other governments, on the alleged ground that the news would spread of itself, a practice which directly tended to the benefit of privateers, and to the injury of neutral commerce.

In regard to breach of blockade, the Court of Admiralty

of Great Britain assumed that the intention of entering into a blockaded port, although not carried into effect, was an illegal act. Sir William Scott, indeed, held that the Admiralty judge was entitled to condemn as lawful prize neutral vessels, which, directing their course towards the blockading line, or approaching the cruisers, made inquiries of them respecting the existence of the blockade (*c*). Moreover, a conditional or eventual destination to a blockaded port makes a ship liable to condemnation, although the master might have been misled by false intelligence concerning the removal of the blockade. Nothing but an extreme case, as, for example, a storm, want of provisions, &c., gives a merchant the right to enter a blockaded port, if it should lie on his way, or only at a short distance out of it; but he must not cast anchor in a place where he might easily elude the blockading squadron. The purchase of ships in a blockaded port is also regarded as strictly prohibited. In short, the prohibitions and suspicions of the Admiralty judge had no limit. All the powerful logic of Sir William Scott would appear to have been directed to the justification of cruisers and privateers in seizing neutral vessels wherever they were met with. Thus blockades, which by other nations have been used as local and temporary measures, were employed by the English as a general expedient for extending their maritime jurisdiction. In their opinion, extensive coasts and whole countries might be declared to be in a state of blockade. This policy had no other object in view than to supply the deficiency of a regular navy by the severity of prize law.

The punishment for breach of blockade is the condemnation of the ship, from which rule Sir William Scott admits of no exception. In his opinion, disputes concerning breach of blockade between the owner and master do not fall within the province of Admiralty judges. One criminal party can-

(*c*) The rule is, that after knowledge of an existing blockade, you are not to go to the very station of the blockading fleet under pretence of inquiry. It may be added that this rule totally deprives the neutral of all power of ascertaining the existence of a blockade by personal inquiry.

(96)

not exculpate himself by throwing the blame upon another. In the opinion of the English judge the master is an agent with full power to manage the ship, and his acts are everywhere reputed the acts of his employer; the owner cannot impugn them anywhere but in his own country (*d*). If there be the least reason to presume that at the time of receiving the cargo on board the existence of the blockade was known, the responsibility then also extends to the owner of it (*e*). The learned judge considered more severity would be justifiable, if the vessel was suspected of a fraudulent deviation in order to approach the blockaded port, for example, under pretence of want of water, provisions, &c. In such cases, he said, the master has probably changed his course to execute the commission of the owner, and to convey the merchandise to an unlawful destination. Under such a supposition Sir William Scott would not, of course, admit any excuse, but confiscated both ship and cargo. This penalty is also extended to ships for *egress* out of the blockaded ports; with the exception of those which had been laden prior to the blockade. The neutral is responsible for this act till the end of the return voyage, for there is no foundation, says Sir William Scott, to consider the vessel free, merely because it has escaped the blockading squadron; the belligerent has full power to pursue it in all directions.

Such being the opinion of Sir William Scott concerning

(*d*) "The act of the master binds the owners as to the conduct of the ship, as well as to penal consequences. The owners of the vessel have appointed him as their agent, and they must in law be responsible for his imprudence as well as his fraud."

(*e*) Certainly, if the "bona fides" of the owner of the cargo is beyond doubt, for example, if the voyage is begun before the declaration of blockade, and the master has prolonged it from obstinacy or caprice, the cargo remains free, but it is not easy to persuade the learned judge of this. With respect to "constructive notice," he does not admit any circumstances in justification, except bad weather. Where the blockade was known at the port of shipment, the master becomes an agent for the cargo; in such case the owners must at all events answer to the country imposing blockade for the acts of persons employed by them; otherwise, by sacrificing the ship, there would be a ready escape for the cargo, for the benefit of which the fraud is intended. *Wildman*, ii. 208.

(97)

blockade, it is scarcely necessary to shew that his interpretation of the law was in direct contradiction to that of European nations. The celebrated judge was himself hardly satisfied with the grounds upon which he proceeded, and sometimes endeavoured to define more strictly the limits of such legal or fictitious blockade (*f*); but as his duty was to protect the "maritime interests" of his country, he had recourse to forced arguments in order to carry out the harsh decrees of the government against neutral merchants or in favour of cruisers and privateers (*g*). Portalis, in this respect, remained more true to his liberal principles, as the ordonnances of the year 1778 did not admit of any extension of contraband of war, and rejected all paper blockades.

All the rules above enumerated would seem to have been quite sufficient for the encouragement of privateering at the expense of neutral nations, but Sir William Scott went so far as to express an opinion, that war ought not to give any advantage to neutral merchants, and that they are not entitled to carry on any trade with the enemy, which is not open to foreigners in times of peace. To this class, for instance, belong coasting and colonial trade. In respect to the former, the court admitted that the navigation from one port of a belligerent to that of another is allowed to neutrals, though if the goods be conveyed along the coast of one and the same state, they are liable to condemnation equally with the ship (*h*). In regard to the latter, Sir William Scott did not for some time apply the rule of 1756, as by the order

(*f*) It is worthy of remark that in some sentences Sir William Scott approached in his views on blockade very nearly to the principles of the "armed neutrality;" thus, in some cases, he required that the cruisers should form an arch round the mouth of a prohibited port, in others he decidedly rejected paper blockade. "A legal blockade cannot exist where no actual blockade has been applied; a mere proclamation that a place is invested is insufficient to constitute a legal blockade."

(*g*) Sir William Scott admitted of exceptions to his rules only for the benefit of subjects of the United States of America, Denmark and Sweden, according to treaties. *Wurm*, Zeitsch. 1852, S. 491.

(*h*) *Wildman*, ii. 154. Sir William Scott adhered to this rule even after the convention of 1801.

H*

of the Privy Council of 1798, it was even permitted to neutrals to convey merchandise to England, or to their own country, from an enemy colony. The convention of St. Petersburg still further extended the freedom of commerce, but the English Admiralty Court was not long confined within such bounds of moderation; Sir William Scott, observing that neutrals purchased colonial products for the purpose of ultimately disposing of them to the enemy, contrived every year to limit the colonial commerce more and more, and, considering it injurious to Great Britain (*i*), at last succeeded in putting an end to it.

It is then evident that the English judge, though adhering to the rules of the Consolato del Mare, endeavoured to cut off all the important branches of neutral commerce. It still farther suffered from his partiality to privateers, as evidenced in his decisions respecting costs and damages. According to his opinion, the privateer, even in cases of restitution, is entitled to indemnification; and the judge can enforce on

(*i*) *Pritchard*, 458—464. In order to prevent the importation of colonial produce of the enemy into the mother country, Sir Wm. Scott, in a rather arbitrary manner, prescribed to neutrals the following rule:—" *The mere touching* at an intermediate port, whether of the country to which the vessel belongs or any other, without importing the cargo into the common stock of the country, *will not alter the nature of the voyage*, which continues the same, and must be considered as a voyage to the country to which the vessel is actually going for the purpose of delivering the cargo at the ultimate port." However harsh was this regulation upon commerce, the English judge was not satisfied with it, but began to condemn as lawful prize all colonial merchandise, if only there appeared a slight suspicion of its being destined for the enemy. Thus sugar, coffee, and other produce, were considered in the prize courts nearly in the same light as war contraband. These decisions of the English judge, limiting colonial commerce, roused public opinion in neutral countries, and principally in the United States of America. Diplomatists as well as statesmen protested against this policy, which gave occasion to many pamphlets. In defence of Sir Wm. Scott appeared a pamphlet by *Stevens:* (" War in Disguise, or the Frauds of Neutral Flags." London, 1806); in favour of the neutrals, those of *Morris* ("Answer to War in Disguise." Boston, 1806) and *Madison* (" Examination of the British Doctrine, which subjects to capture a Neutral Trade, not open in Time of Peace." London, 1806). *Morris*, in his pamphlet, gives in detail the history of the rule of 1756, and also includes the principal decisions of the English judge relating to neutral colonial commerce.

neutrals payment of expenses, if there be the slightest excuse for the seizure of the vessel, the least doubt of the legality of the transaction in which they have been engaged, or any defects in the ship's papers. On the other hand, the learned judge considered the prize courts not legally bound to award compensation to neutral merchants (*j*) for the following reasons:—1. Neutral commerce is only allowed on condition of visitation and arrest on the part of the belligerents. 2. International law only enjoins privateers to pay freight for goods of an enemy; as to other costs (*k*), no mention is made of them. Portalis acted with much more moderation in this respect. As prize judge, he felt it equally his duty to give damages and compensation to both parties, as well for the losses actually sustained as for the "lucrum cessans." In France, however, a decision in favour of neutrals was not always accompanied with costs, because the detention or the loss might have arisen from their own fault. Privateers are responsible for direct violation of the law; neutrals, on the other hand, may by their irregular proceedings give full reason to justify suspicion and mistakes on the part of the belligerents (*l*).

The decision of the court is not considered final, since both privateers and neutrals have the right of appeal. On this account the property in dispute is left untouched for

[(*j*) Since the original publication of this work, Lord Kingsdown, in delivering the sentence of the Court of Appeal in the case of the *Ostsee*, laid it down that, where there was not any probable cause of seizure, the neutral was entitled to restitution with costs and damages. *Moore*, ix. 150.—Tr.]

(*k*) Under the name of international law, Sir William Scott evidently understood the Consolato del Mare; but the learned judge sometimes himself set aside its rules, and did not allow freight to the neutral merchants in cases of coasting or colonial trade, or when they were detected in concealing their papers, &c. All these restrictions seem to be unknown to the Consolato. *Pritchard*, 164—173; *Wildman*, ii. 153—163.

(*l*) L'imprudence des capturés, leur négligence dans l'observation de certaines formes, des procédés équivoques peuvent souvent compromettre leur sureté et faire suspecter leur bonne foi; il peut arriver alors, qu'en examinant l'ensemble des faits, on reconnaisse qu'une prise est invalide, mais on peut reconnaître aussi, que les capturés par leur conduite ont donné lieu à la méprise des capteurs. *Martens*, Merkw. Fälle, ii. 218, &c.

(100)

a time, but may be delivered out on bail at the discretion of the court, and under condition of restitution. The proceedings in the Court of Appeal are similar to those in the Court of Admiralty, but additional proofs are admissible according to circumstances (*m*). Unfortunately, the length of the proceedings and the consequent expenses, particularly in England, render an appeal burdensome to neutrals. We may add that courts of appeal are seldom inclined to reverse the original decision, and on their part may be supposed to lean in favour of the privateers of their own country. Hence the injured neutral has no other remedy than to appeal to his own government. Neutral subjects, however, did not always succeed in obtaining redress, as England seldom made any concessions to diplomatic interference: and, considering the opinions of Sir William Scott as almost infallible, was prepared to defend them by armed force.

In deciding the principal questions of neutrality, Sir William Scott and Portalis were in the habit of referring to international law (*n*); and feeling it their duty to be guided by its principles they relied upon precedents from history, and, in conformity with these, have laid down many important rules,

(*m*) As to the rules of the proceeding in the English court of appeal (which consisted at that time of the Lords Commissioners of Appeals), see *Wildman*, ii. 376. In France the Conseil des Prises, a section of the Conseil d'Etat, was the court of appeal.

(*n*) "The rules of the Court of Admiralty," says Sir William Scott, "consist of international law and treaties. No government is entitled by its own authority to alter the principles of this law without the consent of other nations." *Pritchard*, 3, 163, 312. The courts of common law in England are incompetent to decide causes between belligerents and neutrals. According to ancient custom, at the commencement of war, the English government gives a special commission to the judge of the Admiralty Court to decide questions relating to captures, seizures, prizes and reprisals, according to international law and custom. *Wildman*, ii. 360. As to Portalis, his opinions concerning this subject are expressed in the following words:—"Les lois ou les règles particulières doivent toujours être exécutées de la manière la plus conforme aux principes de la raison universelle, surtout dans les matières appartenant au droit des gens, dans lesquelles les législateurs se sont toujours glorifiés de n'être que les respectueux interprêtes de la loi naturelle." *Martens*, Merkw. Fälle, ii. 225.

(101)

the value of which is indisputable. For ourselves, we are not inclined to attribute to their decisions such universal authority as many publicists do, who endeavour to construct a customary international law upon them, and even give preference to that system rather than to existing treaties(*o*). Examining carefully the English and French practice, we come to the conclusion, that neither one nor the other strictly adhered to the rules of European public law. Sir William Scott seems to have acted in direct opposition to the generally-admitted principles of the "armed neutrality," while Portalis, though more liberal and humane in his judgments, may be considered only as a good interpreter of French ordonnances, and a statesman who gave more regularity to the prize practice of his country.

In fact, the customary law to which the English judge constantly refers, can hardly be considered as of universal operation, for it is not even adopted by all countries; and it may be doubted whether it can be at all an authority for belligerents, being purely English law. However long its precedents may have existed, they are not binding on neutral nations. It may be replied, that Sir William Scott meant by custom the rules of maritime law as contained in the Consolato del Mare, but we have many times observed that the English judge did not strictly adhere to this compilation, but modified and explained it rather in favour of belligerents. Thus the construction of international law, as laid down by him, often appears obscure and vague, for he does not rely on treaties or customs *reciprocally* observed by governments, but chiefly confines himself to such decrees as Instructions to Privateers, Orders in Council, &c., and to the rules laid

(*o*) To this class belong all English jurists of the present century, as *Robinson*, *Chitty*, *Oke Manning*, *Reddie*, and *Wildman*. Their confidence in Sir William Scott is unlimited; they consider him as the "viva vox" of international law, and attribute to his opinions undisputed authority. As to the foreigners who may be considered as his supporters, they are *Jacobsen*, *Bello*, *Kent*, and *Wheaton*. This last, however, quotes Sir William Scott principally because this English judge was held in high consideration in the courts of the United States.

down by the judges who preceded him, from Coke to Marriott. Hence the views of this eminent jurist are not supported by the general convictions of mankind. Deprived of this support, he seldom laid down exact definitions, and consequently his doctrine varied according to the circumstances of war; in short, Sir William Scott gave no security to neutral commerce, but subjected it to the belligerent or to the law of extreme necessity, "jus extremæ necessitatis."

Unfortunately, Portalis was scarcely more independent in the delivery of his opinions; everybody knows that in France judicial authority never attained such weight as in England, where the courts have full power of interpreting the common law and statutes, and of laying down rules in conformity thereto. On the contrary, French judges, in almost all cases, hold strictly to the letter of the law. Under the influence, however, of a temporary modification of the ordonnances of France, Portalis, as we have said, could treat neutral nations with more indulgence than Sir William Scott was disposed to do.

But, contesting the authority of Sir William Scott and Portalis as true expositors of international law, we are far from any intention of disparaging the merits of either of these distinguished jurists and statesmen (*p*). Their names stand high in the history of prize jurisprudence. In their enlarged views, and in the good sense with which they discharged their duties, they surpass all their predecessors. In Sir William Scott, the English bench had one of its most distinguished members. With the advantage of his juridical logic, he entered upon many cases which had not been touched upon or even alluded to in former treaties, and embraced all the principal points in dispute between belligerents and neutrals. On this account his decisions are not only instructive in a scientific point of view, but may afford assistance in the construction of future treaties. As to Portalis, though

(*p*) *Historical Sketches of the Statesmen of George III.*, vol. iii. 91—101. London, 1845. Lord Brougham, in that work draws, probably from personal acquaintance, the character of Sir William Scott as a judge and jurist. As to Portalis, see Revue de Législation, ix. 41.

(103)

the sphere of his activity was more limited, we observe in many of his decisions greater impartiality, and a constant regard to the rights of neutrals, as well as a laudable desire to diminish the severity of maritime warfare (*q*). We may add, that they both fully understood their position, and were never led away in the course of their daily duties, either by feelings of personal animosity, as Marriott sometimes was, or by selfish views, like the revolutionary judges of France, but conferred dignity and honour upon their respective posts (*r*). Certainly they were not free from human error, but before censuring them, we ought not to forget, that the period in which they lived was one of revolution and war; that European nations were influenced by feelings of mutual animosity; that treaties were then but little regarded, and that as Admiralty judges they were obliged to enforce the laws of the belligerents; and here, in our opinion, lies the cause of the apparent partiality of these eminent judges, and of the occasional contradictions to be met with in their decisions.

We are now, we hope, sufficiently acquainted with the principal features of prize practice, as it existed at the

(*q*) He expressed his views in the following terms:—"Les règlements de la course, qui ne portent qu'improprement le nom des lois et qui par eux-mêmes sont essentiellement variables pro temporibus et causis, sont toujours susceptibles dans leur application d'être tempérés par les vues de sagesse et d'équité. J'ajouterai qu'en exécutant des règlements d'une extrème rigueur il faut plutôt restreindre que les étendre, et que dans le choix des divers sens dont ils peuvent être susceptibles, on doit préférer celui qui est le plus favorable à la justice et à la liberté. Le droit ne naît pas des règlements, mais les règlements doivent naître du droit. *Martens*, Merkw. Fälle, ii. 225.

(*r*) Sir William Scott thus defines the duties of an Admiralty judge, in the case of the Swedish ship, the *Maria*, 1 *Rob.* 150. "The seat of judicial authority," he says, "is, indeed, locally here, in the belligerent country, according to the known law and practice of nations; but the law itself has no locality. It is the duty of the person who sits here to determine this question exactly as he would determine the same question if sitting at Stockholm; to assert no pretensions on the part of Great Britain which he would not allow to Sweden in the same circumstances, and to impose no duties on Sweden, as a neutral country, which he would not admit to belong to Great Britain in the same character."

beginning of the 19th century, in England and France. Although the Courts acted with severity against enemy's property, and encouraged privateers by every means in their power, neutral commerce could still exist, but the time soon came when the opinions of Sir William Scott and Portalis were considered too moderate. The enmity between France and England gradually attained such a height, that the rights of neutrality were put in jeopardy, and at last destroyed. This brief period of "the Continental system" (1806—1812) cannot be passed over unnoticed in the history of privateering, as it was the crisis of the long struggle between belligerents and neutrals (*s*).

The peace of Amiens, which for a short time put an end to war, made no provision for neutral commerce or prize law, and did not even allude to the articles respecting neutral rights contained in the treaties of Utrecht. It seemed as if both powers considered the state of neutrality to be henceforth impossible for them, and were only anxious to make preparations for a renewal of the struggle; in fact, hardly a twelvemonth had passed before hostilities were renewed. To protect themselves against the pretensions of these formidable belligerents, the neutral powers lost no time in publishing decrees, by which, under severe penalties, it was forbidden to their subjects to assist either of the contending parties (*t*); but all these measures seem to have been useless, as the more strongly the feeling of enmity reigned the more difficult became the observance of neutrality. On the one hand, Napoleon, having reduced under his power the nations of Continental Europe, demanded their co-operation against England; and on the other, England herself, considering the war with France as one undertaken in defence of liberty and the Christian world, and regarding with distrust those nations

(*s*) The acts which belong to the period of the Continental system may be found in *Martens*, Nouv. Rec. i. 443—549. See also *Comte de Garden*, Histoire des Traités, x. 302—403; and *Reddie*, Researches, ii. 23—68.

(*t*) These decrees (*Martens*' Suppl. iii. 528—557) generally forbid neutrals to take letters of marque from belligerents, and order strict measures to be taken against fraud or error in ship's papers.

(105)

which maintained a friendly intercourse with France, had recourse to measures of a prohibitive character against them (*u*). Thus belligerents, considering the state of neutrality as almost unnatural, began generally to protest against it, and endeavoured to put a stop to neutral commerce altogether. The preparations of Napoleon for a descent on Great Britain, afforded a pretext for this unjustifiable policy; for, seeing the danger which threatened it, the English government declared all the ports from the mouth of the Elbe to Brest (1806) under blockade. In answer to this, the celebrated Berlin decree was published (Nov. 21st, 1806), in which the French Emperor, accusing Great Britain of conduct contrary to international law, declared a general blockade of England, Scotland and Ireland, and, prohibiting all commerce with those countries, subjected to seizure, as lawful prize, all English property wherever it might be found. The judges of the prize courts at Paris and Milan received directions to carry out this decree, which was also communicated to Holland, Tuscany, Spain and Naples, as allies of France, and whose subjects were equally sufferers from the harsh proceedings of England (*x*). Great Britain imme-

(*u*) Among these harsh measures on the part of the English government may be named the blockade of the mouth of the Elbe (1803); on this occasion Sir William Scott directly contradicted himself; formerly he had held that a blockade was a military measure, directed against the port of an enemy, now he maintained the legality of the blockade of neutral territories. *Jacobsen*, Versuch.

(*x*) In explaining the origin of the "Continental system," different authors express contrary opinions. Some of them find that the Order in Council of 1806 sufficiently accounts for it, and throw all the blame upon England; others, as Reddie, look upon the general blockade of the coast, from the Elbe to Brest, as absolutely necessary; for it was a mere precautionary measure against the descent of the French troops intended by Napoleon. They add that England, after destroying the French fleet, was able to direct all her forces to the maintenance of this blockade, and that the Privy Council soon mitigated the severity of their Order; yet, however that may be, one can scarcely agree with such writers as *Piantanida*, *Rayneval*, *Montbrion*, *Hauterive*, who consider Napoleon as an advocate of the liberal principles of neutrality. The true origin of the "Continental system" is to be found in the hostility of the Emperor towards the English, and his desire to annihilate their commerce. The reform of in-

diately had recourse to retaliation, by interdicting, on the 7th of January, 1807, to all nations, any commerce with France. Accordingly, English cruisers and privateers received instructions to give notice of this decree to neutral vessels, and in case of disobedience to capture them. On the 11th of November appeared a new order in Council, whereby the countries which adopted the "Continental system" were declared under blockade, and the ships, which entered into relations with them, lawful prize. On the 25th November of the same year there followed another decree requiring neutrals to take special licences to enable them to trade with the enemy, and for which they were required to pay certain fees. Thus neutral powers ceased to be free, and were placed at the mercy of the belligerents.

By the Milan decree of the 17th of December, 1807, the Emperor of the French inflicted a new blow on the commerce of the world. Every ship coming from England, or in any way connected with that country, was considered as having forfeited its nationality (dénationalisé), and consequently liable to condemnation as lawful prize. It now only remained to induce all European governments to adopt the "Continental system;" in this Napoleon almost succeeded, as some nations were not powerful enough to oppose him; while others, being indignant against Great Britain for the bombardment of Copenhagen, willingly entered into his views. In order to confine the enemy to his own territory, the French Emperor imposed a heavy duty on all colonial produce, and even ordered all English goods found on the Continent to be burnt, which orders were carried out. Such was the abject state of Europe, that no one thought of offering resistance to his will. Auto-da-fés of the commercial inquisition were lighted in many parts of Europe.

ternational law was here a mere excuse; in fact, he cared little about it. The well known Mémoire of the *Duc de Bassano* (1812) proves nothing; for it was published at the end of the "Continental system," in justification of the former conduct of the Emperor. See generally *Comte de Garden*, xi. 1—116.

(107)

It is easy to understand that the "Continental system" opened an extended field to privateers. There was now no difference between them and pirates; not a single merchant-ship was free from the suspicion of the belligerents, who left neutral commerce to the mercy of their privateers. Obtaining large rewards for information against neutrals, they, according to Mr. Baring (*y*), captured and brought in every ship they met with, under the most frivolous pretexts, and Admiralty Courts also acted in the most harsh and inquisitorial manner. While in France they considered the ordonnances of Louis XIV. as too lenient, in England Sir William Scott not only rejected the doctrine of the Consolato del Mare, but even the very idea of neutrality (*z*). In this manner the prize practice, which the English had desired to impose on other nations, was shaken to its foundations, and the customs of the Middle Ages set aside by those very parties who had hitherto been their most zealous advocates.

But all these attempts of the belligerents to interfere with the mutual intercourse of nations, which had for ages been gradually growing up in Europe, and become as necessary as social order itself, were unsuccessful. The "Continental system," being considered an unnatural state, gave rise to general indignation. The severer the decrees, the stronger was the inclination to violate them; neither the power of the French Emperor, nor the subserviency of his allies, could prevent the clandestine importation of prohibited goods. It was in vain that Napoleon threatened with heavy punishment those who traded in English articles, for commerce would exist in spite of his spies and custom-houses, which were

(*y*) *Baring*, "An Inquiry into the Causes and Consequences of the Orders in Council, and Examination of the Conduct of Great Britain towards the neutral Commerce of America." Lond. 1808, p. 94.

(*z*) He said in open court (12th April, 1808) that on the establishment of the "Continental system" neutral ports should be considered as those of an enemy. Some time afterwards this eminent judge confessed that the orders in Council had completely destroyed the prize law of Great Britain. *Jacobsen*, S. 732; *Reddie*, ii. 27, 32, 33.

spread over all Europe. Soon the very authors of these prohibitory measures began to feel the disadvantageous consequences of them, and in order to revive commerce were compelled to have recourse to granting licences. The adoption of this system appears to be a strange anomaly, because licences or permissions to trade with the enemy had hitherto been considered as exceptions to the general rule of war. In the year 1801, Sir William Scott spoke of them as acts "strictissimi juris," to which a liberal construction should never be applied; but after the publication of the French decrees, 1806, 1807, the same learned judge began to look on them in a perfectly different point of view, and to construe them with the utmost liberality. While, in the beginning of the 19th century, a slight inaccuracy in a licence rendered it liable to be impugned, its form was now considered immaterial. The judge allowed holders of licences to import the goods of an enemy in larger quantities, and of different qualities from those specified therein, and even after the expiration of the term for which the licence had been granted. Even those traders who had lost their papers were treated by the court with indulgence (*a*). How can such a change of policy be explained? "By the circumstances of war." Sir William Scott himself frankly admits that nothing but these circumstances could have induced him to deviate from the immemorial precedents and rules of the Admiralty Court. In France the distribution of licences was also attended with abuse and became a system of disreputable traffic and bribery. Speculators were generally permitted to import colonial goods, under the condition of exporting French manufactures, and particularly silks; but as their sale was difficult and almost impossible, the merchant had recourse to different kinds of

(*a*) *Pritchard*, 195—200, and *Jacobsen*, 719—731, give an account of the judgments of Sir William Scott on this subject pronounced by him during the existence of the "Continental system." Licences were delivered not only to neutrals but also to enemy subjects. The number of licences issued by the English increased in different years from 8 to 16,000. In the year 1808 the British government gave general permission to neutral merchants to import corn into Great Britain. *Comte de Garden*, Hist. des Traités, x. 316, n. 1.

fraud, and the government connived at these abuses, as licences were very productive to the public treasury (*b*).

Thus the prohibitory system of the belligerents gave rise to various irregularities and contradictions, but however capricious the belligerents were, other nations did not dare to raise a voice in defence of their rights. True it is, Denmark endeavoured to adhere to the principles of 1780, but unsuccessfully. The Danish decrees on privateering and prize practice, 1807, 1810, contained a heterogeneous mixture of contradictory regulations, and prove only that at the time of the "Continental system" neutral commerce could not exist in Europe (*c*). The same may be said of the declaration of the Emperor Alexander in 1807, who, while appearing to revert to the noble traditions of Russian policy, made injudicious concessions in favour of the "Continental system" by the treaty of Tilsit. The bombardment of Copenhagen, and his indignation against England, were the principal reasons for this declaration, which did not, however, produce any effect, and only afforded the enemies of Russia grounds for accusing her of a vacillating policy.

The influence of the English and French decrees was felt in the most distant countries and even in the New World. Thus the United States of America, after having for some time patiently borne the violence of belligerents, determined to put an end to intercourse with Europe (*d*), the cabinet

(*b*) Dictionnaire de l'Economie politique, i. 182—187.

(*c*) *Martens*, Nouveau Recueil, i. 402, n., and *Jacobsen*, "Bemerkungen über das Dänische Prisenrecht" (Altona, 1808). Both decrees establish the immunity of the neutral flag, but at the same time condemn, as lawful prize, all vessels which have been engaged in trade with Great Britain, and permit privateers to search them if there appear the least irregularity in their papers. Prize proceedings in Denmark are to be determined according to the decree in ten days; it gives neutrals damages, if arrested without reason, but does not admit as evidence any papers unless found on board.

(*d*) The oppression of American commerce increased when the English privateers, in expectation of war, and hoping that the Americans would have, as enemies, no *personam standi in judicio*, and consequently could not defend themselves in court, seized their ships and endeavoured to delay the final adjudication of the cases. It sometimes happened that Sir William Scott, seeing

of Washington having previously endeavoured to open conferences for the revocation of these prohibitory measures, but unsuccessfully, because each belligerent refused to make the first concession. There was nothing, therefore, left for Congress to do, but to prohibit their subjects trading with England, France and their allies, which was carried out by the decree of March 1st, 1809. A short time afterwards Napoleon relaxed his system by making an exception in favour of the Americans. Anticipating reciprocity on the part of Great Britain, a number of merchants of the New World dispatched ships to Europe, but they were soon convinced how vain their expectations had been, as almost the whole of them fell into the hands of the privateers, and on the 30th of May, 1811, were, by the decision of Sir William Scott, declared lawful prizes (*e*). The cabinet of St. James subsequently offered to annul the orders in Council, but this was after the Congress had actually declared war against Great Britain (*f*).

In this second war between England and America we find many interesting facts bearing upon international law. We see also that at this time a more regular prize practice was introduced into the New World. However similar it was to that of England, it still presents some peculiar traits. In the present Essay we will content ourselves with a sketch of it without entering into details (*g*). According to the American

nothing wrong on the part of neutrals, decreed restitution; the privateers, however, appealing to a higher court, the unfortunate neutrals had nothing to do but to enter into a compromise, or, at the risk of delay and its consequences, abide the result. Thus appeals in England instead of promoting the cause of justice only aggravated the sufferings of neutrals. All these facts are collected by Mr. Baring, who may assuredly be considered an impartial witness of the mal-practices of this period. *Wurm*, Zeitsch. (1851), S. 329.

(*e*) *Jacobsen*, Seerecht, 712, 713; *Reddie*, ii. 45—49. To justify these decisions Sir William Scott alleged that England had not received official notice of the revocation of the French decrees in favour of the United States of America.

(*f*) The details of these facts are given by *Comte de Garden*, xiii. 283—352.

(*g*) The reports of the American prize courts were published by *Cranch* and other lawyers after the model of *Robinson*. Some documents concerning prize

(111)

prize judges, international law forms the basis of the jurisdiction of belligerents over neutrals, though we must not therefore conclude that neutrals are bound to submit to it unconditionally, and forfeit their independence. Therefore if (a) the privateer or the Admiralty judge acts unjustly towards foreign merchants, or disregards treaties and customs, their governments are entitled to protect them, and are fully justified in demanding satisfaction from the belligerent; (b) if the vessel is seized within the jurisdiction of a neutral power, the privateer is amenable to it, and the neutral power, whose territory is violated, is competent to adjudge the case and inflict punishment on the privateer for the violation of its territorial rights (*h*).

With respect to evidence, the American judges adopt the view of Sir William Scott, at the same time giving it greater correctness and precision (*i*). All arrested vessels are bound to bring into the prize court the following documents:—Passport or Sea letter, Muster-roll, Charter-party, Bill of Lading, Invoice, Log-book. The production, however, of all these papers would not protect the ship from condemnation, as they may be false; but, on the other hand, the absence of any one of them does not necessarily subject it to condemnation. As to a ship or cargo purchased of an enemy, the neutral is bound to produce the bill of sale, and to prove that it was an absolute and unconditional one. The legality of the sale of the property of an enemy "in transitu" was not admitted by the United States. An enemy's ship or cargo being mortgaged was also subject to condemnation. The prize courts

law may also be found in the American Diplomatic Code by *Elliott*. I have not been able to examine all these books, as they are but little known in Russia. Extracts from them, however, have been inserted by *Wheaton* in his Elements of International Law. As to his "Digest of the Law of Maritime Capture and Prize," it only lately came into my hands. A detailed account of it I have found in *Reddie*, Researches, ii. 229—338. At the time of the publication of this work in Russia, 1855, Dr. *Pratt* had published, in England, Judge Story's Notes on Prize Practice.

(*h*) To this rule the American judges strictly adhered, even without any remonstrance on the part of neutrals. *Wheaton*, Dig. ch. 3, 294, 305.

(*i*) *Wheaton*, Digest, ch. 3; *Reddie*, ii. 304, 305.

(112)

of the United States found it impossible to admit, in such cases, of any exception to the general rules of war (*k*).

With respect to the nationalities of the owner, master and crew, and also of the ship and cargo, the American courts agreed generally with the doctrine of Sir William Scott (*l*), while the opinions of the English judge on war contraband were greatly modified in the New World. Under the name of war contraband, the United States included only arms and ammunition (*m*), and denied to the belligerents the right of enlarging the list of forbidden articles, or of exercising that of preemption in the case of provisions. They also considered illegal the condemnation of a ship on its return voyage. Much as they agree with the British practice, respecting the penalties incurred by neutrals for the conveyance to the enemy of officers, soldiers and despatches (*n*), they differ widely from Sir William Scott's opinion on blockade (*o*). They admit no paper blockade, and do not consider neutral vessels on the open sea (even though destined to the besieged port) liable to seizure, but consider the offence only complete when the master either openly or fraudulently attempts to break the blockading line. They give neutrals full power to approach the blockading squadron, for the purpose of ascertaining the state of the port. In short, American law requires special notice of blockade to every ship approaching the port, and only justifies the seizure of those who attempt to enter it after having been warned. The master not having fallen in with the squadron is entitled to consider the blockade as not existing. Neutral nations, regarding blockade in no other light than as a matter of fact, are not bound to wait for

(*k*) *Wheaton*, El. i. 316—332.

(*l*) Ibid.

(*m*) The judgments in the American courts respecting war contraband are given in the following works: *Wheaton*, Dig. ch. vi.; *Reddie*, ii. 320—327; *Wheaton*, El. ii. 138, and, particularly, 166—169.

(*n*) *Wheaton*, Dig. vi. 8—10; *Reddie*, Researches, ii. 27.

(*o*) The judgments in the American courts respecting blockade may be found in the following works: *Wheaton*, El. ii. 178, 179; Dig. ch. vi. § 114; *Reddie*, ii. 327—333.

permission to enter the port after its termination. The penalty in America for breach of blockade is condemnation of ship and cargo, but the latter, if it belong to third parties, is considered free when its owners are not "participes criminis" with the master. All these latter constructions perfectly harmonize with the spirit of the declaration of 1780.

Besides war contraband and blockade, we should add that the American judges did not acknowledge any arbitrary restrictions of neutral commerce, and rejected the rules of Sir William Scott on coasting and colonial trade.

As to the immunity of the neutral flag, the American courts did not admit it unconditionally, but only in conformity with treaty. True it is, that in the first war with the English (1776—1783), the federal government acceded formally to the "armed neutrality;" when however the principle "the flag covers the cargo" was rejected by France and England, the United States found it incompatible with their interests to adhere to it, and only in the year 1815 they again returned to the liberal principles of 1780.

The reader will, we fear, find this sketch but imperfect, as it gives only the general features, and not the details, of the North American prize practice. One of its best interpreters in the beginning of this century was Chief Justice Marshall, who, although following to a certain extent the English precedents, rejected many of the arbitrary interpretations of Sir William Scott, and paid greater respect to the rights of neutral nations (*p*). From the year 1815 the

(*p*) The English precedents were followed in the United States not so much because they were considered the best interpretations of international law, as from historical associations. This appears from the following words of Chief Justice Marshall. "The United States," he said, "were once a part of the British Empire; the prize legislation of the mother country, having been introduced into all the colonies, was never abrogated; however, it does not follow, that all the incorrect opinions of the English courts have now authority in America. On the contrary our courts ought to examine the rules adopted in British practice, and act according to them only in such cases when they do not interfere with the practice of our law and policy." *Wheaton*, El. i. 301, 331, 332. Thus it is evident that Sir William Scott did not enjoy such undisputed authority in America as his admirers assert.

(114)

influence of English jurisprudence gradually declined, while, as far as we can judge from the treaties entered into by the federal government, the principles of the "armed neutrality" were more strictly maintained.

While the United States were engaged in war with the mother country, great changes took place in Europe. The fall of Napoleon put an end to the unnatural state of international affairs. The "Continental system," with all its arbitrary rules for the oppression of neutral commerce, disappeared, and the further development of the principles of the "armed neutrality," which had been checked by the French Revolution, was fully secured.

PERIOD V.

From the Congress of Vienna to modern Times.

(1814—1854.)

The establishment of the political system at the Congress of Vienna opened a new period in the history of Europe. The most prominent feature of this period is its pacific character. War, which formerly caused general disturbance, now became more rare and limited in its operations. The principal labour of diplomacy consisted in anticipating, or at least checking, any tendency to hostilities, in preserving the "status quo," and upholding alliances and commercial relations. Such a change in external policy could not but confer essential benefit on mankind, and, in fact, during the forty years the intercourse of nations has been greatly extended. Christianity and civilization have penetrated the most distant countries of the world, and international law has made rapid progress. In proof whereof we may cite the abolition of the slave trade, the revocation of the antiquated and barbarous custom of the "droit d'aubaine," the liberation of commerce from the shackles of the mercantile system, the opening of navigable rivers for the use of all adjacent countries, and the admission of international copyright by treaty. Among the benefits of this period may also be mentioned the improvement of maritime law, and the diffusion of the principles of the "armed neutrality." The system of the "Consolato del Mare," which unnecessarily augmented the cruelties of naval war, was apparently abandoned, together with the harsh decrees of the Revolution and of the Empire.

In confirmation of this view, we will now examine the more important treaties of this interesting period. Beginning with

Europe we find that, in addition to Russia (*a*), France now became a zealous defender of the "armed neutrality." She not only adopted the principles of 1780 in her treaties (*b*), but avowed her intention of observing them in her relations with all states without distinction (*c*). The immunities of neutral commerce were also admitted by Greece, as a new member of the political system (*d*). The only exception in favour of the "Consolato del Mare" is the treaty of Great Britain with Portugal (1842), whereby it appears that the English still continued to adhere to the system of the Middle Ages (*e*). But this exception scarcely affords any reason to doubt the acceptance of the principles of 1780 as a general law of Europe and the civilized world, since no other government than that of Portugal renounced the immunity of its flag. France and the United States even foresaw the necessity of retaliation against such a system, and were, it appears,

(*a*) The last occasion on which Russia declared her views respecting the rights of neutrality was the treaty with the United States in 1854. Both parties admit the rule "le pavillon couvre la cargaison et ne la confisque pas," and bind themselves to apply it, under condition of reciprocity, to all nations.

(*b*) See the treaties of France with the Brazils, 1826, 1828 (*Martens*, N. R. vi. 868, viii. 60); with Bolivia, 1834 (*Annales maritimes et coloniales*, 1837, p. 680, 2de partie; with Texas, 1839 (*Martens*, xvi. 2, 287); with Denmark, 1842 (*Murhard*, Nouveaux Suppl. ii. 81), and in particular with Venezuela, New Grenada and Ecuador, 1839—1846 (*Murhard*, N. R. v. 165, 402, vii. 613). Besides the principles of 1780 the French treaties likewise recognise those of the second armed neutrality concerning the freedom from visitation of ships sailing under protection of convoy.

(*c*) See the declaration of Count Molé published on the occasion of reprisals against La Plata. *Ortolan*, Règles internationales et diplomatie de la Mer, ii. 335.

(*d*) See treaties of Greece with Prussia, and the German Zollverein, 1839; with Holland and the Free Cities, 1843 (*Murhard*, N. R. i. 580, v. 5, 480). Without enumerating in detail the rights of neutral commerce they give an exact definition of war contraband (dans le sens le plus restreint, consacré par le droit des gens), and reject paper blockade; but the treaty of Prussia with Denmark (1818) confirms the laws of the armed neutrality in their full extent. *Martens*, N. R. iv. 527.

(*e*) *Murhard*, N. R. iii. However this treaty apparently is only the renewal of the Convention of 1810. *Martens*, N. R. iii. 194.

prepared to have recourse to strong measures (*f*); hence it may be confidently asserted, that should the courts of the English admiralty ever attempt to apply in matters of prize the doctrine of the "Consolato del Mare," the principles adopted by other nations would not thereby be shaken, but the attempt would rather prove injurious to Great Britain herself. However, since the Navigation Act of Cromwell was repealed, it was not difficult to foresee that England would change her policy with regard to neutral commerce, and in fact the British and French declaration (March 28th, 1854) not only acknowledged the immunity of the flag, but also the inviolability of the cargo, "le pavillon couvre la cargaison et ne la confisque pas" (*g*). Thus the most implacable opponent of the "armed neutrality" was at length induced to yield to the public opinion of Europe.

The obligatory force of the principles of 1780 was also firmly established in America, being accepted by the most important maritime power, the United States, and acknowledged by the rest of that continent. All the treaties of this kind, whether entered into by the American States one with another, or with Europe, present a most striking resemblance: thereby showing that the nations of the New World adopt uniform rules for neutral commerce. In proof of this, we will refer to the text, and take into consideration some other documents of the American diplomacy.

1. Neutral nations, according to the opinion of American statesmen, are not bound to submit to the system of the "Consolato." It finds no support in the philosophy of law,

(*f*) In all their treaties the United States of America insert the following clause: "Stipulations, declaring that the flag shall cover the property, shall be understood as applying to those powers only who recognise this principle; but if either of the two contracting parties shall be at war with a third, and the other neutral, *the flag of the neutral shall cover the property of enemies, whose governments acknowledge this principle, and not of others.*" This is also introduced in the French treaties (see note (*b*), p. 116); where an evident allusion is made to England, as this power alone for a long time persisted in refusing to admit the immunity of the neutral flag.

(*g*) The analysis of this declaration in an international point of view will be found in the Edinburgh Review for July, 1854, pp. 193—225.

and although it has obtained a practical authority from former usage and by its introduction into some treaties, yet in fact it is upheld solely by the physical force of the belligerents. A neutral government, acting honourably, is fully entitled to have due respect paid to its flag, and a belligerent has no right to withhold it (*h*); therefore in their treaties the United States adhere to the principle, as an immutable law of maritime warfare, "the flag covers and confiscates the cargo"(*i*). If, however, a neutral government should permit one of the belligerents to apply to its subjects the doctrine of the "Consolato," in such case the other also may do the same, in order to preserve the balance of power. From Mahommedan States, America, following the example of Europe, required greater privileges for neutral commerce, namely, the complete immunity of both the flag and cargo (*k*).

2. The term "war contraband," in all treaties of the United States, is confined to arms and ammunition. Goods not manufactured for warlike purposes are considered free. Every neutral merchant, after surrendering the contraband, has a right to continue his voyage without molestation, and is only bound to proceed to the nearest port of the belligerent, when the prohibited articles form the bulk of his cargo, and the cruiser has no convenient room for them on board. In either case the neutral ship remains free from arrest and capture.

3. Blockade is considered broken, when a neutral merchant, having received special warning of it (which is usually marked on the muster roll), endeavours by force or fraud to

(*h*) All the statesmen of America from Jefferson to Webster maintained these principles. See particularly the dispatches of J. Q. Adams, formerly Minister for Foreign Affairs. *Wheaton*, El. ii. 134, 135.

(*i*) But this last rule, le pavillon confisque la cargaison, as we have said in note (*a*), p. 116, is abandoned in the last treaty with Russia, 1854.

(*k*) See treaties of the United States of America with Algiers, 1815, and Morocco, 1835. *Martens*, N. R. v. 596, xiii. 685. In the treaties with Christian powers, although neutral cargo on board enemy's ships is considered lawful prize, yet when laden prior to the commencement of the war, cruisers are directed to leave it untouched.

(119)

penetrate the blockading squadron. The ship, however, which has entered the port prior to the blockade, not only is considered free from capture, but has full right to put to sea with the goods taken on board previous to its commencement; and even if the cargo is taken in during the blockade, this is no ground for declaring the ship lawful prize, although the belligerent may compel her to return to the port whence she came. In short, no one but a refractory master is exposed to inevitable capture.

4. The former harsh manner of conducting visitation is abolished, neither are neutrals any longer bound to come on board the cruiser with their papers. With respect to ships under convoy, they are perfectly free from visitation, according to the rules of the second armed neutrality.

5. Every neutral ship which sails for an enemy's port must be furnished with a passport and other documents, in the absence of which she is liable to be seized, although she might be released by the prize court, on the owner producing proofs of her nationality and the legitimacy of her commerce.

6. The Admiralty judge is bound to give to the neutral a copy of his judgment, with his reasons whereon it is founded, which the neutral, if dissatisfied, may submit to his own government (*l*).

These rules were zealously supported by the United States, and so far generally admitted, that no other government of the New World adopted the principle of the "Consolato" (*m*).

(*l*) See treaties of the United States with Sweden, 1818 and 1827 (*Martens*, N. R. iv. 251, vii. 271); with Spain, 1819 (v. 342); with Columbia, 1824 (vi. 984); with Central America, 1825 (vi. 826); with the Brazils, 1828 (ix. 54); with Mexico, 1831 (x. 323); with Chili, 1832 (xi. 438); with Bolivia, 1836 (xv. 113); with Ecuador, 1839 (*Murhard*, N. R. g. iv. 299), &c.

(*m*) Of the treaties which the American nations have agreed to amongst themselves, or with Europe, the following are the most important:—Columbia with Holland, 1829 (*Martens*, N. R. ix. 576; *Murhard*, N. Suppl. i. 691); Mexico with the Free States of Germany, 1828 (*Murhard*, N. Suppl. i. 684); with Prussia, 1831 (*Martens*, N. R. xii. 534); and with Austria, 1842 (*Murhard*, iii. 432); the Brazils with Prussia, 1827 (*Martens*, N. R. vii. 470); with the Free Cities (ib. vii. 310); and with Denmark, 1828 (ib. vii. 628); Venezuela with the Free Cities, 1837 (*Martens*, N. R. xvi. 239); New Granada with Sardinia,

(120)

Thus the principles of 1780 form the basis of all new treaties respecting neutral commerce. The same spirit pervades the practice of belligerents. All the decrees published by them since the Congress of Vienna secure the freedom of the flag, strictly define war contraband, and abrogate arbitrary search.

Even blockade at the present time ceases to be the powerful means of oppression it formerly was to neutrals. In proof of this may be cited the decrees which France published previous to the commencement of hostilities against Mexico and La Plata. Upon that occasion the French government directed the commanders of the blockading squadron and the prize courts to observe the following rules: (a) A blockade is reputed valid, in relation to neutrals, only after it has been notified to them; (b) If the vessel approach the port in ignorance of the blockade, the cruiser, without arresting it, is bound to apprise the master of the circumstance; (c) For this purpose a note is made on the muster roll of the neutral ship; (d) If after this notification the vessel should approach the blockaded port, it may be lawfully seized (*n*). The United States of America acted upon similar (*o*) rules at the time of the last war with Mexico, and also when they blockaded Vera Cruz and Buenos Ayres. Still more moderate in her demands, as a belligerent, was Russia, when she blockaded the Dardanelles and Bosphorus, in the year 1828. This

1847 (*Murhard*, xi. 281); and the Brazils with Uruguay, 1851 (Annuaire des deux Mondes, 1851, 1852, pp. 981—983). All these treaties are more or less similar to the before-mentioned treaties of the United States, and are based on the principles of the "armed neutrality."

(*n*) *Ortolan*, Inter. ii. 334; *Martens*, N. R. xv. 803, &c.

(*o*) See instructions to the commanders of the American fleet, May 14th, 1846 (*Murhard*, N. R. ix. 167). In them, besides the special notification of blockade (warning) which is required, a fortnight for leaving the port is allowed to vessels that had entered it previous to its establishment. The respect which the prize courts of the United States at that time paid to the rights of neutrals may be seen from the examples cited by *Wurm* (Zeitsch. für die g. Staatswissenschaft, 1852, S. 494, &c.). See also the decrees of the republic of Chili, 1838, and of Denmark, 1848 (*Martens*, N. R. xv. 504; *Wurm*, Zeitsch. 1851, 474).

blockade was established for no other purpose than that of preventing the importation into the capital of Turkey of war contraband and provisions, and consequently had a strictly local character (*p*). In short, the vague doctrine of blockade, upheld by Marriott and Sir William Scott, was now decidedly rejected by the general opinion of Europe and America. England herself seemed to abandon it when, on the occasion of the Danish war (1848—1850), she declared the illegality of any blockade not supported by a sufficient fleet (*q*). It is true that the Brazils, Portugal, Spain, and some other countries, endeavoured in their wars to revive former abuses, but unsuccessfully (*r*). Neutral nations adhered to the opinion that a blockade is a local arrangement, requiring notification, and that the belligerent country has

(*p*) See the letter of Vice-Admiral Heyden to the commanders of the foreign fleets in the Levant, October 6th, 1828 (*Lesur*, Annuaire historique, 1828, App. 126—128). In order that neutral commerce might be disturbed as little as possible the blockading squadron was directed, 1st, To permit ingress into the Dardanelles and Bosphorus to all neutral vessels not laden with war contraband. 2. To allow free egress from Constantinople to all ships not engaged in the conveyance of troops, arms, and provisions to the enemy. 3. To be moderate in the exercise of the right of search. 4. To make use of force only against those who resist or attempt to break the blockading line. With respect to the blockade of Trieste by Sardinia in 1848, see *Wurm*, Zeits. 1851, S. 322, 323.

(*q*) *Murhard*, N. R. i. 542, iv. 467—486; *Wurm*, Zeits. 1852, s. 501, 502. In the declaration of the 28th March, 1854, England also admitted the necessity of the blockade being effective.

(*r*) The following circumstance was the cause of collision between Brazil and neutral powers. At the time of the war against Buenos Ayres, 1825, the Brazilian admiral, Lebeau, declared all the coast of La Plata, of twenty miles, to be blockaded. As he had then only one corvette, two war brigs and some gun boats, France, England and the United States immediately protested against the measure. The matter was ended by giving full compensation to the neutral merchants, and the right of "paper blockade" was formally renounced on the part of the Brazilian government. *Lesur*, Ann. 1827, App. 167; 1828, App. 191, 192; *Martens*, N. R. viii. 60, x. 18. The pretensions of Spain at the time of a war with South America, and of Portugal in the year 1833, met with no better success. *Murhard*, N. Suppl. iii. 212, 213, and *Wurm*, Zeits. 1852, 487, &c. It is curious to notice that in all these disputes England was on the side of the neutrals, and, in opposition to her former practice, united with other states in insisting on the reality of the blockade.

only a right to condemn as lawful prize those ships which wilfully attempt to break the blockading line.

Thus we see that the most recent decrees of belligerents, in questions of neutral commerce, harmonize. This fact will probably afford the reader sufficient reason to anticipate the complete and universal adoption of the principles of 1780. Indeed, they have energetic and powerful supporters, who persist in enforcing them upon other nations. We can even say, that from 1815 to the present time neutral commerce has not met with any serious interruption, and the slightest attempts of belligerents to extend the right of capture have not only uniformly failed but met with general reprobation.

Such being the spirit of treaties, decrees and internal legislation, the Admiralty Courts can no longer arbitrarily deprive neutral merchants of their ships and cargo, but must decide in conformity with international law. We have seen that on the breaking out of the American war, the coalition of neutral states induced Marriott to mitigate the severity of his judgments. Our age affords even less opportunity for abuses in prize practice. In order to appreciate the difference, we must bear in mind that the armed neutrality was then in its first stage of development; but now the arbitrary power of belligerents having been checked, all nations are agreed that treaties and general customs should serve as the only guides for Admiralty Courts (*s*). In fact, in all the maritime wars since the Congress of Vienna, arbitrary proceedings of prize courts have almost ceased; selfish or false interpretations of the principles of neutrality, and the despotic acts against neutral commerce, even if they have not been totally aban-

(*s*) It is remarkable that the United States were never willing to acknowledge the authority of the judicial decisions laid down at the time of the Continental system, and even demanded their revocation, as well as compensation for their subjects, from almost all European nations. *Lesur*, Ann. 1831, App. 206, 210. With the same energy did the American government, at the time of the South American war, protest against the malpractices of the Spanish prize courts. A curious diplomatic correspondence on this subject will be found in *Murhard*, N. R. iii. 180—220.

(123)

doned, have occurred more rarely. We may further add, that the so-called mixed commissions now often serve for the final settlement of disputes concerning maritime prizes between neutrals and belligerents. This new organ of jurisdiction consists of members chosen by the mutual consent of governments for the purpose of awarding compensation to merchants for losses and damages inflicted by the unjust or erroneous decisions of Admiralty Courts (*t*). It becomes expedient therefore, in our present treatise, to define more completely the character and functions of this new tribunal. But in order, on the one hand, to avoid mistakes in the definition of its attributes, and, on the other, to show its relation to the Admiralty Courts, it must first be agreed on what foundations, and within what limits, belligerents have a right to exercise prize jurisdiction over neutral subjects. This question is justly considered one of the most intricate of international jurisprudence, and, from the very middle of the eighteenth century, has been a subject of controversy. Writers on this question may be divided into two parties, the one rejecting the authority of Admiralty Courts over neutral nations, while the other, on the contrary, maintains that a "forum competens" for cases relating to naval prizes can only exist in the territory of the belligerent power. To the former party belong Hübner, St. Croix, Wurm, &c. They assert that the belligerents have only a right to deal with the neutral merchant, when taken within the limits of their territory; that is, in their inland or adjacent seas; but, as to the other cases, the prize jurisdiction does not belong to them, because, 1st. The open sea is considered free for all nations, and subject to none. 2. Ships are usually carried away by force, and consequently against the will of the owners. 3. No one ought to be a judge in his own case.

(*t*) Mixed commissions are the mere creations of treaties. See those of North America with England, France, Holland, Denmark, Portugal, Sweden and Naples, *Lesur*, 1831, App. 206–210; *Martens*, N. R. (v. 400, vii. 350, 380, x. 598)—of England with Spain, Brazils and La Plata—of France with Brazils and other countries, *Martens*, N. R. vi. 246, viii. 56, 60, x. 542.

These writers further add that Admiralty Courts not unfrequently give severe judgments against neutrals, and they therefore contend that all cases of this kind should be brought before mixed commissions (tribunal mixte), composed of plenipotentiaries selected from the contending parties (*u*).

The second school regards the subject in quite a different point of view; and looking on the "pia desideria" of Hübner as impracticable, submits to the jurisdiction of the belligerents as a matter of course, and urges in support of its theory the following reasons:—1st. A privateer is responsible to no other government than the one from which he received his commission (Martens). 2nd. The decisions of the Admiralty Court are binding on neutrals, according to the rule "actor sequitur forum rei," the privateer in this case being the defendant (Tetens and Rayneval). 3rd. Every capture, like a siege, a blockade, or other military operation (un acte de guerre), being the act of the belligerent, he alone is responsible for its consequences (Lampredi and Massé). 4th. Every neutral subject who violates his duty is "de jure" deprived of the protection of his country and is liable to be dealt with as an enemy (*x*) (Hautefeuille). Looking impartially on both schools, it is evident that the latter is rather weak in

(*u*) Concerning Hübner, see note (*h*), p. 60. His doctrine is critically examined by *Hautefeuille*, Droits et Devoirs, iv. 306—312. Mixed prize courts, according to the idea of Hübner, ought to consist of commissioners from neutral and belligerent powers; to them should be added the consuls of that government whose subjects are the owners of the vessels captured. De la Saisie des Bâtiments neutres, ii. 44—69. *St. Croix* proposes, on the breaking out of a war, to establish a kind of amphictionic maritime court for all European nations (Histoire de la Puissance navale de l'Angleterre, Paris, 1786). *Wurm* suggests to refer all cases of neutral prizes to the arbitration of third powers, or to the award of mixed commissions (Staatslexicon, 1849, xiii. 144). See also *Jouffroi*, Droit des Gens maritimes, Berl. 1806, p. 288; *Nau*, Völkerseerecht, S. 215.

(*x*) We content ourselves with giving the conclusions of these several jurists, without attempting to enter into the details of their doctrine, as they frequently use the same arguments. See *Reddie* (Researches, i. 402, 417, ii. 121, 125, 216, 226); *Wurm* (Staatslexicon, xiii. 144); *Hautefeuille*, Droits et Devoirs, iv. 294--322.

(125)

theoretical views—in fact, the arguments of Lampredi, Tetens, Rayneval and Massé hardly touch the point, but are forced and unsatisfactory. In the majority of cases in the Admiralty Court the neutral merchant is, in point of fact, the defendant, while the privateer is the plaintiff; moreover, what analogy is there between a blockade and the seizure of an unarmed ship? The conclusions of Hautefeuille and Martens are more just, but they do not remove all doubts concerning the limits of prize jurisdiction. Thus, in a theoretical point of view, the first school seems to be distinguished by advanced opinions and supported by the general principles of justice, although practice is in favour of the second, as the authority of the Admiralty Court has been acknowledged by all nations, from the Middle Ages.

Here, then, we come to the question, is the institution of mixed commissions favourable to the views of Hübner? We find no difficulty in answering this question, there being an essential difference between the mixed commissions of our day and the prize tribunals he advocates. Mixed commissions are appointed only in time of peace. Without the intention of restoring the prizes which have been adjudged they do not rescind the sentence in cases once decided, their duty only being to compensate neutral subjects for the injury or damage they may have sustained in the preceding war. On the contrary, Hübner and his followers give the mixed commission full power of jurisdiction over belligerents and neutrals, and make it the regular organ of judicature. Thus, according to the ideas of Hübner, all the calamities of neutral nations would be removed, but his plan has never yet been thoroughly carried out. Prize jurisdiction still belongs to belligerents; the States of Barbary only have hitherto adopted mixed prize tribunals, and have given a voice in them to foreign consuls (y). But

(y) See treaties of Tunis and Tripoli with France (1830, 1832), and of Tunis with Sardinia (1832), *Martens*, N. R. x. 49—57; xiv. 21. In Greece at the time of the war of independence there was also established, at the request of the principal European powers, a mixed prize tribunal for reviewing the decisions of the ordinary courts and for restoring to neutrals their vessels which had been

(126)

we can hardly infer, as some jurists of the second school do, that the authority of the belligerents in prize matters is absolute. To admit this erroneous view would amount to giving one nation legislative power over another, to abandoning the commerce of the world to the mercy of belligerents, and almost to destroying the very idea of neutrality. On the contrary, universal practice proves that prize courts, though an organ of belligerents, have a peculiar character differing widely from that of the other branches of judicature. In fact their power is confined within certain limits, principally with regard to other nations. Being appointed by belligerent governments, they administer justice to their own subjects according to the constitution of the country, to the enemy according to the general laws of war, and to neutrals according to treaties and customs. Although Marriott and Sir William Scott entertained singular views about international law, they did not doubt the correctness of this doctrine. It is evident then neutral merchants come within the jurisdiction of the Admiralty Court upon the same principle on which they are subject to visitation and arrest. But this jurisdiction, as well as all other rights of the belligerent, is to be exercised in conformity with the law of nations. Neutral governments are only bound to acknowledge it under condition of due respect being paid to their rights, and that treaties and customs are strictly observed (*z*). It may be contended that prize courts in reality were guided principally by rules of their own, and by the decrees of belligerents; but this objection is not so strong as is generally supposed, for we know from history that neutral nations only submitted to the

unjustly seized. The existence of this court however was of short duration. See *Wurm*, Zeitsch. 1851, S. 397; Neueste Staatsacten, x. 57—362; *Lesur*, Annuaire, 1827, pp. 141—143, App. 1828, p. 454; Staatslexicon, xiii. 145.

(*z*) *Rutherforth*, Institutes, ii. ch. 9, S. 19; *Wheaton*, Elements, ii. 49—51; *Heffter*, Völkerrecht, S. 172, and in particular *Oppenheim*, System des Völkerechts, S. 320—326. In the opinion of the last author prize jurisdiction necessarily belongs to the belligerent (dem Staat für und durch den der Krieg geführt wird), who gives special commissions to prize courts to administer international justice according to treaties and customs. See also Edinburgh Review, July, 1854, pp. 197, 198.

prize law with reference to the formalities of the process, while the principle, upon which the sentence was to be founded, depended upon the mutual consent of nations. In this work we have had occasion to show, that even in the 15th century, when governments were not strong enough to protect their own merchants, and ideas of international justice were imperfect, even then an unlimited power in prize cases was hardly conceded to belligerents. The principles on which neutral ships were made lawful prize were laid down in treaties or by international customs. From the middle of the 17th century, when governments more strictly defined war contraband and blockade, and recognized the freedom of the neutral flag, prize jurisdiction was still more restricted. It is true that belligerents often refused to observe generally-admitted principles; this irregularity, however, prevailed only so long as the neutrals acted without concert. Unfortunately, before the balance of power was firmly established on the seas, arbitrary systems, subversive of the rights of neutrality, grew up in the prize courts under the influence of mercantile jealousy, but every independent power strongly protested against these exorbitant pretensions.

In 1780 when an opportunity presented itself of curbing the tyranny of belligerents, and Russia was enabled to come forward as a defender of international law, it became necessary to lay down the true principles of prize jurisdiction, and though the revolutionary wars prevented for some years their salutary adoption, they have at last attained almost universal recognition. Every impartial inquirer who directs his attention to the more recent facts in the diplomatic history of Europe and America can hardly fail to conclude that the decisions of Admiralty Courts are not "ipso jure" obligatory on neutral subjects, but only receive their final sanction when in conformity with treaties or customs, and the principles of universal justice. The last resort for the settlement of disputed questions concerning neutral prizes is negotiation. The merchants who are aggrieved by the decisions of the Admiralty Courts are entitled to appeal to their own governments. From the Middle Ages to the present time no nation has ventured to question this right. Hence we can readily explain the expediency of mixed commissions, for as long as the Admiralty Courts act in conformity with international law towards neutral merchants, their decisions are binding upon both parties; but when they act in opposition to treaties and customs, or in an oppressive manner, or adopt arbitrary rules and interpretations, an independent government is entitled to demand satisfaction for its subjects. In such cases, mixed commissions may be the best means of preventing hostilities between nations, and serve as very proper organs for bringing disputes to a friendly termination. Should a nation decline to avail itself of these institutions, it would in fact amount to rejecting negotiations, good offices and mediation, and producing immediate war (*a*). To prevent this, mixed commissions have, since 1815, been frequently resorted to by the governments of Europe and America (*b*), and have been found to be not only useful but expedient. In fact up to the present time they have never been prejudicial to the belligerent parties, for they neither deprived them of any essential right, nor interfered with the usual course of prize procedure, as they were generally appointed after the conclusion of peace, when the angry passions of contending parties had subsided, and when all questions could be deliberately taken into consideration and impartially settled. It may be supposed indeed, that their salutary jurisdiction will extend still more generally, and that their decisions will supply whatever is deficient in treaties in

(*a*) See the conferences of different governments respecting the establishment of mixed commissions in *Murhard*, N. Supp. iii. 180—220; *Wheaton*, Elements, ii. 45—58.

(*b*) Mixed commissions however can hardly be considered as institutions of modern times; they were even made use of in the Middle Ages in prize cases, as for instance when a ship had been illegally captured during the time of an armistice. Mention of them is made in some acts of the 14th century. See treaty of the year 1310 between the German Empire and France (*Dumont*, i. 1, 358), and a letter of Edward II. to Hakon of Norway of the year 1316 (*Dumont*, i. 2, 31). Subsequently this institution having disappeared during the time of the cruel commercial wars, was revived again in the middle of the 18th century.

reference to prize matters, and consequently promote the improvement of international law. The extension of the liberal principles of neutrality also inflicted, though indirectly, a great blow on the barbarous customs of maritime war. Amongst the more important results of the present period must be noticed the gradual decay of privateering. We have remarked, that even in the 17th and 18th centuries this institution had become very injurious to the civilized world; in fact it could only flourish so long as belligerents oppressed neutral commerce, and partiality reigned in Admiralty Courts. We have also seen that the declaration of 1780 gave the first blow to privateering, from which it recovered with difficulty. Even the violent edicts of the Revolution and Empire revived it only for a few years; the prevalence of the "Continental system" was its last brilliant epoch, though true it is, at the beginning of the contest for the independence of the Spanish colonies and that of Greece, it reappeared and soon degenerated into piracy (*c*). In short, the conclusion of general peace in 1815, was a signal for the decay of this institution. In fact, while in former times the commencement of a war gave adventurers even among neutral subjects

(*c*) On privateering in the Spanish American colonies, see *Lesur*, Annuaire hist. 1818, App. 313, 320, 321; 1819, pp. 403, 419, 420; 1822, pp. 598, 722; 1824, p. 686; 1825, p. 632. Already in the year 1821, piracy in the Gulf of Mexico and Sea of the Antilles had reached such vast proportions that the Spanish king suspended the grant of letters of marque. After this, privateering was suspended at Buenos Ayres, and before the conclusion of the war had almost disappeared. At the time of the Greek revolution, privateers, as we have said, took to piracy; infesting small and almost inaccessible bays, they attacked merchant ships without distinction. This weak government endeavoured in vain by the decree of the 8th of June, 1826, to check these pirates, and prohibit the construction of small privateering boats known by the name of "mystics, params and klefttines." At Egina, Hydra and other islands there were shortly afterwards formed numerous societies for the purpose of plundering merchants, and which found protectors or associates in the prize courts. Upon this England and France dispatched their fleets in order to destroy these nests of pirates, and induced the Greeks to abandon privateering as injurious to international commerce. *Lesur*, Annuaire hist. 1826, pp. 428—430, 441; 1827, pp. 399—430. See the letters of Admiral Codrington and De Rigny to the Greek government as well as the instructions given to the English and French commanders, in *Lesur*, 1828, App. 141—143.

(130)

an opportunity to procure commissions (lettres de marque), all treaties made since the Congress of Vienna forbid any person to carry on privateering in the service of a foreign country. In the Middle Ages privateers were also employed in time of peace by the naval powers to make reprisals, but this custom became obsolete even in the 18th century. At all events neither England at the time of the rupture with Holland (1832), with New Granada (1836), with Naples and Buenos Ayres (1839—1841) (*d*), nor France at the time of the rupture with La Plata and Mexico, nor any other states, have had recourse to privateering, but have confined the taking of prizes to their own ships of war. Privateering therefore is no longer considered an institution necessary for maritime war, as it was during the last century. In fact, France at the breaking out of hostilities with Spain, 1823, declared her firm intention of not issuing letters of marque and adhered to it, though the enemy gave commissions to his subjects to seize French merchant vessels (*e*). In the Russo-Turkish and Anglo-Chinese wars captures were also confined to ships of war (*f*). Subsequently, in the year 1846, when a quarrel arose between the United States and Mexico, the newspapers alluded with much apprehension to the prospect of the renewal of privateering. In fact the Mexican general Almonte proceeded to issue commissions at Havannah, and threatened to circulate them in Europe; but these threats were of no avail, since all governments bound by treaties, forbade their subjects to enrol themselves as privateers against North America. In England, where privateering formerly flourished, the sale of Mexican commissions was noticed in parliament, unanimously discountenanced, and consequently prohibited by the government. Only in Spain one adventurer equipped a vessel for a privateering expedition, but he was

(*d*) *Martens*, N. R. xiii. 54; ix. 1, 138; *Ortolan*, i. 386—396.

(*e*) Letter of Chateaubriand to La Ferroney, 21st April, 1823 (Congrès de Verone, ii. 8, Brux. 1838); *Lesur* (1823), 239; *Wurm*, Zeitschr. (1851), S. 317.

(*f*) At the beginning of the war between England and China, when Sir Robert Peel asked whether the government intended to make use of privateers, Lord Russell answered in the negative. *Wurm*, Zeitschr. (1851), 318—322.

(131)

arrested and convicted on charge of piracy. Even in the United States the counter proposition of the President concerning the establishment of privateers produced no result; but on the contrary, Congress sanctioned new and more stringent measures against piracy (*g*). Finally, neither in the wars between Austria and Sardinia (1848—49), nor in that between Denmark and Germany (1848—50), was privateering had recourse to (*h*). In short, since the Congress of Vienna none of the maritime powers of Europe and America have made use of privateers. All international wars have terminated without their assistance; they have made their appearance only in exceptional cases, as in civil wars, and even then met with universal reprobation, and were condemned by public opinion.

Sceptics, for the most part, look upon these events as fortuitous, or attribute the decay of privateering only to the pacific character of that epoch; but we cannot agree with them, for many governments have declared their full and unreserved readiness to abolish privateering (*i*), and some have formally renounced it, while private individuals, having ceased to be occupied in it, have conceived a disgust against its pursuit. Privateering is now considered to border closely on piracy, and to be inconsistent with the spirit of Christian civilization and the higher principles of morality. Publicists,

(*g*) *Wurm*, Zeitschr. (1851), S. 318—322.

(*h*) *Wurm*, Zeitschr. (1851), S. 322—327; see *Bülau*, Jahrbucher, 1849—Die Kaperei im Seekriege. In the declaration of the 28th and 29th of March, 1854, England and France both expressed the same determination not to issue commissions to privateers.

(*i*) When France declared in 1823 that she had no intention of issuing letters of marque against Spanish commerce, the President of the United States of America made a proposition to the European powers to put an end to privateering by general consent; but this proposition, although favourably received in some quarters (see *Lesur*, Annuaire hist. (1823, 619—796; 1824, 683), had no immediate result. Afterwards the United States made a similar proposition to the Congress of Panama. *Lesur* (1826), 583; *Ladd*, Essay on Congress of Nations, Lond. (1840), pp. 15, 16. Up to the end of the Crimean War, only the States of Barbary, Tunis and Tripoli had formally renounced privateering by treaty, on terms of reciprocity. See treaties of Tunis and Tripoli with France (1830—1832), and with Sardinia (1832), *Martens*, N. R. x. 49—57, xiv. 21.

statesmen and all the leading men of the age unanimously denounce it, and have enlisted public opinion on their side. This general opposition deserves our attention, and we will now proceed to trace and explain the cause of it.

Some doubts about the utility of privateering even sprung up at the end of the 18th century. Besides the theoretical opponents and critics, to which class belonged many moralists, philanthropists and zealous partisans of the armed neutrality (*k*), even practical lawyers have discovered that this institution is productive of little advantage to belligerents. Thus, Lampredi, the well known defender of the system of the Consolato, admitted that the motive which weighed most with privateers was gain rather than patriotism. Martens, the impartial inquirer and calm historian, takes the same view, and says that "glory and duty alone instigate the officer to take up arms in the cause of his country, honour being considered by him as a sufficient reward for the labours and dangers which he encounters, while a privateer does not care about the result of the war, nor very often about the good of his country; his chief aim being self-interest, and gain his only reward. Accordingly, it has been found that the best means of stimulating privateers is to promise them all the ships and goods they may take, and to deprive them as seldom as possible of their plunder" (*l*).

But notwithstanding the inquiring spirit of the 18th century, the majority of the then publicists and statesmen were rather inclined to encourage privateering. Supported by the traditions of the Middle Ages, it appeared to many nations an efficient, and, to some, an indispensable instrument of maritime warfare. This was particularly the case in Great Britain, where names of famous privateers, from the time of Elizabeth to Cromwell, were very popular; and in France,

(*k*) *Büsch*, Bestreben der Völker, S. 287—310; *Galiani*, Dei Doveri dei Principi, x. s. 2; *Totze*, La Liberté de la Navigation, p. 226; *Montbrion*, De la Prépondérance de la Grande Bretagne, Paris, 1805, p. 236—239.

(*l*) *Lampredi*, Du Commerce des Neutres trad. par Peuchet, p. 166; *Martens*, Essai, s. 6, pp. 38, 39. See second additional note by the author, p. 145.

(133)

where Louis XIV. made privateering a favourite occupation with sailors and inhabitants of the coast. Only when protracted and almost uninterrupted wars (1793—1815) had nearly annihilated general commerce,—when privateers were chiefly engaged in plundering neutral ships, and when at last, under the influence of the "Continental system," they threatened to put an end to the intercourse of nations altogether,—the prejudice in their favour received a violent shock. The majority of the publicists of the 19th century have come to the conclusion that this system not only brings no benefit to the belligerents, but may be ruinous to the peace of the world. Intending to examine the arguments of both parties, we shall begin with those of its supporters. The reasons they allege are the following:—1. Privateering, particularly for nations that have no considerable fleets, serves as a school of maritime war. Many of the distinguished admirals of Holland and England received their education in privateering expeditions. 2. It affords to individuals an opportunity of taking an active part in hostilities, and, while enriching them, it brings profit to the treasury, as well as diminishes the expenses of Government by rendering it unnecessary to fit out so many ships of war. 3. As commerce with the enemy is prohibited "de jure," and, according to the exigencies of war, cannot be left free, we must admit that privateers are among the best instruments of surveillance over merchants, as they have no motive to conceal the guilty, but look to obtain a reward by delivering them into the hands of justice. Hence the greater the extent to which general commerce is carried on, the more need have belligerents of their services (*m*).

But however strong these arguments may appear they will not bear criticism, for we can hardly admit that pri-

(*m*) *Jacobsen*, Seerecht, S. 583; *Lebeau*, Code des Prises, iv. pp. 42, 43. One of the most zealous supporters of privateering was the French lawyer Valin, who not only justifies all the acts of privateers, and highly extols the *noble* character of this occupation, but considers every censure of it as the senseless talk of pseudo-philosophers and false patriots.

(134)

vateering is the best or even an indispensable school for maritime war. In fact, some European nations have never had recourse to privateering, and yet have maintained considerable fleets, and have produced distinguished naval commanders. As an instance, we may here cite Russia. Certainly there was a time when corsairs were considered bold and experienced navigators; but we can hardly thence infer that the progress of navigation always depended, and must depend, upon the prevalence of piracy. The same may be asserted of privateering; for, in the times of anarchy and private feud, it was the principal school of maritime warfare, although it subsequently became useless. The best, if not the only means of obtaining practical skill in this art, is now regular naval service. Privateering would be of little avail against an armed enemy in the present advanced state of military science. The history of the 18th and 19th centuries affords too few examples to give us reason to think that privateers are capable of undertaking great naval operations (*n*), or giving material support to the regular navy (*o*). We may even say, that they studiously avoid encounters with cruisers, and only pursue their favourite occupation of plundering defenceless merchant ships.

No less untenable are the other arguments in favour of privateering; for instance, that it sometimes enriches individuals. This is correct, but can hardly furnish a strong argument in its favour. As to the benefits accruing from it to the public treasury, they are by no means considerable; for if the equipment of vessels of war be attended with greater expense, the prizes taken by them are generally appropriated by the

(*n*) The expedition of Dugay-Trouin against Rio Janeiro in the time of Louis XIV. is usually cited as an instance to the contrary, but this is not very correct, as we know from history that it was carried on with the assistance of the royal army and navy.

(*o*) *Martens* says, On oblige même tous les armateurs de prêter secours aux vaisseaux de guerre de leur souverain, dans les occasions; mais il est rare d'en voir les effets; il l'est moins sans doute de les voir disparaître à l'approche d'un danger, qui ne leur offre pas l'amorce d'un butin considérable. Essai, s. 14, p. 59; see also *Rayneval*, De la liberté des Mers, i. ch. 38, p. 309.

(135)

Crown to the benefit of the state; while, on the contrary, privateers are only bound to surrender to the treasury a very small percentage of their plunder. The surveillance of the enemy's commerce, assumed by privateers, also has its drawbacks, and often leads to the perpetration of serious offences. We learn from history that privateers were not usually satisfied with their direct profits, but carried on an illicit trade, and even smuggled into their own country forbidden goods, under the disguise of lawful prize, which no severity of punishment (*p*) was altogether sufficient to prevent. Such abuses flourished more than ever under the "Continental system." In short, the laws of war were never so strictly observed by privateers as their supporters affirm; but, on the contrary, instigated by the thirst of gain, they more wantonly transgressed the limits of humanity and justice towards the enemy and neutrals than any responsible officer of the regular navy would ever venture to do.

If privateering does not answer the exigencies of national economy and war policy, still less can it be defended on the ground of international justice; in fact, nearly all the jurists of the 19th century are opposed to it. Thus Rayneval looks upon privateering as an immoral pursuit (*q*), and Reddie, with all his partiality for the Consolato, and the practice of the British prize courts, admits that privateering is not only useless

(*p*) *Martens*, Essai, s. 35, pp. 104, 105.

(*q*) We quote here his own words upon the subject: Des particuliers s'enrichissent aux dépens d'autres particuliers, et tout le mal retombe sur le commerce et sur les paisibles négocians de deux nations ennemies . . . . . Voilà ce que c'est la course, et elle n'est rien autre chose. Je passe sous silence la manière irrégulière et souvent féroce avec laquelle se conduisent la plupart des corsaires, les vexations qu'ils font éprouver aux neutres, et les querelles très sérieuses qu'ils provoquent (Institutions du Droit de la Nature et des Gens, iii. xiv, p. 266). *Pinheiro Ferreira* (Manuel du Citoyen, p. 601), Sartorius (Organon, S. 153, Geng, 1837), and all the advocates of perpetual peace, are equally against privateering. *Marchand* (Nouveau projet de paix perpétuelle, 1842, p. 84) calls it sea robbery, and can discover no use in it, "puisque les pertes sont réciproques, qu'elles ne peuvent hâter le terme des hostilités, et qu'enfin elles rendent les peuples ennemis longtemps encore après que leurs gouvernements sont réconciliés." See also *Ladd*, Essay on Congress of Nations, Lond. 1840, pp. 8, 26.

for belligerents, but even injurious to all civilized nations. In his opinion, as expressed in his "Historical and Critical Researches," the putting an end to privateering is the only reform of naval warfare possible at the present time, which is conformable to the requirements of universal justice. Its abolition can never act injuriously to the belligerent, nor yet give any advantage to the neutrals, as privateers do not form an integral or substantial appurtenance of war. Unfortunately it is not so easy to give up this institution at once, as it would require the general concurrence of all nations. One nation cannot renounce privateering while others continue to make use of it. According to the same authority, and in some degree to prevent abuses arising out of the system, naval officers should be appointed for the purpose of exercising surveillance over privateers (*r*).

But the most decided opponents of privateering are found among the jurists of continental Europe. Thus Pütter considers this institution not only inconsistent with the principles of morality, but also with the spirit of European public law and the general rights of neutral nations. He says that, "It is not difficult to understand the cause of its existence up to the present time. Nations had recourse to it in order to destroy the commerce of their rivals, to put an end to the sale of their goods, and to secure the market to themselves." These mercantile calculations he considers erroneous, and, in the name of international law as well as for the honour and welfare of humanity, demands the abolition of privateering, and expresses a hope that the European powers would declare it piracy (*s*).

(*r*) *Reddie*, Historical and Critical Researches, i. xviii, xix, (Introd.); ii. 391 393, 574. This necessity has been long felt by some nations; for instance, in Holland a special functionary was appointed to each privateer, whose duty it was to draw up reports on the visitation and arrest of vessels; and although this officer was originally paid by the admiralty, yet afterwards government allowed him to receive a per-centage on the captures, thereby destroying his independence. See *Martens*, Essai, S. 16, p. 64, note.

(*s*) *Pütter*, Beiträge zur Völkerrechtsgeschichte (Leip. 1843, S. 209 (ein Vorschlag zur Güte). The protests of Asher against privateering are equally energetic; see his Beiträge (Hamb. 1854), S. 1–5.

(137)

Some French authors go still further. They denounce not only privateering, but all capture of private property at sea. Rayneval himself does not find any justifiable reason why a defenceless merchant should be considered an enemy, and be despoiled of his ship and cargo (*t*). The same thoughts are expressed with greater perspicuity and boldness by Vincens. "It is evident," he says, "that, in continental wars, European nations, in consequence of a tacit understanding amongst themselves, (the solidity of which is secured by the march of civilization, and the spirit of philanthropy,) avoid as much as possible unnecessary cruelty. In fact, though invading armies are generally supported at the expense of the country through which they pass, and contributions levied on cities and provinces, all these exactions of the enemy are made on the local authorities, while private property is generally respected, and plunder punished as an offence against the laws of war. At sea the case is different. There all property belonging to an enemy is reputed lawful prize, and plunder is allowed, not in exceptional cases only, nor under pretext of self-preservation, but as a general rule. Formerly even the goods of an enemy merchant were for a long time seized, in neutral ships, which could not be suspected of any hostile intentions. For this special purpose, belligerents employed not only regular fleets, but also privateers. All which evils, according to Vincens, are useless, and should be avoided, for privateers are as unable to render assistance to a regular navy in war as the merchant ships they capture. In short, many customs of the Middle Ages that are now considered to be immoral in continental war still exist in favour of privateers. Vincens even asserts that maritime captures are not done away with altogether, only because one nation has hitherto considered the loss of another an advantage to itself.

(*t*) Pourquoi donc les pille-t-on sur la mer, qui est un élément libre ? Et ce pillage quel rapport a-t-il avec le but de la guerre, avec les principes du droit des gens ? Institutions, iii. xvi, 166. A well known English periodical, The Edinburgh Review, from the very time of its commencement denounced the capture of private property at sea on almost the same grounds (vol. viii. pp. 13—15).

(138)

This view according to him does not deserve criticism: men engaged in business understand well that the commerce of different countries is closely interwoven, the bankruptcies of merchants in one nation being sensibly felt by those of another (*u*). Massé, a countryman of Vincens, also takes the same view, and sees no difference between privateers and pirates. The seizure of merchant ships is, according to him, a disreputable practice; therefore, we must regard its abolition as a reform that would be worthy of an enlightened age like the present. Let us hope, exclaims the French jurist, that higher views of morality and a feeling of common interest will concur in putting an end to this barbarous system (*x*).

Privateering has as few supporters amongst statesmen as amongst jurists; at least, not one of the eminent politicians of the 19th century has defended it; whilst, on the contrary, many ministers and diplomatists, as Adams, Webster, Count Arnim, Lord Aberdeen (*y*), &c., have spoken and written against it. Even Napoleon, as is evident from his writings, is inclined to admit more humane principles of maritime war (*z*).

Thus almost all the political thinkers and practical men of this age are agreed that the existence of privateering does not harmonise with the present state of civilization. Amongst the advocates of this system, Kaltenborn, Hautefeuille and

(*u*) *Vincens*, Exposition raisonnée de la Législation commerciale (Paris, 1821), livre xii. ch. 17, 18.

(*x*) *Massé*, Le Droit commercial (Paris, 1844), i. pp. 153—4, 162—3. Nearly the same ideas occur in a pamphlet on Maritime Law by Naville (Paris, 1840), pp. 48, 49. He is of opinion that, with the present extension of steam navigation, privateers, if allowed so to do, might entirely destroy international commerce; consequently that the abolition of privateering becomes absolutely necessary for the welfare of mankind.

(*y*) *Webster's* Works (Boston, 1851), vol. iii. p. 12; *Wurm*, Zeitschr. (1851), S. 314, 326, 327; *Kaltenborn* (Bülau Jahrbücher, 1849), p. 193. *Lord Aberdeen* calls privateering "the most intolerable relic of a barbarous age." Economist, 1854, n. 581.

(*z*) Il est à désirer qu'un temps vienne, où les mêmes idées libérales s'étendent sur la guerre de mer, et que les armées navales des deux puissances puissent se battre sans donner lieu à la confiscation des navires marchands, et sans faire constituer prisonniers de guerre de simples matelots du commerce ou les passagers non militaires. Mémoires, iii. ch. 6, § 1. See *Ortolan*, ii. 41.

(139)

Ortolan may be noticed; not one of whom, however, defends it absolutely and in all respects. As to the first of them, he is influenced by the hope of seeing in Germany a maritime power, and proposes to form a naval militia out of privateers; but considering how irreconcilable these reforms are with the nature of privateering, we can only say that, up to this time, they have never been realized (*a*). Hautefeuille, though a zealous defender of the liberal principles of neutrality, considers that privateering is not contrary to international law, so long as it is directed against the enemy, and that it becomes injurious only when it serves as an instrument of oppression against neutral commerce; therefore he thinks that neutral nations may demand from belligerents perfect freedom from visitation by privateers (*b*). But we may ask Hautefeuille, on our part: Is it possible to employ privateers solely against the ships of the enemy, and at the same time to prohibit to them the visitation of neutrals? It is evident that enemy's ships, in order to avoid arrest and confiscation, would protect themselves under a neutral flag, and the same altercations and disputes of which Hautefeuille is afraid would occur. Thus his views seem to be contradictory, and inadmissible in practice. The proofs which Ortolan adduces in defence of the seizure of private property at sea seem to be stronger and more consistent. In opposition to Rayneval, Vincens, and Massé, this practical man expresses the opinion that there is an essential difference between maritime and continental warfare. On land the belligerent fully attains his aim by the conquest of the enemy's territories, and has no occasion to touch private property. On the contrary, in a maritime war we see peculiar phenomena; in it there is no question of conquest unless the enemy undertake a descent on the coast. In the meantime, it is necessary here to inflict as much injury as possible on the adversary in order to compel him to make peace. Some people think that it is quite sufficient for this purpose

(*a*) *Kaltenborn*, Die Kaperei im Seekriege, S. 193—202, 216—228.
(*b*) *Hautefeuille*, Droits et Devoirs, i. 340—41.

to capture enemy's ships of war. But the enemy may detain his navy in inaccessible ports, avoid engagements and cover the sea with merchant vessels alone. In such cases, if we admit the immunity of these last, maritime war having no object should be renounced. At the same time, the seizure of merchant vessels is perfectly justified, in the opinion of Ortolan, by their very quality. A commercial ship cannot indeed be compared with a fort or magazine, but still may directly serve hostile purposes, its crew consisting of men trained and capable, at the first call of their country, of taking part in naval engagements. Thus, the following reasons may be alleged in favour of the capture of private property at sea:—1. A merchant navy by its equipment is easily convertible into an engine of war. 2. If we admit the immunity of merchant ships and the private property of the enemy, the object of maritime war cannot be attained. The enemy without bringing out one single man-of-war will remain unhurt, and derive from the commerce of his subjects a constant supply of means for continuing the struggle. These two reasons, as Ortolan thinks, not only explain the difference between maritime and continental warfare, but may convince us that the immunity of private property at sea can never be allowed, since otherwise maritime war would be an imperfect war (une guerre imparfaite), and hardly come under the description of a war at all (*c*).

In defending, however, with all the power of his practical mind, the necessity of allowing the capture of private property at sea, Ortolan does not find that the proofs in favour of privateering are so conclusive; on the contrary, he concedes that the practice of it is injurious, and can only be justified in extreme cases, as, for instance, in a contest between a secondary and a great maritime power, when granting commissions to privateers is the only means of placing the combatants on equal terms (*d*). Therefore, if the

(*c*) *Ortolan*, i. 41—49, 56—57. Wheaton concurs in opinion with Ortolan in the principal points. Elements, ii. 17.

(*d*) *Ortolan*, i. 57, 59; *Wheaton*, Elements, ii. 19.

(141)

capture of private property at sea is to be permitted it does not follow that privateering is an important or substantial instrument for that purpose; the advantage of this institution appears still more doubtful when we take into consideration the fact that the subjects of the belligerents usually suspend their mercantile operations during war, and that privateers principally attack neutral merchants. It may therefore, without hesitation, be affirmed that the age of privateering is over, never to return; for privateers can no longer take an active part against an armed enemy and are only resorted to by the belligerents as a mode of retaliation; and even cases of this kind, it may be added, are of a very rare occurrence (*e*). Almost all the maritime powers of Europe and America have, in a regular navy, a more efficient instrument of war. Certainly, when recourse is had to militia, landwehr, or general armaments, merchant ships might also be employed in naval expeditions; but even on such occasions the experience of the last three centuries shows how easily they degenerate into pirates (*f*). The spirit of our age decidedly demands the abolition of privateering. It may be done away with by general treaties, or disappear, though more slowly, by tacit consent (tacito consensu), as many former abuses of war have imperceptibly done.

We cannot however fully agree with Ortolan that the capture of merchant ships is an universal custom between nations. Certainly there was a time when belligerents, in their efforts to interrupt all trade, declared, so to say, against each other a general interdict (aquæ et ignis interdictionem), as a necessary accompaniment of maritime war, when neutral commerce was persecuted as much as that of the enemy is now, and when the principle "la robe de l'ennemi confisque celle d'ami" found many supporters. But all these abuses in the practice of Christian nations have been mitigated since

(*e*) *Wurm*, Zeitschrift (1851), S. 327, 333; Edinburgh Review, July, 1854, 222.

(*f*) We may here mention as historical proofs the Gueux de Mer, the South American corsairs, and the Greek pirates of our own times.

the middle of the 18th century, and chiefly by the powerful coalition of neutrals in 1780, known as the "armed neutrality." At the present time not only the rights of neutral commerce are more generally secured, but even enemy merchants are left free at the commencement of war to return peaceably within a certain term to their native country. The whole property of an enemy is no longer liable to seizure; private debts and the sums deposited in public and private banks are by many treaties excepted (*g*). Nor are decisions of Admiralty Courts considered as irrevocable titles for property of prize, but require to be confirmed by a treaty of peace. Besides, if we read history we find that European governments have frequently, at the termination of a war, restored one to another the ships taken from their subjects, or have established mixed commissions for the purpose of ascertaining the damages incurred by the merchants, and the amount of compensation they were entitled to, or have submitted prize questions to arbitration (*h*). From all these facts we may justly conclude that maritime warfare may be modified or improved under the influence of civilization, as much as continental warfare has been; and that the belligerents are now prepared to admit, if not as a general rule, at least as an exception, the immunity of private property at sea. Ortolan we think looks on the mercantile navy with too much suspicion (*i*); in fact, so long as privateering lasted,

(*g*) *Wheaton*, Elements, i. 279—334.

(*h*) As examples may be cited, the convention between France and Spain in the year 1823. *Martens*, N. R. vi. 386. England also, at the conclusion of the war with Holland, 1832, restored to her all the Dutch vessels that had been taken. *Martens*, N. R. xiii. 97, 98. As to the other exceptions, see *Martens*, N. R. xvi. 2, 611; and *Wurm*, Zeitschr. (1851), 322, 323.

(*i*) He writes in this manner. Dans l'hypothèse d'une guerre où l'Angleterre serait une des parties belligérantes, trouvera-t-on injuste que l'autre partie s'empare des navires de la compagnie Anglaise des Indes, parce que la destination de ces navires est spécialement le commerce? Mais ces navires sont organisés militairement; ils font partie intégrante de la force publique Britannique; cette compagnie commerciale tient à sa solde et à son service des officiers de guerre, des troupes de toutes armes; en un mot elle fait le commerce à main armée. *Ortolan*, Règles internationales, ii. 44. But is this remark applicable to all merchant ships? Ortolan himself doubts it. In fact, we

(143)

merchant vessels might sometimes serve as instruments in an attack on the enemy, but since this institution has fallen into disuse, there is no longer any pretext for despoiling the owners of private ships of their property.

Thus, without allowing full freedom of commerce between enemies, as some publicists are inclined to do, we are far from sharing Ortolan's views on maritime war, and from looking upon the capture of merchant ships and cargo as the necessary consequence of it. Admitting that all states regularly adopt this practice, we may easily grant that they are guided chiefly by the principle of retaliation, and adhere to their former customs only, because they have not yet had an opportunity of consulting the true interests of nations. The temporary detention of the property of the enemy is quite sufficient for the purposes of the belligerents, and as to the condemnation, it is more injurious than beneficial, unnecessarily adding to the cruelty of war.

This last opinion is supported by Martens, Linguet, Jouffroy, Heffter, and other authors of the positive school (*k*), being more satisfactory in theory, as well as confirmed by the history of the last fifty years. The rigorous measures against private property had no other purpose than to encourage plunder, and were pursued to their full extent only as long as war continued to retain a mercantile character; at the present time other principles are coming forward. Now maritime war is confined to regular navies, privateering has everywhere ceased, and there is little reason for thinking that the practice of condemnation of merchant ships will be

cannot admit that the mercantile navy is fully efficient for active service in war. We think that there are branches of navigation and commerce of an entirely specific character; as, for example, fishing, the immunity of which has been generally acknowledged in times of maritime war, see *Heffter*, 137.

(*k*) *Martens*, Essai sur les Armateurs, s. 45. This author looks upon maritime capture as contrary to the spirit of the present European private law. Heffter takes an extended view of the subject. Völkerrecht, S. 130, 132, 139, 140, 175, 192. He proves very clearly that, by international law, war, at the present time, gives only actual possession (vera possessio), but not the legal property. See also *Jouffroi*, Le Droit des Gens maritime universel (Berlin, 1806), p. 332. *Linguet*, Ann. marit. vi. 104; *Asher*, Beiträge, S. 30.

(144)

long maintained (*l*). Belligerents now have fewer motives to give the entire property in their prizes to cruisers, as they formerly did to privateers, since they limit both the expeditions against commerce, as well as the number of captures, thereby manifesting their willingness to mitigate the calamities of maritime war (*m*). These noble efforts of the principal European governments, tending to improve the condition of mankind, command the warmest sympathy of Christians and philanthropists. Let us hope that sooner or later they will attain the wished-for success.

(*l*) How little these customs are applicable to the present state of civilization, a Belgian political economist, Molinary, clearly proves. See Journal des Economistes, Août et Septembre, 1854.

(*m*) The first step to reform has been already taken in the New World by a treaty between Brazil and Uruguay, by which they renounced the right of capture of private property. This treaty was concluded in the year 1851. Annuaire des deux Mondes, 1851—1852, p. 981—983.

SECOND ADDITIONAL NOTE BY THE AUTHOR.

Page 133.

Cauchy, in his Memoir recently read before the Political Academy of Paris (Séances et travaux de l'Académie des Sciences morales et politiques, Juillet 1866, pp. 110—116), gives some new information about the history of privateering, and traces the gradual decline of this institution in France from the middle to the close of the 18th century. It appears from the facts collected by him, as well as by others, that the wars of Louis XIV. were the last in which French privateers acted vigorously against the enemy. Thus, in the war of 1691—1697, 4,200 English ships were captured by them. As the British commerce had not reached at that time such proportions as it subsequently did, this number of prizes was certainly very considerable. With respect to their value it amounted, according to St. Croix, (Histoire des Progrès de la Puissance navale de l'Angleterre, ii. 85,) to thirty millions sterling.

Unfortunately we do not find in the interesting paper of M. Cauchy any statistical accounts relating to the war of the Spanish succession. It is known only that French privateers were as numerous in it as in their former contests with the maritime powers, and inflicted on the enemy no less injury. Martens goes even so far as to assert, that "cette guerre est peut-être la seule dans laquelle de tels armaments ont décidé quelque chose." But already, in the seven years' war, the number as well as the value of captures sensibly diminished. On the 12th of July, 1757, it was reported in England that from the breaking out of hostilities only 772 ships had been seized, though the letters of marque had been distributed six months before the declaration of war. The number of prizes taken from the enemy by the French was still less considerable, and did not then exceed 637 merchant ships and privateers. During the whole American war (1776—83), the French corsairs captured 566 ships, valued at about twenty-eight million livres. The six years of the revolutionary war under the Convention and the Directory were still less profitable to privateers. In vain the government encouraged them by all the means in its power, and gave them a liberal reward even for illegal captures. The number of prizes up to 1799 amounted only to 2,658 ships. If we suppose that the majority of them were made on the enemy, it must still be said that his loss amounted only to one-tenth of that suffered by him in 1691—97, as the British commerce now extended from 300,000 to 1,500,000 tons. It is to be regretted that we have not sufficient statistical data to prove by the number of captures that privateering was for a long time principally directed against neutrals. However this may be, Franklin is perfectly right in affirming that the injury inflicted on the enemy by corsairs would be considerable only at the breaking out of a war, when merchants are taken by surprise, but that it greatly diminishes during the course of it. In armed expeditions, or in active service against the belligerent navy, privateers

(146)

seldom took any important part. In fact, such heroic deeds as those of Dugay-Trouin and Jean Bart were rare even in the time of Louis XIV. As to the privateers of the French revolution, we scarcely find among them any great warriors, with the sole exception of Surcouf, who can be compared with those mentioned above. Since the Congress of Vienna no more fitting occupation was left to privateers than the slave trade. Accordingly many adventurers of that description, French, Spanish, and Portuguese, resorted to it, and carried on their piratical practices in distant countries inhabited by the oppressed negro race. Thus in the course of centuries the character of privateering had greatly changed for the worse. In the Middle Ages it served as a practical school of maritime warfare, in the 19th century it degenerated into a most disreputable traffic. Before concluding our remarks we may express sincere regret that a full and authentic history of privateering has not yet been written. The materials for such a work lie dispersed in western Europe, and are hardly accessible to a Russian inquirer.

POSTSCRIPT.

From 1854 to 1866.

The Crimean war is still fresh in the memory of the present generation. As a full description of its great events lies beyond the scope of the present work, it might be sufficient for our purpose to consider only such of them as relate to maritime international law (*a*). We cannot, however, omit noticing the peculiar character of its naval operations. So far as they were directed against governments (and for the greater part this was actually the case) they seem to have been unavoidable, and the prompt conclusion of the peace was chiefly due to their efficiency. In fact that war, destructive as it was, did not last longer than two years, and naturally terminated with the capture of Sebastopol. We must here do full justice to the generous conduct of the belligerents, as well towards the subjects of each other, as with reference to neutrals. Legal piracy was much more circumscribed, and the rules of capture were more relaxed in this war than in the struggles which took place among the European powers during the 18th century and at the beginning of the 19th. The suspension of privateering, the permission given to enemy's ships to return to their own country without molestation during six weeks from the commencement of hostilities, and the recognition of the immunity of the neutral

(*a*) The diplomatic documents of that time, such as the treaties, declarations and decrees, &c., of belligerents and neutrals, may be found in the valuable collection published in Hamburgh by *Dr. Soetbeer* (1854—6), under the title "Sammlung officieller Actenstücke in Bezug auf Schiffahrt und Handel in Kriegszeiten." The introduction to it contains the remarks of the learned author on the present state of international law. "Grundzüge des Seevölkerrechts der Gegenwart."

(148)

flag, are undoubtedly very liberal measures, and do honour to the enlightened spirit of the age. But it cannot be said that the Western powers, allied with Turkey, went so far in their concessions as to do away with all those harsh customs of maritime warfare, which seem to be incompatible with the present state of civilization. The destruction of private property belonging to the enemy was still carried on to a very great extent, and, we may add, often with little advantage to the interested parties. Thus the depredations of the English cruisers in the neighbourhood of the Black Sea and that of Azoff as well as of the Baltic, and even in the vicinity of Archangel, having brought ruin on poor fishermen and inoffensive traders, could not but leave a painful impression on the minds of the population, without impairing in the least the resources of the Russian government. The same may be said of the ravages committed by the belligerents in their descents upon the coasts. In many cases, of course, it was impossible to prevent the perpetration of great atrocities, and though some commanders did their utmost to spare the inoffensive enemy, their good intentions were generally ineffectual. The fire set to public buildings and warehouses naturally extended to the neighbouring dwellings, and sometimes whole villages were reduced to ashes. Accordingly the otherwise pacific inhabitants were forced to take up arms in defence of their homes. It is also to be regretted that such exemptions from war, as were then made for the Russo-American territory by an arrangement of the belligerents, was not extended to other localities lying at some distance from the seat of operations. The bombardment of fortified places like Sebastopol, Sweaborg and Cronstad could be carried on without proceeding to the general capture of the enemy's ships and goods. Precedents for the localisation of maritime war were to be found in the recent policy of France and some other powers. From 1815 there occur many instances of hostilities successfully conducted on that principle. Thus was fought the celebrated battle of Navarino. The same may be said of the coercive blockades of La Plata,

Mexico, &c. In short, when war becomes concentrated in its object, when the principal instruments of attack as well as of defence are directed by belligerents to one and the same point, the extension of hostilities brings no profit whatever to the contending parties. In favour of this view may be adduced not only motives of humanity, but likewise the lessons of experience. It cannot, however, be denied but that during the Crimean war, some ameliorations were introduced into prize procedure (*b*). In fact its forms were greatly simplified, and the business of Admiralty Courts was dispatched with greater expedition. It may be noticed, that more was done by England for the satisfaction of neutrals at that time than by France, where, even in former days, they had been treated rather favourably. According to the instructions given to the British prize tribunals, the standing interrogatories are to be administered to the crew within five days after notice has been given of the arrival of the cruiser with the captured ship (*c*). In the absence of any claim within that period the court is bound to issue a formal monition, and then to proceed to the adjudication of the case. When, however, doubts arise or further proof is required, time may be granted by the judge to a party on application to the court. Three months are allowed for the appeal from the Admiralty Court to her Majesty in Council, six or twelve months, according to distance from Vice-Admiralty Courts. England and France also, on the 10th of May, 1854, entered into an arrangement relative to joint captures (*d*).

As to evidence, the British Admiralty Court allowed the

(*b*) The reports of cases decided in the Admiralty Court and the Court of Appeal (1854—56) are edited by *Dr. Spinks* of Doctors' Commons. We are much indebted for this valuable collection to the kindness of *H. C. Rotheray*, Esq., the registrar of the Admiralty Court. As to the decisions of the Conseil des Prises of Paris, they may be found in the 2nd edition of the treatise on prizes by *De Pistoie* and *Duverdy* (1859). *Dr. Soetbeer* in his Grundzüge gives also an admirable review of the most important judgments delivered in England and France on maritime captures.

(*c*) An Act of Parliament on this subject was passed June 2nd, 1854.

(*d*) *Spinks*' Appendix, ix—xiii.

interested parties to produce all kinds of testimony, verbal or documentary. In the opinion of the court this rule was adopted for several reasons, and principally because the prize court, having no municipal character, and being concerned in the transactions of different nations, could never construct a code in conformity with their various rules, and consequently might do injustice by rejecting some proofs recognized as admissible in other countries. We cannot, however, say that neutrals derived much benefit from this apparently liberal doctrine, or that the court unreservedly adhered to it.

The restrictions on further proof still continued in force against real or suspected *mala fides;* an equitable title to property did not satisfy the court in all cases, a legal title to it being sometimes required (*e*).

In order to lay before our readers the innovations introduced into the prize practice of England and France between 1854 and 1856, we now proceed to review the more important cases relating to neutrals.

The first circumstance to be noticed here is the assurances given by the governments of both these countries that a liberal interpretation should be put upon all the declaratory acts of the belligerents respecting trade with the enemy, as well as general commerce in time of war. We must add, however, that many disputed questions of international law having been omitted in these declarations, extensive power of interpretation was still left to the judge. Our readers may imagine that this discretionary power was rather to the advantage of cruisers than to that of neutrals. In fact, the opinions of a judge on such points must always, to a certain extent, be liable to question, since, as a subject of one of the belligerent powers, he may naturally be supposed to have a bias in favour of his own country. The truth of this remark was once more confirmed by the experience of the Crimean war. The former practices of the British Admiralty Court, and

(*e*) The opinions of the Court on evidence are fully stated in the case of the *Francisca, Spinks'* Rep. pp. 137, 138. See also previous case of the *Ida*, ibid. p. 34.

(151)

principally those of Sir William Scott, so far as they were not abrogated by the recent orders in council, were revived to the detriment of neutral commerce. Thus, in determining the national character of persons, the court seemed to manifest a leaning in favour of cruisers. Knowing, as we do already, how much neutrals are interested in this question, it was unfortunate that the personal qualifications of neutrality had never been accurately defined in treaties. This important omission had afforded Sir William Scott a good opportunity for laying down his own theories upon the subject; and these theories, during the Crimean war, were rather adhered to than relaxed. The principle that in time of war a person is to be considered as belonging to that nation where he is resident and carries on his trade appeared to the court almost conclusive (*f*), yet in the case of the *Ernst Merck* we observe a slight modification of it. The court there considered that a national character, acquired by occupation only, could be changed with greater facility than one arising from birth or long residence. However this may be, this difference, though admitted by belligerents, is of little consequence to neutrals. The learned judge added, that at all events a national character must remain, until another is *bonâ fide* acquired (*g*).

The rules laid down by Prize Courts, on the national character of ships, seems to be still more severe and arbitrary. The ordonnance of 1778 (art. 7), forbidding the sale of this kind of property by the enemy to neutrals, was applied in France during the Crimean war with the same rigour as on its first appearance. The English tribunals, though admitting in theory the bonâ fide neutralization of merchant vessels, also looked on it with great suspicion. Even the transfer of ships to neutrals before the commencement of hostilities (imminente bello) was considered as a colorable or fictitious sale, depriving the belligerent of his rights; at least the new owner seldom succeeded in proving the contrary, the pre-

(*f*) *Spinks'* Reports, pp. 10, 45, 109, 276, 336; *Soetbeer*, Grundzüge, i. pp. 21, 22.

(*g*) *Spinks'* Reports, pp. 102, 103.

sumption of the judge against him being so strong, that the absence of a single paper led to condemnation (*h*). In short, all the transactions of neutrals with the enemy were put under the control or supervision of belligerents for the purpose of preventing frauds. It can hardly be affirmed that the British courts exercised this power in a mild or tolerant spirit during the Crimean war. The opinions of Sir William Scott on the transfer of property from the enemy to neutrals (see above, Period IV. page 89) were constantly referred to and implicitly followed. The court, in extolling them "as the delight and admiration of the world," seemed to have forgotten that their authority, uncontested as it was in the eyes of belligerents, had never great weight with neutrals. We cannot, then, wonder that from the very beginning of the war the United States protested against the practice adopted by the British and French courts with reference to the neutral character of ships. "The exercise of commerce by every nation is one of the incidents of its sovereignty," the American attorney-general said in his report to his government (7th August, 1854). "This sovereign right is not to cease whenever any two other nations go to war. A belligerent cannot annul sales of its enemy's ships to neutrals; to do so is to usurp the jurisdiction over the business of other nations." Without denying that the title of a neutral purchaser should be absolute and bonâ fide acquired, Mr. Cushing assailed the doctrine of Sir William Scott, according to which the very fact of the sale *in transitu* was a presumption or evidence of *mala fides*, and concluded that "the belligerent, who claims to take property from the neutral as enemy's property *must prove* the invalidity of the possession as well as of the contract (*i*)." Unfortunately neither France nor Great Britain

(*h*) *Spinks*, p. 16 (The Johanna Emilia), 67—80 (The Ocean Bride), 98—104 (Ernst Merck), 104—111 (The Soglasie), 264—276 (The Baltic), 276—281 (The Nina), &c. The French cases (The Orione, The Christian, The Alexander) are reported by *De Pistoie* and *Duverdy*, ii. 499, 502, 503 (2nd edition).

(*i*) The report of *Mr. Cushing* may be found in the collection of *Dr. Soetbeer*, 182.

(153)

have altered their practice since this statement of international law was published. The complaints against the severity of the courts continued to be heard to the end of the war. The absence of reciprocity and the difference of treatment practised towards cruisers and neutral merchants were particularly observable in the judgments of the Admiralty Court. For instance, it allowed captors to prove the copartnership of the enemy in vessels, bearing the neutral flag, and to claim his part as a good prize, but did not extend the same favour to neutrals in corresponding cases (*k*). The very exemption of a neutral cargo from condemnation, though fully conceded by England in 1854, was counteracted by the general prohibition of sale *in transitu*, and neutrals accordingly suffered from this restrictive interpretation of the court. Great objections, also, have been raised by the court against the validity of any bonds or liens affecting the cargoes captured on board enemy's ships (*l*).

In the interpretation of blockade, the British Admiralty Court followed its own precedents rather than the liberal principles of 1780. As an instance of this may be mentioned the celebrated case of the *Francisca* (*m*). When examining that case, the court expressed its resolution to act in strict conformity with the decisions of Sir William Scott, not solely on account of their authority in England, but also " because they were adopted as a part of the law of nations." From this point of view, as we have said before, many unsettled questions of international law were regularly decided in favour of belligerents. Thus the testimony of the commander-in-chief, as to the sufficiency of the blockading force, is reputed by the British court to be the best, and sometimes conclusive evidence. The distance of the squadron from the blockaded port does not affect in the least the legality of the measure; even the occasional absence of the cruisers from

(*k*) *Spinks*, Reports, 49 (The Primus) and 57 (The Industrie).

(*l*) *Spinks*, p. 27—37 (The Ida), 39—42 (The Fidentia), 42—48 (The Abo), 60, 65 (The Johann Christoph). See also the observations of *Soetbeer*, Grundzüge, pp. 25, 26.

(*m*) *Spinks*, p. 113—161.

(154)

the station appears to be permitted. The Judge assumed, also, that a blockade de facto needs no notification, and adopted all the conclusions of his predecessor in regard to constructive notice. Notoriety, according to both these Judges, precludes neutrals from approaching the port on any pretext whatever. Individual warning is requisite only as an exception to the rule. These opinions opened the door to presumptions, and by throwing the *onus probandi* on neutrals gave the court a favourable opportunity to condemn all the ships whose masters could not prove their ignorance of the blockade.

Belligerents were thus enabled to extend their operations without incurring any responsibility for the efficiency of the measures directed against universal commerce. Only capricious permission of ingress or egress was reputed to be illegal. As to the blockade itself, the court did not appear to be very strict in its estimate of the means necessary for its maintenance, for it observed that it could see no reason why three or four steam-vessels should not be sufficient to blockade an extent of eighty-five miles of coast. The treaties of England with Sweden (1661) and Denmark (1670), containing very liberal interpretations of blockade, it considered as privileges incompatible with international law. It must be added, however, that some of the decisions of the British Admiralty Court were overruled by the judicial committee of the Privy Council (*n*).

The principles of blockade, as stated by that committee in the appeal in the case of the *Francisca*, may thus be summed up. The exclusion of neutrals from a blockaded port rests, not on any unlimited right of belligerents to cripple the enemy's commerce, but on the same grounds as the prohibition of contraband trade. Both these restrictions on the general intercourse of nations appear to be founded on the same reasons, viz., that the interference of a neutral with the naval operations of a belligerent being irreconcilable with a state of war, cannot be permitted under any pretext what-

(*n*) *Spinks*, p. 287 – 305.

ever. Proceeding to the definition of blockade, the judicial committee pronounced their opinion, that the prohibitory measures of the commander should be absolute. Accordingly, when exceptions are made by belligerents in behalf of their own subjects, or of their allies, the blockade ceases to be valid against neutrals; otherwise its partial relaxation might be alleged as proof that the interdiction of the port to commerce did not exist. If a modified blockade is to be enforced at all, justice seems to require that its intended modification should be notified to neutral states. The committee came also to the conclusion that the condemnation of a neutral ship for the breach of blockade should be established on more solid grounds than those admitted by the court below. A ship cannot be condemned unless, at the time of the offence, the port of her destination was legally in a state of blockade, and was known to be so by the master or the owner. The fact of knowledge must be one which admits of no reasonable doubt. Presumptions in such cases should not be carried too far. Without requiring special notification, the committee laid down some restrictions, rather adverse to the doctrine of paper blockades. "The notice of the blockade must not be more extensive than the blockade itself. A belligerent cannot be allowed to proclaim that he has extended the blockade to several ports of the enemy, when in truth he has only blockaded one." In fact, "if he could do so, such a course would be attended with the grossest injustice to neutrals. Consequently a neutral is at liberty to disregard a notice of this description, and is not liable to the penalties attending a breach of blockade, for afterwards attempting to enter the port which is really blockaded."

So far their lordships have mitigated the former rules of the English prize courts. The French government did more for the satisfaction of neutrals, by requiring from cruisers a special notification of blockade to every ship bound to the prohibited port (*o*).

(*o*) This liberal policy was adopted by France from 1830. The despatch of

(156)

The decrees of belligerents (1854) having omitted to define contraband of war, we find no change made by prize courts in this branch of law; it must be added, however, that few cases of this description are reported. In one of them brought before the Conseil des Prises of Paris, *Vrouw Howina*, it was laid down that saltpetre, when an enemy's property, or destined to his ports for the use of his naval and military forces, should be condemned (*o*). At the same time the court intimated their opinion, that the very transport of contraband by neutrals could no longer be permitted on the high seas with impunity. Any concealment or fraud committed by the trader may here give rise to presumption against him on a suspicion of his *bona fides*. Nothing but documentary evidence can satisfy the court that the prohibited article is not enemy's property. Otherwise, or when more than three-fourths of the cargo are contraband, the ship itself is liable to condemnation. The case of *Margarete Zéloni*de was decided on the same grounds (*p*). We have reason then to conclude that the rules of the ordonnance of 1778 relating to this subject continued in force notwithstanding the liberal concessions which had been made by France to neutrals in subsequent treaties. All transport of enemy's troops was very strictly prohibited during the Crimean war. The case of the *Creta* may serve as an instance of this. This ship, having on board 270 Russian officers, was captured on the way from Japan to Ayen and condemned by the prize court of Hong Kong. The plea of the master that he acted from motives of humanity, and a desire to save the passengers from shipwreck, was rejected by the court, as it appeared from his papers that he was to receive from the enemy a remuneration for his services (*q*).

Costs and damages were allowed to captors by prize courts

the Minister of Foreign Affairs to the Conseil d'Etat on this subject, may be found in the work of *De Pistoie & Duverdy*, i. 371 (2nd ed.)

(*o*) *De Pistoie & Duverdy*, ii. 523—526.

(*p*) *Soetbeer*, Grundzüge, ii 16.

(*q*) Ibid.

as liberally as before. The general rule of the Consolato del Mare with reference to freight also continued to be enforced on neutrals. They paid it for their cargo in cases of condemnation as well as of restitution. The French practice differed little from that of the English in this respect. The case of the *Orione* (*r*), decided by the prize council of Paris, shows this. On the contrary neutrals were but seldom, and then only sparingly, reimbursed their losses. This absence of reciprocity has from time immemorial been the principal subject of complaint on the part of neutrals against belligerents. In fact, if they are not to be remunerated for the damages and sufferings inflicted on them by captors without any reasonable cause, what justice can they expect from prize courts? As long as the captor runs no risk whatever in seizing any ship, how many inducements has he not to commit arbitrary and violent acts. The truth of this remark is attested by the conduct of English cruisers in the Crimean war. They were left almost free from responsibility in arresting neutral vessels which were suspected of breaking blockade. A most remarkable case of this description, that of the *Ostsee*, may here be cited (*s*). This ship was seized in the gulf of Finland before either Cronstadt or Sweaborg was really blockaded. The court, while fully admitting the evident injustice of her seizure, declined at the same time to condemn the captors in costs and damages, adding, that to do so would amount to "the extremity of the laws of nations, which ought by no means to be adopted as a general rule." In order to justify himself in public opinion, the Judge said that Lord Stowell, during the seventeen years he presided in the court, had condemned the captors in costs and damages in only about ten or twelve cases, *not one in a thousand.* Happily neutrals appealed against this judgment. The Judicial Committee having on that occasion reviewed the whole question of costs and damages (*t*), laid down the following rules

(*r*) *De Pistoie & Duverdy*, ii. 499; *Soetbeer*, i. 37.
(*s*) *Spinks*, pp. 174, 175.
(*t*) Ibid. p. 175—193.

for the future guidance of prize courts. In the opinion of the Committee the restitution of a ship and cargo may be attended with three consequences:—

1. The claimants may be ordered to pay to the captors their costs and expenses;
2. The restitution may be without costs; or,
3. The captors may be ordered to pay costs and damages to the claimants.

The first consequence may be applied with justice only to cases when a ship, by her own misconduct, has occasioned her capture. The second, when she has become involved with little or no fault on her part in such suspicion as to make it the right or even the duty of a belligerent to seize her. The third, when a belligerent has seized the ship at his own peril without any probable cause (sans cause raisonnable). Having cited in favour of their view the opinions of English, French and American jurists, the Committee add that neither in the texts nor in the precedents has it ever been stated that, in order to condemn captors in costs or damages, vexatious conduct on their part must be proved, or that honest mistake, though occasioned by the act of the belligerent government, can relieve them from their liability to make good to a foreigner and neutral the damage which by their conduct he has sustained. The captors act always as the agents of the state, which must be ultimately responsible for their acts. Prize courts are in duty bound to afford remedy and give redress to individuals for all the wrongs they have suffered from captors.

Having considered all the circumstances of the case, the Committee came to the conclusion that costs and damages should be awarded more liberally than had been hitherto customary, adding that, upon more diligent search, it appeared that they had formerly been decreed on restitution more frequently than had been supposed. This relaxation of the rule was likewise adopted in order that the English practice might be in conformity with that of France and the United States of America.

(159)

The Committee observed, that captors having a great interest in increasing the number of prizes, the temptation to send in ships for adjudication was already sufficiently strong of itself. " Is a captor to be permitted to say to the captured, You have nothing to complain of; I had a right to take my chance; go about your business and be thankful for your escape." The Committee came to this conclusion in favour of neutrals, in full expectation that the same principles would be adopted by other belligerents in behalf of English subjects when they were neutrals. It cannot, however, be said that all the doubts upon the subject were cleared up by this decision.

In a subsequent case, that of the *Leucade* (*u*), the court expressed its regret that the Court of Appeal, having abandoned the former practice, had left out of view many difficult points of the question. According to the learned Judge, it would be very important to ascertain how far the captor's evidence as to the facts of the actual capture should be admitted.

The court laid down here some new interpretations and distinctions. Feeling it its duty to look to the preservation of belligerent rights, it expressed its concern about the maintenance of blockade, if the costs and damages were to be accorded to neutrals without giving the captors an opportunity for explanation. Such a course appeared to it not only unjust in itself but detrimental to England. The court added that it should still follow, as to what might be left in doubt by the Committee, all the principles established by Sir William Scott.

It may be supposed from the subsequent case of the *Fortuna* (*v*), that costs and damages were only allowed to neutrals in strict conformity with the ruling of the Superior Court, and we must, therefore, conclude, that notwithstanding the reversal of the judgment in the case of the *Ostsee*, the English

(*u*) *Spinks*, p. 217—238. (*v*) Ibid. p. 307—313.

Admiralty Court is not likely to extend the principles laid down by the Judicial Committee in that case.

Dr. Soetbeer, of Hamburgh, in his remarks on maritime international law, says, that the English Admiralty Court still seems to be disinclined to vary its former practice. Now as long as the probable cause of the detention of ships is left to the interpretation of belligerents, neutrals will in all probability be generally condemned in costs, otherwise the captors would be deterred from acting with their former zeal (*v*). We cannot but subscribe to this opinion. In fact, the fair treatment of neutrals is hardly to be expected from judges, who hold the opinion that it is to the interest of their country, when at war, to cripple the enemy's commerce by every means in their power. The whole doctrine of costs and damages rests on no other foundation. The courts have established it for the sake of the belligerent, in order to assist him in the prosecution of his main object. Before it, not only considerations of mercy but even those of strict justice fade away. As long as such harsh views prevail, a neutral will naturally be considered by the court in the light of an abettor of the enemy. On the contrary, the cruisers who act with energy meet with great favour and are rewarded for their services at the expense of a foreign claimant.

Such was the state of the prize practice during the Crimean war.

We now come to the Congress of Paris. Amongst its acts, the declaration of the 16th of April, 1856, assumes a prominent place. The members of the congress concluded their work of pacification by adopting the following principles of maritime international law :—

1. Privateering is and remains abolished.
2. The neutral flag covers enemy's goods with the exception of contraband of war.
3. Neutral goods not contraband are free under the enemy's flag.

(*v*) *Soetbeer*, ii. 17.

(161)

4. Blockades, in order to be binding, must be effective, that is, maintained by a force sufficient really to prevent access to the coast of the enemy.

These four principles were proposed by France after a previous consultation with England, and unanimously adopted by all the contracting parties. M. Walewski observed on that occasion, "that the Congress of Westphalia having sanctioned the liberty of conscience, and the Congress of Vienna the abolition of the slave trade as well as the free navigation of European rivers, it would be worthy of the Congress of Paris to put an end to the dissensions between belligerents and neutrals by the establishment of an uniform system of law for a time of war." He seemed to expect that the declaration would contribute as much to the general improvement as to the satisfaction of the world (*x*).

Unfortunately subsequent events have proved that these expectations were too sanguine. In fact, the declaration of Paris cannot be considered as an act embracing the whole subject of belligerent and neutral rights. We find in its meagre contents nothing but such provisions as were already made in former treaties by the majority of nations. As to the most intricate and disputed questions of prize law it leaves them still unsettled. In the second and fourth articles of it are recapitulated (and very imperfectly) the principles of 1780; the third extends to all neutrals the privileges already

(*x*) The declaration of the 16th April, as well as the protocols of the Congress relating to it, may be found in the Sammlung of *Dr. Soetbeer*, neue Folge, iii. No. 187—192. The subsequent negociations upon it are fully set forth in two recent works on the reform of maritime capture. The first of these was published in Hamburg, by Prof. *L. K. Ægidi* and *M. A. Klauhold*, under the title "Frei Schiff unter Feindes Flagge." The second, read by *M. Cauchy*, before the French Academy in 1866, appeared as a pamphlet a few months ago in Paris (Du respect de la propriété privée dans la guerre maritime). Both the works abound with diplomatic and other documents. We are much indebted to these publications for the contents of the following pages. *M. Cauchy* is also known as the author of a larger work on maritime international law, which appeared in 1862, in two volumes, under the auspices of the same celebrated Academy (Académie des Sciences morales et politiques).

accorded by Mahometan powers to their allies, and only the first is really an important innovation or an improvement of international law. But the abolition of privateering, great blessing as it was, could hardly satisfy public opinion. European nations having been prepared for it by its gradual decay, looked for something more. A step further in the same direction was now required. The members of the Congress might have proceeded at once to put an end altogether to the capture of private property at sea. In order to limit the number of captures, it was necessary to revise carefully the whole prize law. The establishment of a general peace being very favourable to such a work, it might have been more successfully accomplished by a congress than by the separate efforts of statesmen, or by protracted negotiations. The diplomatists of 1856 were probably well aware of the necessity of this reform. In fact, not only neutrals but all inoffensive traders with the enemy required now a more efficient security from plunder. Accordingly the abolition of privateering appeared to them a matter of no great importance, for, expecting to be treated by cruisers with the same rigour as before, they could hardly regard it as an improvement. It must, indeed, be added, that the policy of France as a belligerent power from 1815 was more liberal in that respect than the law sanctioned on the 16th of April, 1856. So far back as 1823, she made the first step towards the abolition of maritime capture (*y*). The same proposals might have been made to the Congress. Why the French government omitted to do so we cannot tell. Probably it dispaired of persuading the other contracting powers to adopt more advanced views on the subject. However that might have been, the Congress of Paris rendered (very tardily) justice to the "armed neutrality," and inflicted a fresh blow on the barbarous practices

(*y*) *Ægidi* and *Klauhold*, Introduction, pp. viii, ix; document lvi. 5. Here is inserted the communication of *M. Chateaubriand* to the United States upon the subject, 29th Oct., 1823. The circular note of the French government, dated 12th April, 1823, may be found in *Cauchy* (Annex. to the Mémoire, No. 5).

of the Consolato. The adherence of England, and the subsequent, almost unanimous, approval of the declaration by the governments of Europe and South America, impart great value to it in the eyes of the whole civilized world. The Congress proclaimed the four principles to be indisputable, and at once declined to admit of any amendments into the text of the declaration. Consequently Spain and Mexico refused to accede to these engagements, alleging that they were not prepared to abolish privateering.

But the Congress, having irrevocably condemned this institution, did not interfere with them, in the hope that they would eventually follow the better course of policy. In short, no pressure was put upon any power, but at the same time no partial exception could be made to the general rule. In our opinion the Congress acted very prudently in proposing to other powers to adopt the declaration as a whole, otherwise the results already obtained by it might have been frustrated or have entailed new difficulties.

A more dangerous opposition to the Congress came from other quarters. The projected improvement of international law did not satisfy the United States, probably because it was made without their participation. In fact, the first proposal for abolishing capture of private property at sea belongs to a diplomatist of that country, namely to Franklin. His "quaker notions" were subsequently revived, under the President Munro and his secretary of state, John Q. Adams. So far back as 1823, Mr. Rush, the American ambassador in London, received in his instructions a project of a treaty to be concluded with England concerning captures. In that project not only privateering was condemned, but also further measures were proposed for the mitigation of cruelty in war. According to the American government, the trade with the enemy might be made perfectly free and unmolested by the mutual consent of the belligerents. But at the Conference held on that occasion on the 3rd of July, 1824, the English ministers declined to enter into the proposed engagement, and the subject was dropped. The efforts of the

(164)

American government to conciliate to its views some other cabinets of Europe were also met rather coldly. Even Russia, warmly approving the desired reform (comme un titre de gloire pour la diplomatie moderne), replied that in order to effect it the consent of other nations should be first obtained. (Note of Count Nesselrode, 1st February, 1824.) After an interval of nearly twenty-five years, the negotiations upon the subject were reopened between the United States and the provisional governments of France and Germany, under the unfavourable circumstances of the general revolution in Europe, but were soon interrupted. In short, this American propaganda of liberal principles of maritime war had no success up to the Congress of Paris, and seemed at last to have been abandoned (*z*). The eventual suspension of privateering during the Crimean war was indeed even regarded unfavourably by the United States. "The renunciation of this custom," said President Pierce in his message to the Congress, 4th of December, 1854, "is naturally desired only by nations having a large regular navy; but to adopt it, as a rule of international law, is to leave us in time of war at the mercy of the great maritime powers" (*a*). All these precedents concurred in determining the American government to oppose the declaration of Paris. Accordingly, when it was submitted to the approval of the United States, they did their utmost to dissuade minor powers from adopting it (circular note of Mr. Marcy, 14th July, 1856), and made the following objections to its contents:—Mr. Marcy regretted that the four principles were inseparable. This condition appeared to him onerous for his country. But the greatest danger, according to the secretary of state, might be expected from the application of the first principle. Privateering, he said, cannot be abolished without going at once a step further; that is, with-

(*z*) At least the treaty between Uruguay and Brazils of 1851, as well as that of 1856 between Costarica and Granada, by which they abolished the right of maritime capture, seem to have been made without any participation of the United States. *Ægidi* and *Klauhold*, documents, N. lviii.

(*a*) *Cauchy*, Séances et travaux de l'Académie, 1866, Juillet, p. 82.

(165)

out proceeding to the abolition of capture, otherwise all the independent nations would be obliged to create a large navy or to surrender their commerce and navigation into the hands of the great maritime powers. In order to meet this difficulty, the cabinet of Washington proposed to add to the original text a new clause, tending to the immunity of private property from seizure in time of war, with the sole exception of contraband. (Note of Mr. Marcy to Mr. Sartiges, 28th July, 1856.)

It is curious to note that the new proposals of the United States seemed at first to have some chances of success, and to find a favourable reception in the official circles of England and France. In fact, Mr. Walewsky, in his conversations with the American minister, gave him to understand that the Emperor was rather inclined to enter into the views of the American republic. Lord Palmerston himself stated in his speech at Liverpool (7th November, 1856) that the relaxations of international law might perhaps be extended so far, that private property should no longer be the object of aggression in maritime war. As to Mr. Cobden's opinions on the subject, they perfectly coincided with those of Mr. Marcy (*b*). Even the *Times* newspaper advised the ministers to take the American note into serious consideration, and suggested the adoption of the proposed innovations (*c*). President Pierce himself announced in the next annual message (2nd December, 1856) the formal accession of Russia to the American policy, and added that assurances of a similar purport had been received with respect to the disposition of the Emperor of the French.

But at the very beginning of the next year it again appeared that the authors of the Congress persisted in their original resolution. Accordingly no further communications

(*b*) See his letters of Nov. 8, Dec. 8 and 15, 1856, in the documents collected by *Ægidi* and *Klauhold*, N. xi.

(*c*) Three years afterwards the *Times*, having changed its views again, opposed the American scheme. See the leading article upon the subject, Dec. 7th, 1859.

from Paris or London came to Mr. Marcy respecting his note. The cause of this revulsion of feeling has not yet been sufficiently explained; it depended perhaps on the more careful consideration of the new plan by England and France, or, as some suppose, on Mr. Marcy's own procrastination in giving Mr. Mason full powers to act; the public opinion at that time seemed to be very wavering and unsettled upon the question. Even in America the reform found but few warm friends and supporters. A pamphlet, directed against it by an English barrister, made some sensation at New York, and found adherents (*d*). Before the opening of the next spring the government of President Pierce came to an end. Having received, too late, a favourable answer from Prussia, and sent his project to Paris, Mr. Marcy retired. With the accession of Mr. Buchanan the affairs assumed a different aspect. General Cass was named the secretary of state; it appeared that he did not agree with the views of his predecessor. Accordingly American ministers received instructions to suspend, until further orders, the negotiations.

In the course of the same year, 1857, Mr. Lyndsay called the attention of the House of Commons to the unsettled state of maritime international law after the declaration of Paris. The debates on that subject brought into full light the unwillingness of the English government to adopt the American scheme. Lord Palmerston appeared almost to retract his speech at Liverpool; Lord John Russell even suggested that England had taken, perhaps, an imprudent step in signing the declaration itself. After some discussion the motion of Mr. Lyndsay was withdrawn (*e*).

In 1859, the Italian war broke out; the principles of the 16th of April having been carried out by all the parties engaged in it, neutrals had now hardly any reason to com-

(*d*) *R. W. Russell*, The New Maritime Law, Review of Mr. Marsh's Letter to Mr. Sartiges, New York, 1856.

(*e*) The account of these debates on the 14th of July, 1857, may be found in the documents collected by *Ægidi* and *Klauhold*, N. xii. For the previous discussion on the declaration of Paris in the House of Lords, see *Hansard*, vol. cxlii. p. 482.

(167)

plain of the conduct of belligerents, even the subjects of the enemy were treated rather leniently; thus the embargo laid by Sardinia on Austrian ships at the commencement of hostilities brought after it no condemnations, and had only the effect of a temporary measure. The rumours spread about the extension of contraband proved also to be erroneous. Soon afterwards England and France declared war against China; it is remarkable that the right of maritime capture was totally suspended on that occasion. The western powers allowed the trade with the enemy to go on without any hindrance whatever from cruisers (*f*). These last relaxations of maritime law were received with still greater approval by the commercial classes of Europe. The public surmised that the general improvement of it, though inevitably postponed, might in time succeed. Had the views of Mr. Marcy been pursued then in America, they might have found more support on this side of the Atlantic than in 1856. Unfortunately General Cass, by his circular note, rather raised new difficulties than brought the affair to a satisfactory issue. For this note, large, obscure and learned, as a second-rate German book might easily be, discovered the selfish views of the American government. Liberal professions on the law of maritime captures are here made rather awkwardly and to no purpose. General Cass goes further than Mr. Marcy in his objections against the principles of the 16th of April, and at the same time defends privateering as a necessary instrument of war for the United States. According to him, the whole law of contraband and blockade must be thoroughly revised; he says, that in order to interdict the access of an enemy's port to neutrals, belligerents should invest it by sea and land, otherwise blockade is nothing but an abuse of power; as to other reforms, it is difficult to guess in what they should consist. General Cass seems to lose himself in vague generalities. In short, the public opinion

(*f*) *Ægidi* and *Klauhold*, documents, N. xxxix. The note of France to the Hanse towns on this subject bears the date of the 30th June, 1859; that of England, of the 4th July, 1859.

(168)

of Europe was much perplexed by this extraordinary document, and clung to the original scheme of Mr. Marcy, notwithstanding the uncertainties of American policy. As long as the Italian war lasted, the agitation about the reform of maritime law went on in the chambers of commerce. The Hanseatic Towns, and principally Bremen, took the most active part in it. It was then expected that a second Congress would be held in Paris for the settlement of Italian affairs. Accordingly great efforts were made to introduce before it the question of belligerent and neutral rights. Acting under the impulse of his countrymen, Mr. Geffeken, the Hanseatic minister in Berlin, addressed a memoir upon the subject to the court of Prussia, 14th November, 1859, and went to Holland with the special purpose of persuading the Dutch government to appear as the representative of the secondary states upon the question before the Congress. In fact, Baron Golstern, the minister of foreign affairs at the Hague, acceded to this proposal, and sent a circular note asking the interested parties to give him power to act in their name. Unfortunately, excepting Denmark, Hanover and the Hanseatic Towns, no other power gave a cordial support to Holland. It must be added that the expected Congress did not take place. The only result of the treaty of Zürich for maritime international law is its third article, in which stands the following clause:—" In order to mitigate the evils of war, and in derogation to general rule, the Austrian ships already captured, and not yet condemned by the prize court, will be fully restored" (*g*). About the same time we observe in England the first signs of a literary and political movement in favour of the abolition of maritime capture. The warmest friends of this reform were of course shipowners, whose interests coincided with the perfect immunity of private property in time of war. Their views found an echo in the

(*g*) The same provisions may be found in a decree of the French emperor, published after the Mexican war (March 29, 1865). Exceptions are here made only against ships laden with contraband, or having violated blockade. *Cauchy*, Doc. N. 12.

(169)

chambers of commerce and with some influential organs of the press. The question was also ably discussed at the annual meetings of the Social Science Association (*h*). When General Cass published his celebrated note, Mr. Lyndsay addressed to Lord John Russell a letter upon the subject, and recommended the English government to enter into a compact with the other powers of Europe upon the basis of Mr. Marcy's original proposals. In his opinion the concurrence of the United States to such an arrangement would be now unimportant. England might leave them alone as in 1856, and act according to her own interest. Lord John Russell promised to reconsider the question, though he avowed that the course of policy recommended to him was liable to grave objections. In 1860, at the end of the session, the select committee on merchant shipping presented to the House of Commons a report on belligerent rights at sea, to the same effect. In conclusion the committee said, "that the time had arrived when all private property, not contraband of war, should be exempt from maritime capture (*i*). In the course of the same year Mr. Lyndsay, in order to ascertain the state of the public opinion in America, went to the United States and made there speeches upon the subject before the chambers of commerce. At the opening of the next session another member of the House of Commons, Mr. Horsfall, asked the secretary of state whether the English government felt disposed to act according to the suggestions of the committee. Lord John Russell replied, that since the appearance of the note of General Cass, he thought it not advisable to continue the discussion of belligerent rights with America, adding that the adoption of the new rule proposed by the committee

(*h*) See the Transactions of the Society for 1860, pp. 163, 279; 1861, p. 748, 793; 1862, p. 896; 1863, pp. 851, 878, 884; 1864, pp. 596, 656. The most interesting papers on the subject are from the pen of *Mr. Beach Lawrence* (of the United States), *Mr. J. O'Hugan* (of Ireland), *Mr. Lamport*, *Mr. Ashworth*, and others.

(*i*) The letter of *Mr. Lyndsay*, and the report of the committee, may be found among the documents collected by *Ægidi* and *Klauhold*, N. xiv. xl.

would tend rather to the prolongation than to the shortening of wars (*k*).

The greatest event of 1861 was the breaking out of the American civil war. From its very commencement it assumed an international aspect. The whole Christian world felt itself concerned in the final struggle between liberty and slavery. To this must be added the unusual character of hostilities in the United States, the sufferings of European commerce, and the distress of England caused by the interruption of the cotton trade. The general security was also menaced by new contests and difficulties about maritime international law. Neutrals attempted in vain to stand aloof from interference and to maintain an impartial attitude. It now appeared that the conduct of the American government towards them did not exactly correspond with its former declarations. The affair of the Trent and the blockade of the whole Southern coast proved that the United States were as much inclined to the unlimited extension of belligerent rights as all the great maritime powers. The somewhat hasty recognition of the state of war by England and France made the matter still worse. The people of the North could not bear it patiently, and felt their pride wounded. Their irritation was of course communicated to the government. The Confederates on their side made great efforts to maintain their independence and to find support in Europe. According to our custom, we shall not here speak of such events of that war as bore upon the parties immediately engaged in it. Our chief interest lies with its foreign relations ; first, it must be observed, that the struggle with the Confederates made the United States better appreciate the value of the declaration of Paris, as their recent imprudence in having rejected it now brought forth its bitter fruits. In fact, privateering revived in the South to the great detriment of Northern commerce. At the same time, the rebel government subscribed to the other principles of the 16th of April, relating to neutral com-

(*k*) The account of this debate is also given by *Ægidi* and *Klauhold*. See documents, N. xli.

(171)

merce. In order to frustrate the designs of the enemy, President Lincoln resolved to make amends for the past, and tried to renew with the European powers the negotiations on the subject interrupted by his predecessor. Accordingly instructions to accede fully to the declaration were dispatched to the American ministers at the courts of London and Paris, but this change of policy came too late; England and France having reason to doubt its sincerity were not prepared to accept it. The arrière pensée of the president, who expected that after signing the proposed engagement they would treat Southern privateers as pirates, was perfectly understood by the diplomatists. Before affixing his signature to the act, M. Thouvenel observed, that the French government did not intend thereby to undertake any engagement which should have any bearing direct or indirect on the internal differences then prevailing in the United States. A similar clause was added by Earl Russell (*l*). The American government felt itself offended by this novel and anomalous proceeding, and immediately broke off the negotiations. Even the treaty made then with Russia (24th of August, 1861) upon the subject was subsequently suspended, and did not receive due ratification.

In the meantime the necessities of war led the United States to the formation of a regular navy and to the construction of iron-clad ships. In consequence of these innovations the plan of Mr. Marcy in favour of privateering and against the first principle of the declaration of Paris had lost its force, and a new and most destructive instrument of maritime war being thus discovered, it was understood that privateering could no longer serve for the defence of American traditions, and still less for aggressive purposes. The old men-of-war were superseded by Monitors, which required for their management experienced mechanics. The difference between

(*l*) See the correspondence of England with America on maritime international law (1862), N. 28. For the communication of these documents, the author is much indebted to *H. Farrer*, Esq., of the Board of Trade, and begs here to express his acknowledgment with his best thanks.

(172)

the commercial and regular navy now became greater, and naval operations could be conducted more efficiently against continental armies or besieged towns with the new engines adapted to this purpose, than with the comparatively less formidable instruments of former times. In short, maritime warfare assumed quite a different aspect. The capture of the private property of the enemy by cruisers or privateers appeared to be an insignificant mode of coercion, at least for those who had in their hands a more formidable means of destruction and devastation.

On the other side the Confederates, being a weaker party, had no other means of harassing the enemy than by making depredations or attacks on his commerce, and consequently resorted to the aid of privateers or cruisers. These adventurers acted in the American civil war as in the Middle Ages, i. e. at their own risk and peril, like pirates. The blockade of the Southern coast intercepted their communications with their country, left them almost without control, and prevented their obtaining regular commissions. Accordingly, they dispersed themselves over distant seas, and destroyed or appropriated their captures without any adjudication by a prize court. The subjects of the federal government having in this manner lost a large amount of their floating capital, were compelled to put their goods under the protection of neutrals; the revival of privateering, however, soon led to greater embarrassments. It was discovered that the Confederates had given directions for the construction of steamers in Liverpool and Birkenhead, apparently for trading purposes, but in reality with the intention of employing them against the enemy. In fact some of these steamers, the *Florida*, *Georgia*, *Alabama* and *Shenandoah*, having secretly made their escape from British ports, were subsequently fitted out as cruisers: public opinion in the United States could not of course look on such proceedings but with indignation, and accused England of conniving with rebels. This bitter reproach, directed as it was against the whole nation, evidently goes too far. But it can hardly be denied that sympathy for the South was at that time openly professed by many influential members of the British community, and even by some organs of the press. It must also be added, that the English government failed to enforce international duties on its subjects, and displayed a degree of indecision in its conduct nearly to the close of the war. The chief responsibility, however, attaches to the shipbuilders who, for the sake of their own profits, were almost ready to involve their country in the greatest peril.

The indecision of Earl Russell with reference to the *Alabama*, also forms a great contrast to the conduct of the Duke of Wellington against the Portuguese rebels in 1828. Both these statesmen had to deal with the same foreign enlistment act, but they acted very differently. The great Duke felt no doubt about his duty to repress the violation of that act, and having sent a squadron to Terceira against the ships that had arrived from England with hostile purposes, enforced with the greatest energy the strict observance of the sacred duties of neutrality; on the contrary, the proceedings against the *Alabama* were conducted in such an unsatisfactory manner, that the ship was permitted to go away under the command of an Englishman, to the reproach of the British name and honour, and to the abuse of its hospitality. The results of this negligence are sufficiently known. The affair of the *Alabama* led not only to protracted negotiations, but greatly endangered the friendly intercourse of the two countries. The case of the *Shenandoah* increased still more the irritation of the Americans against the English. Even the prosecution of the *Alexandra* and the seizure of the "battering rams" cannot be considered satisfactory. The partial and tardy interference in both cases was due less to the energy of the British government, than to the incessant demands of Mr. Adams, the minister of the United States in London. On the contrary, the Lord Chief Baron, when summing up in the first case, expressed an opinion rather favourable to the relaxation of neutral duties, namely, by saying that he saw no reason why ships of war should not be allowed to leave English ports, as freely as arms and other articles of war contraband destined for the use of the belligerents (*m*).

At all events the British government was in the American civil war called upon to discharge the duty of a neutral, and ought to have duly considered what had been her own conduct when a belligerent. It must be confessed that the appearance of England in this new character was somewhat unusual, and consequently rather awkward. As the United States had in their turn recourse to paper blockades and other violent measures, as they had introduced into their diplomacy the passions of an internecine struggle, the English could now understand how delicate the position of neutrals towards belligerents is, and how hard it is for a government, having any respect for its own dignity, to disregard the sufferings of its subjects, when they are treated unjustly and without mercy by a foreign power on no other ground than the so-called "jus extremæ necessitatis." It seems as if the importance of the principles of 1780 were now for the first time fully appreciated by the statesmen and jurists of Great Britain. At least very few of them were still inclined to uphold the universal authority of Lord Stowell, and to maintain the right of Great Britain to enforce on the rest of the world its own peculiar views of international jurisprudence. To this latter party belongs also the author of the brilliant letters of Historicus (*n*), who may be considered as an opponent of the "armed neutrality." But even he made some reluctant concessions in favour of its views, or prudently passed over in silence the irregularities and inconsistencies of the British practice.

As to other independent men, they have accepted the

(*m*) The international questions connected with all these cases are more fully stated by *Mr. Langel*, a French publicist, in his Essai on confederate cruisers. See *Revue des Deux Mondes*, Juillet, 1864.

(*n*) Among many pamphlets written on the American side against Historicus, the most interesting are those of Mr. *Geo. Bemis*. See his *Precedents of American Neutrality*, Boston, 1864, and *Hasty Recognition of American Belligerency*, Boston, 1865. Lately there appeared a third pamphlet by the same author.

liberal principles of 1780 and 1856 sincerely and unreservedly. It is be regretted, however, that English jurists were rather too late in recommending the milder course of policy to their countrymen with reference to belligerent rights, for had they done it sooner it probably might have prevented the contests for the maintenance of maritime law and the effusion of blood in 1800. Mr. Fox was not, perhaps, altogether wrong in his single advocacy in favour of the first "armed neutrality." The American civil war once more proved to England and to the world that the best rule for foreign as well as internal relations is still to be found in the old maxim, of doing to others as we would they should do unto us. May this divine maxim never be deviated from by powerful nations.

As to the advocates of the full immunity of private property from capture, their number in England rather increased than diminished during the American civil war. The most interesting publication of this kind appeared in 1862. It was an anonymous pamphlet directed against the opinion of Earl Russell, that this reform would reduce the power, offensive and defensive, of all states having a military as well as commercial marine. The author commences with a short review of the improvements in carrying on warfare, and asserts that the prevalent tendency of modern times is to consider it as a contest of governments, not of nations. Attacks on private property appear to him incompatible with the present state of civilization. Such property on land being held sacred, at least as a general rule, the author sees no sufficient reason to except the merchant ships of the enemy from the benefit of this policy. In fact, if the great end of war be the reduction or exhaustion of the military and naval forces of the belligerents, why should they be plundered? Of course, if they carry provisions for the combatants, they may be subjected to capture, but even in such cases the right of pre-emption seems to be quite sufficient for the purposes of war. The principal objects which, according to the author, England may now hope to attain by means of capture are—

(176)

1. The destruction of the enemy's commerce; and 2. The better manning of her navy by the attractions of prize-money. After discussing the first point, he is decidedly opposed to it; in his opinion the British flag is likely to suffer more than any other by captures. He also justly observes that by seizing enemy's ships, England would be frequently plundering her own merchants or capitalists, and thereby indirectly injuring herself to a very considerable extent. Even if these ships are driven off the sea, the enemy's commerce will not be put an end to, but only pass into the hands of neutrals. The arguments of the author are chiefly founded upon facts and confirmed by the experience of the Crimean war. He concludes that the right of maritime capture is not only useless but very obnoxious, for it does not mitigate or abbreviate wars by impairing the active forces of the enemy, its effect being to produce irritation between different nations, which prolongs hostilities; the enemy being more annoyed than injured by it. Experience generally is in favour of the author's views. "The French revolutionary war came to an end when the resources of France in men and money were exhausted;" and this exhaustion was due to her gigantic military efforts rather than to the interruption of her commerce. The author goes so far as to recommend that the general trade of the enemy should continue uninterrupted, reserving to the government the power of stopping it, if necessary, in any special case (*o*).

Soon afterwards the reform of maritime warfare became the subject of new discussions in the House of Commons (11th and 17th March, 1862); they are interesting for us not so much on account of their result as from the opinions of some influential members of the House expressed on that occasion. The original motion, made by Mr. Horsfall and seconded by Mr. Cobden, was to call the attention of the government to the unsettled state of maritime international law concerning belligerent rights. Accordingly Mr. Liddell suggested that a Congress should be convoked in order to

(*o*) In 1866 there appeared a second edition of this pamphlet.

(177)

ascertain whether other powers were inclined to grant immunity to private property of the enemy at sea. Sir G. C. Lewis met these proposals with his usual scepticism, and went so far as almost to deny the validity of any engagements made for a time of war. Mr. Baring felt it his duty to combat the extreme opinions held by that eminent statesman, and said, very truly, that England, being the greatest commercial power, is more interested in the abolition of captures than continental nations. The able speech of Mr. Lyndsay was almost to the same effect. Lord Palmerston appeared as the chief opponent of the motion, as well as of the projected reform. His arguments, however, against it seem not very happy. He still held sacred the old doctrine, that the destruction of enemy's commerce is the chief aim of maritime war. In his opinion the respect of private property at sea would reduce hostilities to a mere exchange of diplomatic notes. The noble lord succeeded for the moment, and Mr. Horsfall withdrew his motion (*p*).

Three years more elapsed before anything was done either by England or by the United States for the improvement of maritime international law. The American war only added fresh difficulties to the question of neutrality which was still pending. The two countries seemed disinclined to make any concessions to each other; the mutual animosity between them went on increasing. It might be even expected that they would sooner or later have come to open hostilities. At the close of the civil war, Mr. Adams renewed in London his demands of compensation for the losses American citizens had sustained by the Confederate cruisers, and offered to refer the question to arbitration. The English government, however, after some hesitation, declined to accede to these proposals. In the meantime the House of Commons made one more ineffectual attempt to accelerate the reform of maritime warfare. The animated discussion on the 3rd March, 1866, led to no more important results than that mentioned above. It deserves

(*p*) The full account of these debates is given by *Ægidi* and *Klauhold*, N. xlviii, xlix.

(178)

our attention only because it elicited with greater clearness the views of the ministry and of political parties on the subject. The debate originated upon a motion made by Mr. Gregory. He moved an address to the Queen, praying that her Majesty would be pleased to use her influence with foreign powers in order to put an end to maritime captures. This motion was strongly supported by Messrs. Liddell, Baxter, Torrens, Buxton and Laing. The Lord Advocate and Attorney-General opposed it more on the grounds of expediency than on those of law. The former even admitted that private property ought not to be made the subject of capture or destruction, particularly as the result accruing therefrom was utterly disproportionate to the loss sustained by the individual owner. Having added that an arrangement might be made for limiting captures in such cases, he objected to it only because it would cripple the strength of the English nation for attack and defence. In his opinion the only way to deprive war of its terrors was to avoid that which could occasion hostilities. The Attorney-General also excused himself for not using legal arguments upon the subject, and considered it a question of policy. In his point of view the American blockade appeared only as a powerful means for the speedy termination of that war. He thought the objections raised by merchants as well as jurists against the efficiency and the universal extension of that blockade were unimportant, and maintained that maritime captures would continue as long as other belligerent rights, because merchant ships and mercantile navy were easily convertible into engines of war. As to the difficulties of the proposed change, they seemed to the Attorney-General almost insurmountable. The new rule, according to him, would never be observed, even when accorded by general treaty. He despaired of securing its validity amid all the accidents of war. At all events, when enemy's ships were seized upon suspicion, this rule would be called in question and practically set aside by the belligerents. The Attorney-General also thought it impossible to apply to the enemy all the limitations that apply to neutrals, as well as to afford them the protection of prize courts; and at the close of his speech expressed a hope that changes to that effect would only be made in obedience to sound public opinion.

Thus the English ministry declined to undertake the solution of the problem in which the commercial interests of Great Britain were principally and deeply concerned. The first step for securing the immunity of private property from capture had been taken elsewhere, for the Italian government had fearlessly adopted this rule from the 1st January, 1866, upon the sole condition of reciprocity (*q*).

The full report of this debate is given in the *Times* of 3rd March, 1866.

In the same year this example of humanity and justice, which had been given to the world by this now free nation, found followers in Europe. In fact, when the last German war broke out, both Austria, by the decree of the 13th, and Prussia, by that of the 19th of May, adopted the Italian scheme (*r*). As far as we know, the belligerent powers strictly observed this new rule and found it sufficient. In short, the experiment was made successfully, and hostilities were carried on by regular navies without any disturbance to enemy's commerce. This circumstance deserves to be carefully weighed by other nations. The German war in that respect stands alone in the annals of war, and is the first international one limited to operations between *combatants*, without being accompanied by useless depredations on defenceless merchants. Unfortunately having, as far as it depended on them, destroyed legal piracy, the three powers just mentioned could not contribute much by their efforts to a

(*q*) See the articles 211, 212, of the code for mercantile marine of that kingdom, published June 25, 1865. *Ægidi*, doc. N. li. Condemnation is reserved only for the breaking of blockade as well as for war contraband. In both cases, however, the enemy will be treated according to the same principles, as neutrals.

(*r*) These decrees may be found among the documents collected by *Ægidi* (N. lii, liii), and are inserted in the Mémoire of *M. Cauchy*, p. 259—262. Séances, 8 & 9 livraison.

general reform in maritime warfare. The obstacles to it seem still to be great, and can hardly be overcome by the Continental governments of Europe. The consent to an arrangement of belligerent rights and neutral duties between England and the United States should be first obtained, for it would be premature and almost useless to hold a Congress on maritime international law without their participation. Unfortunately the dissensions caused by the American civil war still menace the peace of the world. In order to put an end to these difficulties, and to prevent the occurrence of still greater evils, both the interested parties are in duty bound to make mutual concessions. The new ministry in England seems to be rather inclined to an honourable settlement of the *Alabama* affair, and even to the revision of the existing statutes on neutrality. The appointment of a commission of Jurists for the latter purpose in 1866 may be considered as a favourable omen. It is probable that this commission will suggest some amendments to the Foreign Enlistment Act, in which neutral duties are neither sufficiently recognised, nor adequately defined (*s*). In fact, the relaxation of these stringent duties appears to have been the principal cause of all the present difficulties The incursions of the Fenians may be, at least partly, traced to the same source. The late proposal of the American Congress to suspend the legislative Acts of the country having reference to neutrality was also made with no other view than that of retaliation.

It was not long ago reported that a second and more important step had been taken by the Cabinet of St. James' towards the settlement of the difference pending between the two countries. The English ministry made a counter proposition in favour of arbitration. We hope it will be accepted by the United States with good will, and prove satisfactory to the interested parties.

(*s*) Whereas in the American Act of 1818, sects. 10 and 11, these duties are strongly enforced on shipbuilders and shipowners, the British Act of 1819 contains no corresponding provisions. For further information on this subject, see Law Magazine, Feb. 1867, p. 270—272, and papers read before the Juridical Society by Messrs. *Kerr* and *Reilly*, vol ii. art. vi.

(181)

But all these specific modes and contrivances to get out of embarrassments act only as palliatives, and are resorted to by politicians rather tardily and with some reluctance. An enlightened statesman can render greater service to his country and to the rest of the world by preventing, as far as it lies in his power, differences from occurring between independent nations. England and America have had experience enough to understand that the principal point of their disputes generally turn on those rules of international law which relate to maritime war and neutrality. It is high time for both governments to think seriously what is the best course to pursue under these circumstances. We have already said in our Introduction that, in our humble opinion, nothing can contribute more to the peace of the world than an impartial and careful reconstruction of those rules. Should, then, two great maritime powers assume the initiative in such a work, its ultimate success would be fully secured. They might adopt a uniform maritime law for the time of war, embracing neutral duties as well as belligerent rights, captures and prize procedure. Here the principal problem for solution is to determine exactly in what cases private property should in future be subjected to seizure and condemnation. As they are the greatest commercial countries, England and America are better prepared to devise a practical scheme on that subject, and to amend the customs of the Middle Ages, which, being no longer adapted to the exigencies of our times, serve only to obstruct the free intercourse of nations at sea. The reform in the law of maritime warfare so much desired by the rest of the world is in the hands of the great Anglo-Saxon family. Having contributed so much to liberty and civilization, it can confer on the world new benefits by securing justice and general freedom on the great highway of nations. The uniform law laid down by the common action of England and America may not only settle for a long time their present difficulties, but may be submitted to a general congress of Christian nations and elaborated into one universal maritime code. More than eighty years ago the founders of the

(182)

"armed neutrality" had such a project in view, but the time had not then arrived for the realization of their "pia desideria." Even now much good feeling, sincerity and forbearance are requisite, in order, in the solution of the problem, to give general satisfaction. However, labours, preparatory to such a step, commenced in 1780, and though interrupted by subsequent events were resumed in 1814 by proceedings in the same direction, viz., by separate treaties, negotiations, mixed commissions, &c. In our time, when the more intricate points of the subject are better understood, when belligerents as well as neutrals have almost exhausted their respective remedies, common legislation on maritime war seems to be of the utmost importance to general security. If England and America are inclined to live on terms of peace and impart the same blessings to the rest of the world, they can hardly do anything better than promote, by all means in their power, the codification of maritime international law.

Our expectations may be too sanguine. The prospects of a reform lie yet in the future, and the future is hidden from us all. It often brings with it new complications and delays. However, we still look forward with confidence in its promises. In all probability the time is not far distant when a maritime code will be drawn up, though perhaps only in the form of a project. But there is no apparent reason to despair of its being accepted in an improved form, when public opinion urges so strongly its necessity, when jurists of different countries agree in their views upon the subject, when the best statesmen are inclined to amend the existing laws and to bring them into harmony, when, in short, the interests of mankind are understood to coincide with this reform. The growing tendency to it seems to us irresistible, the natural course of events has hitherto been favourable to the mitigation of capture, and the immunity of private property was partially observed in the last German war. This movement cannot cease until belligerent rights are reduced to their minimum, i. e. to the "jus extremæ necessitatis," in the proper sense of the term, until

(183)

enemy merchants are placed on an equal footing with neutrals, under the sole condition "ne se bello interponant" (*u*), until the rights of pacific traders on sea are secured in the same degree as those of the unarmed inhabitants of the continent. Such may be the provisions of the future code! It has been very truly observed in some recent publications on the subject, that these rules are required not only by humanity but also by Christian justice (*v*). As to neutral rights and duties, there is no other way for the clear definition of them, than to follow the principles of 1780 to their ultimate results, as expressed in treaties from that to the present time. As, however, treaties are silent on some questions, recourse may be had to the judgments of different countries in prize cases. But these rules ought to be followed with great circumspection, as they have been laid down by belligerents alone, and very often to the detriment of neutrals. We hope that very few of them will enter into the international prize code without modification. At all events it is necessary to compare the dicta of the best English, French and American judges, before coming to the conclusion about and the adoption of any restrictive rule for neutral commerce. The very existence of the Admiralty Courts, at least in their present constitution and exclusive dependence upon belligerents, ought to be the subject of the most serious consideration (*x*). The

(*u*) This expression is used by *Bynkershoek* in his *Quæstiones juris publici*, Lib. 1, c. ix.

(*v*) Such seems to be the opinion of Sig. *Ercole Vidari*, as expressed in his pamphlet: *Del rispetto della proprieta privata dei popoli belligeranti*, Milano, 1865. We know this publication only from extracts of it given by *M. Cauchy* (annexes, No. 23), who comes himself almost to the same conclusion. (See his Memoir, p. 267—9.) The capture of private ships, according to him, cannot be justified on the same grounds as the condemnation for importing war contraband or breach of blockade. In the two last cases a private individual is punished for direct interference in war, while in the first he suffers without any reasonable cause, and only as an imaginary enemy. We must add that, more than ten years ago, Dr. *Asher*, of Hamburg, defended with great force nearly the same views. See his *Essai sur le droit maritime*. Hamb. 1856.

(*x*) The most recent work embracing the laws of neutrality came from the pen of Dr. *Gessner*, under the title *Le droit des neutres sur mer*. The views of this learned gentleman are those of the advanced German school. He also

maritime code will necessarily curtail in some degree their almost unlimited power of laying down rules about costs and damages, as well as on evidence, and of interpreting the law of blockade and war contraband in favour of cruisers. As to the questions of nationality, they will be set aside altogether if the enemy merchant is to be considered as neutral. Condemnation itself will probably be reserved for few cases, such as transport of troops, spy-services, and other fraudulent actions of private individuals. In short, it will be maintained only as a just punishment against transgressors of neutral duties.

Having given in this Postscript the more important results obtained during the last twelve years in the law of maritime capture, we beg to conclude our work with a few additional observations. Its appearance before a larger and well-informed public makes the author sincerely regret that he could not make it more perfect. Some errors will be easily discovered in a book embracing such a vast historical subject. However it may be, we have tried all the means in our power to contribute to the improvement and codification of general prize law. The men, who may be called upon to give advice or aid to governments in the practical solution of this problem, will find here, we hope, some information on the questions connected with it. In writing about war and neutrality we have had in view only the peace and general security of the world. In our humble opinion, nothing but the strict observance of international justice can lead to mutual confidence, now as greatly endangered between the principal powers of Europe as in their relations with America. Our attention has been chiefly directed to the principles of 1780 for a very obvious reason. We find in them rules of conduct better adapted to the necessities of the present age, than any other. If these principles served some temporary political purpose, it proves nothing against their intrinsic value. The

advocates a reform in maritime warfare as well as the establishment of international prize courts suggested by *Hübner*. This valuable work deserves the attention of English and American jurists.

(185)

Northern coalition of 1800 is dissolved, and we heartily wish it may never be revived. England herself was lately called upon to defend neutral rights, and having failed to perform the corresponding duties (as in the case of the *Alabama*), greatly suffered for it. An armed neutrality may serve equally for all nations, and is more efficient than an unarmed one. At the present time the principles of 1780 may be directed to still higher purposes, i. e. to the pacification of the world. In this point of view they should, and we trust they will, be better appreciated by the British public. If they have more value in the eyes of a Russian jurist, it is only because they have made his country appear as an impartial arbiter in disputed questions of international law, and perform her duty to the general satisfaction of continental Europe. The best periods of Russian history were, in our opinion, those in which the sovereigns and statesmen of that immense country were animated by the cosmopolitan spirit of Christianity. It enabled them to confer the greatest benefits on their own subjects, as well as on the world at large. An international jurist of Russian origin cannot look indifferently on such moral triumphs as were won in 1780 by the justice, impartiality and moderation of his countrymen. No nation can be afraid of or suffer by glorious conquests of that description. They are gained without bloodshed, and turn sooner or later to the advantage of mankind. International jurisprudence, founded by a man of such large and benevolent views as Grotius, makes every one, whatever may be his creed, capacities, or political opinions, work for it in the same spirit. Our voice is too feeble and distant to be heard in all the countries concerned in the reform of maritime law, but we are happy to offer our humble contribution to the common stock of knowledge, and to do our utmost in furthering the interest of civilization throughout the world.

KHARKOV, RUSSIA,
25 March,
6 April, 1867.

ADDENDA TO THE POSTSCRIPT.

Note (*h*), p. 152. As the cases brought before the Judicial Committee after 1856 are not reported by Dr. Spinks, I could not of course take them all into my consideration. But I have found subsequently in the collection of Dr. Soetbeer (Nachtrag 1) an interesting case of the *Ariel*, 25th March, 1857, from which I see that their Lordships have modified or relaxed the rules laid down by the Admiralty Court concerning the sale of enemy's ships to neutrals. In their opinion the bill of sale ought to be considered in the same light as a conveyance of freehold or leasehold estates. In all these documents the purchase-money is always mentioned to have been fully paid, and yet there may be a collateral instrument showing that nothing has been paid, or the whole or part of the money may be left upon mortgage. Their Lordships also came to the conclusion that liens, whether in favour of a neutral or enemy's ship, or vice versâ, *are equally to be disregarded* in a prize court. I see also from the cases of the *Gerasimo*, *Aspasia* and the *Achilles* (25th March, 1857, Soetbeer, ibid.), that the doctrine of the learned Judge of the Admiralty Court on nationality has been reconsidered by their Lordships and interpreted more in favour of neutrals.

INDEX.

PAPERS READ BEFORE THE JURIDICAL SOCIETY

VII.

A BIOGRAPHICAL NOTICE OF THE LATE PROFESSOR WURM

By PROFESSOR KATCHENOVSKY

[Read 7th March, 1859.]

The science of international law lost, a few weeks ago, one of its most distinguished expounders and commentators. On the 2nd of February last, died, in Holstein, the celebrated publicist of Hamburgh, Dr. Wurm. His name belongs not only to his own country, but to all the civilized world. During the last twenty-five years he took the leading part in the discussion of all great questions of European policy, was the constant and impartial observer of diplomacy, the able defender of international rights, and one of the most intelligent organs of public opinion. His death is, therefore, an important event in the annals of science; he left after him a void; his scientific place can hardly be filled by another. Feeling a high and sincere respect for the merits of this eminent man, I thought it my duty to communicate some facts relating to his biography, and to give a general sketch of his works. These facts were collected for the most part by my personal inquiries and observations during a month's residence in Hamburgh last year.

Though there are few striking events in the life of Dr. Wurm, it is worthy of attention in many respects. We find in it, on the one side, proofs of the vigour and variety of his talents; on the other, it reflects the great aspirations and tendencies of our age. The most instructive part of this life for us is that which is connected with his activity as a publicist. It is interesting to know the causes that led him to the study of international law.

Dr. Wurm was born in Würtemberg, at Tübingen, in 1803. His father was a theologian, and desired, as many fathers desire, that his son should embrace the same profession; but, having found afterwards that he was averse to the study of theology, gave him up to follow his own inclinations. With all the energy of his youthful mind, Dr. Wurm attached himself to the classical literature of Greece and Rome — the ancient historians, poets, and orators, became his favourite companions; he acquired, at the same time, the knowledge of Hebrew — a language perfectly understood by his learned father. It seemed that our future publicist was destined to cultivate philology and history. But it was not so decreed. During his travels in Switzerland he made the acquaintance of an intelligent Englishman, Mr. Greaves, who persuaded him to go to this country, and gave him his aid in obtaining the place of tutor in a private school at Epsom. His residence in England gave another direction to the studies, and changed the ideas, of Wurm. He saw before him a practical people, endowed in the highest degree with the instinct of self-government, and enjoying the blessings of freedom. Political questions acquired now great interest in his eyes, and he returned to Hamburgh quite another man. One of his first duties was to acquaint the Germans with the social life, with the institutions, and with the literature of England. For that purpose he conducted a periodical — the *Hamburgh Reporter*. Some years since was undertaken by him another publication in the German language, under the name of "Critical Additions to the Hamburgh commercial paper (*Borsenhalle*)." During this period of his life occurred the revolution of July, in France. Its influence was felt through all the continent, and produced great excitement in the minds of the German people. The fear of a general war, and the retrograde tendencies of governments, more and more directed all the attention of Dr. Wurm to questions of public and international law. He was led to their study almost against his will, by the force of circumstances; and became attached to them, not by sudden caprice or by ambition, but by the growing importance of the subject. His position at Hamburgh gave him the best qualification, and the best opportunities, of performing the difficult task of an international jurist. In fact, it is hardly possible for an intelligent man to be indifferent to the interests of peace, of general commerce, and of navigation, after naturalizing himself in that Hanseatic city. The prosperity of Hamburgh as a free and commercial town is closely connected with the liberty of Europe, and with the stability of international law. Only in this cause can we find the explanation of a singular phenomenon, that at Hamburgh have flourished so many distinguished publicists in the 18th and 19th centuries. All these men were faithful supporters of free trade, and friends of the liberal principles of neutral commerce. Here, at Hamburgh, appeared some sixty years ago, the curious pamphlets of "Old Busch" (as he is called) against the arbitrary prize decisions of Dr. Marriott, the piratical decrees of the French Directory, and the continental system of the Emperor Napoleon. This remarkable man, seeing the oppression of commerce during the endless revolutionary wars, consecrated all his life to the defence of international law from the tyranny of maritime powers. The Hamburgh people, in the simplicity of their merchant souls, could not appreciate the generous instinct from which the learned old man took to his heart this subject; they were surprised, and sometimes angry, at seeing his intervention in their affairs, and rendered him justice only after his death. The testimonial of their thanks is the modest monument erected to his memory at Hamburgh. Dr. Wurm was a great admirer of Professor Busch, and became one of his ardent followers. Both in the same degree, and with the same devotion to their cause, fought for freedom of commerce, contributed to the prosperity of Hamburgh, and, as far as they could, promoted its interests. There is, however, some difference between them. Generally speaking, Busch was less prepared for the duties of a publicist: in his pamphlets appeal rather the qualities of a generous patriot than of an historian or a diplomatist. On the contrary, the works of Dr. Wurm exhibit the most thorough comprehension of European policy, and a vast erudition. In reading these works we come to the conclusion that the author had the talents of a great statesman. His knowledge of the diplomatic history of Europe can hardly be equalled; he surpassed in it many, if not all the publicists of our age. No important precedent escaped his careful research; he observed the fluctuations of international policy with wonderful accuracy and attention. If he was deficient in abstract reasoning, he excelled on the other side in practical sense, and in appreciation of facts. It would be difficult to sustain with him a polemic on this field.

Professor Wurm never undertook to write a comprehensive work on international law. All his contributions to this science consist of essays or treatises on various subjects, written chiefly for German periodicals. They embrace many important questions of peace and war, and give the most valuable information on the state of international law in the present century. I will enumerate here the principal or the best of them, and indicate where they are to be found, because, unfortunately, they are not yet collected. He contributed to the Political Dictionary (*Staatslexicon*) of Rotteck and Welcker, two essays on prize law and reprisals; to the Political Review of Tübingen univcrsity (*Zeitschrift für die gesammte Staatswissenschaft*), a series of articles on the state and application of international law during the war between Denmark and Gcrmany, and an essay on the rank and precedence of diplomatic agents; to the German Quarterly Review (*Deutsche Vierteljahesschrift*), a treatise on international commerce, his last work on special reprisals (September, 1858), and many others. Of the pamphlets published by him separately, the most remarkable are on the Sound dues and Stade dues, which essays are published in the blue books of the House of Commons; two series of letters on the Danubian question (1855, 1858, Leipzig), the diplomatic history of the Turco-Russian war, and the memoirs or letters addressed to Lord John Russell on the law of neutral commerce, and to Lord Palmerston on the Schleswig-Holstein question. I do not mention here his numerous works on German affairs, as they have a more local importance.

From this enumeration we see what a laborious life was his; the learned professor never ceased to work; even during his illness, not being able to write, he dictated to his wife. Many valuable works he left unfinished, and among them a history of England from 1815, a sketch or the treaties relating to the slavetrade, an essay on mediation and arbitration, and perhaps others. It would be worth while to publish all these posthumous papers; undigested as they are, they would be of great use for future inquirers, and particularly for an historian of international law, to whom they would furnish a precious collection of facts and precedents.

It would be too long to give a detailed account of each of the works of Professor Wurm. I have no intention to criticize them here; but I should add a few words to their general characteristics, given before. I have said that the chief merit of Dr. Wurm consisted in his knowledge of diplomatic history. This knowledge served him as the best guide in treating international law. He gave no peculiar attention to theory; his illustrations are eminently practical. We can say, without exaggeration, that he gave the initiative and a great impulse to the study of state papers, and laid the foundation of a modern school of publicists different from the former. In another paper, read before this society, I treated of the works of Professor Martens, and said what influence they had on international jurisprudence. The method of Martens degenerated in process of time into the mere compilation of treaties, and led to the decay of the scientific spirit. Professor Wurm, by his works, accomplished a great and beneficial change in this respect, and, we may say, restored to the science its former dignity. Standing on practical ground, he never contented himself, like the successors of Martens, with the statement of facts, but appreciated their historical value with critical judgment. It is true that he seldom arrived at philosophical results, but this circumstance cannot diminish his merits in our eyes. If he did not lay down principles, he certainly aided in elaborating them. Thus he solved a part of the scientific problem, and left the other to political philosophers.

As I said before, Dr. Wurm possessed the qualities of an eminent publicist, and was better prepared for his task than many others of the same profession. With profound erudition in history and general literature, he combined great knowledge of European languages — English, Dutch, and French were quite familiar to him; he read with facility Italian, Spanish, Danish, and Swedish books. In his library I found almost all valuable publications upon international law, diplomatic documents, pamphlets, and some manuscripts of historical value; in a. word, his library was as an international observatory, from which he observed with wonderful impartiality and acuteness all the phenomena of diplomacy, all the events and occurrences of the world. His correspondence with some statesmen gave him useful information from many countries. He followed the movements of cabinets, and knew some secrets and intrigues hardly known to any other publicist. I was struck by his energy and vigilance; he knew no fatigue, and watched carefully the interests of Europe and of civilisation.

Professor Wurm contributed to the science of international law, not only by his works, but also by his lectures. He selected every year some important subject of European policy, and delivered his opinions upon it before the Hamburgh public. I attended several of these lectures, and feel it my duty to say that they were as instructive as full of interest. The oratorical powers of Dr. Wurm were very considerable; it is true that his voice was not strong; but it is no less true that he spoke with talent and with animation. His style was as clear in speech as in writing. During the last year, the subject of his lectures was the history of British domination in India. I could speak a longer time of this remarkable man. His talents were so great, his knowledge was so extensive, the charm of his conversation so uncommon, that we can apply to him the words of the poet — "Age could not wither him, nor custom stale his infinite variety." But as I proposed to myself to give but a short sketch of his scientific life, and to render justice to his eminent works on international law, I shall conclude with a few remarks. In studying the biography of almost all the men who have given a great impulse to this science, we find that they were less appreciated by their contemporaries than they deserved, and often were persecuted for their opinions. Even posterity has sometimes treated them with indifference. In a word, their profession could hardly satisfy their ambition, or even serve their pecuniary interests. When I compare the splendid monuments erected to generals and admirals in many towns with the modest tomb of Hugo Grotius — when every parish has its great men, but the resting-place of true greatness is hardly to be found — I appreciate more the modest devotion of those who can work for science and for humanity, without other prospects of reward but the respect and gratitude of the friends of civilisation. Let us then pay them, gentlemen, our tribute of sympathy! They have left us good examples — a love of truth, a sincere desire of peace, a brotherly feeling to all the Christian family, a great respect for right and for justice. Dr. Wurm was distinguished by these qualities in no less a degree than other international jurists; he worked honestly and conscientiously; he obeyed, during all the struggles and excitement of our age, the sense of duty; he was persecuted for his liberal opinions; he was suspected and misrepresented in his feelings. .May he rest now in peace, and let us not forget his works and his merits! May his successors study international jurisprudence with the same spirit of impartiality and toleration; may the words *Immer wahr*, which I have read on the seal of his letters, become their true device, and guide them in the paths of science!

[LETTER OF PROFESSOR KATCHENOWSKY]

[The materials which follow are taken from George W. Hastings (ed.), *Transactions of the National Association for the Promotion of Social Science 1860* (London, John W. Parker, Son, and Bourne, 1861), pp. xxv-xxvi. The Fourth Annual Meeting of the National Association was held at Glasgow from 24-29 September 1860 inclusive. Professor Kachenovskii had written to the General Secretary of the Association, George W. Hastings.[1]]

A resolution was passed by the [National] Association [for the Promotion of Social Science], constituting a Sixth Department, to embrace the subjects of Trade and International Law, and it is believed that considerable results will follow from this extension of our programme.

The resolution was passed in consequence of representations made by foreigners at the Meeting, among them MM. Desmarest and Pagès. The following letter on the subject was received from Professor Katchenowsky, of the University of Kharcov, Russia, and was read to the Association: –

Kharcov, 22*nd August* (3*rd Sept.*), 1860

MY DEAR SIR, –

In offering you my best thanks for the invitation to your annual meeting you honoured me with, I regret very

[1] George W. Hastings (ed.), *Transactions of the National Association for the Promotion of Social Science 1859* (1860), p. xxxiii.

sincerely my being not able of leaving Russia for the present year. You may be assured that nothing but public duties could retain me here, and that I shall avail myself of the first opportunity for attending a congress of the National Association for Promotion of Social Science. However long is the distance lying between us, you will not doubt of my sympathy to your Association, and of my best wishes for the success of the present meeting. I shall be happy in communicating to my countrymen its proceedings and results as far as they will reach me by newspapers or otherwise.

I take now the liberty of offering you some suggestions concerning your programme. Extensive as it is, it does not include one of the most important branches of social science – I mean the international law of Europe and America. There are many topics in it worthy of your consideration. By discussing them you will touch some vital questions of general interest, and direct the attention of the Continent of Europe to the proceedings of your Congress. In the present state of things international jurists and publicists have no common centre for action on public opinion, and cannot interchange their ideas, however profitable it may be for the world. In fact, you will not deny that the relations between the different communities grow every year more complicated. I do not intend to speak here of political relations. They are to be regulated by mutual agreement of different powers and governments. I mean to call your attention to the growing importance of social relations, whose existence now is felt by everybody. It is no exaggeration to say that we see in the nineteenth century a new phenomenon in social life, appearing almost unexpectedly under the influence of modern inventions — such as electric telegraphs, railways, steam navigation, &c., and favoured by the natural course of events. A new society, embracing all the Christian nations, and connecting them by mutual ties of interest and humanity, is firmly established in Europe. It would be idle to contest this fact; it would be late to resist its effects and consequences. It was decreed by Providence. We are obliged, on the contrary, to conform ourselves to the necessity of changing our former conduct, and to promote the improvement of international law. It is not to be obtained more by individual exertions of Governments or by separate efforts of diplomacy; it is required, as the French say, "*par la force des choses*", or "*ex necessitate rerum*", and should be done by public exertion or by public opinion.

I will try to prove this by facts. You know, for instance, the imperfect state of private international law. There is no civilized Government that does not acknowledge it; but you shall hardly find two or three Governments acting upon the same principles in its administration; every one of them follows its own inclinations and traditions. I do not speak here of insignificant differences in the formalities of contracts or of modes of acquiring property. I mean the most important relations between the members of different communities. I do complain of their being uncertain, left to arbitrary provisions, and subject to many local exceptions. In my opinion, the establishment of *uniform rules* for them is an absolute necessity. The international jurists of Europe had felt long ago the absence of those rules, but their voice was too feeble to be heard, and up to the present day the security of foreign relations is depending more upon general conscience and humanity that upon strict and well defined law. Now, it is high time to think of the future, and to find efficient remedies for this bad state of things. Public opinion cannot be longer indifferent to the growing complications of private international law. We are not able even to enumerate here the number of its victims who suffer and incur heavy losses in foreign countries from mere ignorance of local habits and provisions, who become engaged almost by surprise in the most long and expensive lawsuits, and who vainly cry for help in their unexpected difficulties. Diplomatic agents and consuls, even, with the best intentions, are incompetent to provide for the state of things depending not on their will, and having its foundations in the *routine* or practice of past ages.

I think, then, that your Department of Jurisprudence will promote the general good by taking this subject into their profound consideration, and by enlarging their programme accordingly. I see that *adaptation of law to social changes* does enter into the plan of your occupations. It seems, then, that my humble suggestion goes not contrary to the general views of that Department. There is, in fact, no other branch of law less adapted to social changes than private international law. May your Congress become a powerful organ for its improvement, and proclaim to the world its general and beneficent principles! They are already elaborated by international jurists, and require nothing but to be discussed and adopted by a respected body of statesmen and social philosophers. The most important questions to be resolved are those of foreign jurisdiction, of extradition, of laws of succession, of contracts, and of validity of marriage in foreign countries. To these may be added others of the same description.

The opinions I express here are not products of my own imagination. My views of private international law find echo with many English publicists and statesmen. The necessity of uniform rules in it is acknowledged by all those to whom this subject is particularly known. From the latest works written upon it in England, those of Sir G. Lewis (on foreign jurisdiction) and of Mr. Westlake, express in other and better words the same feelings. But I have no need to assure that you will find in England great numbers of competent men who will lead this matter to the most satisfactory conclusion.

As to my suggestions, if you find them worthy of consideration, you will be so kind as to communicate them to the juridical department. I am very sorry of being not able to discuss all doubtful points in the present letter, written in haste (as otherwise it should not reach you in due time); but I hope to develop my views on a future occasion if it shall be required, and to forward another paper upon this subject.

I am, my dear Sir, yours faithfully,
D. Katchenowsky

G. W. Hastings. Esq.

DISSERTATION ON WAR AND PEACE, BY BASIL MAHNOFSKY

ST. PETERSBURGH, 1803

D. I. KACHENOVSKII

[The present work was communicated to the Peace Society in London, England, on 18 May 1858, and appeared in *The Herald of Peace*, 1 June 1858, pp. 71–72. One must assume that the Peace Society and/or its printer experienced difficulty with Kachenovskii's handwriting, for the individual to whom he refers is Vasilii [Basil] Fedorovich Malinovskii (1765–1814). They read the "li" as an "h" – WEB]

This curious work consists of two parts: in the first the author speaks of the evils of war; in the second of the blessings of peace.

Chapter I. The practice of war, and the general opinion of its necessity.

Our short life is full of many necessary evils. Should we add to them the unnecessary evil of war! The habit of it makes us indifferent. We are short-sighted and do not feel our cruelty. War is the brutal force of wild beasts, combined with the art of destroying the life and happiness of man. War is a monster whose footsteps are stained with blood. It deprives the nations of their repose, and shortens their life.

It is time now to abolish the practice of settling international disputes by the sword. We think to mitigate war by humanity and moderation; but this humanity is the humanity of an executioner, who makes choice of the

> instruments of death, not to spare the life of his victims, but to shorten it. Why so deceive ourselves by such ideas? Nothing but opinion of the necessity of war makes war necessary. We think that we cannot live without war, because it existed everywhere and in all ages. But man is free; he has reason and will, he has liberty of judgment and of action to change his habits. If we compare the Western nations with the ancient, we will find many changes made not only in laws, usages and arts, but even in religion itself. The ancient world adored war; its gods were heroes and warriors. But our God is God of peace and love. Christianity commands us to love our neighbours without distinction of nationality.

So begins our author his work. We have not space for the complete translation of this book; we will follow the general ideas, and give a few extracts of the most remarkable sentences, of Mr. Mahnofsky. After the introductory remarks he explains the historical causes of the existence of war in Europe. In his opinion there were only two principal impediments to 'general peace — ignorancc and superstition. "Civilization", says he, "shall enlarge our views and make us understand that the interests of every state or kingdom is bound with the general welfare of Europe. Europe is now sufficiently prepared for peace. Her inhabitants are united by science and commerce, by similar laws and manners; they profess the same religion; their languages have more or less a common origin. The name of European should be respected in all the parts of the earth.

In the second and third chapter our author refutes the common prejudice in respect of war, and proves that this evil can produce nothing but evil. We shall not repeat the words of Mr. Mahnofsky about this subject; they express only the ideas familiar to the men of the Peace Society. It is unnecessary to add, that he has no sympathy with aggressive policy. He thinks that the glory of nations consists not in the conquest they make upon their neighbours, but in those peaceful conquests by which man subdues nature and promotes civilization. “The true force of a kingdom”, says he, “is the happiness of the people, the mutual tie of the inhabitants and their confidence in the government. Englishmen are respected in Europe, not for their wars, but because they have great statesmen, civil and social virtues, and public spirit”.

In the fourth chapter are expressed the opinions of our author about greatness and heroic virtues. He thinks that conquerors and generals do not promote the general improvement, but serve only as instruments of ruin and death. The true greatness is determined not by the numbers of fought victories, but by the number of useful services to mankind.

Chapter the fifth is the most eloquent and beautiful. It treats of the miseries of war. “We pride ourselves”, says Mr. Mahnofsky, “that we are humane in war and spare the vanquished foe”. To refute this opinion, he gives a description of some remarkable sieges and battles. His remarks on the extent of pauperism and the increase of taxes and of military budgets in modern Europe, are very interesting. He expressed the desire that regular armies may be diminished.

In the sixth chapter, Mr. Mahnofsky compares the miseries of war with the advantages of peace. “The governments”, says he, “live now in constant fear of war, and have no leisure for the elaboration of laws and for the improvement of society. The public money is employed, not for the real wants of the people, but for military purposes”.

In the seventh chapter our author speaks about diplomacy. “This art has retained till the present time its original features, and consists in lies and intrigues. Its instruments are official and secret spies. The mutual animosity and rivalry of nations, is nourished by a certain class of publicists and pamphleteers; some of them are corrupted by the courts and by ambitious men, — these are of the most dangerous class; the others are the fever-minded patriots who think that the love to the country consists in the indiscriminate hatred of all foreigners; and the third pursue their occupation from the mere love of scandal. All these men forget their duty to society, and instead of promoting peace, inflame the passions of the communities.

In the second part of the work the author speaks of the means leading to the general pacification of mankind. These are: 1, Sanction of international law by the consent of all the civilized world, (chapter the first). 2, The confederation and the convocation of an international congress, (chapter the second). The principal duty of this congress is the prevention of war. "The limits of nations shall be determined by the congress, and cannot be changed without its approval. All international disputes are to be settled before this tribunal".

In the last six chapters Mr. Mahnofsky develops his general ideas, and discusses the principal questions that are to be determined by the congress. He thinks that its authority and attributes cannot prejudice the independence of nations. In resuming his principles, the author concludes that universal peace is the consolidation of society. If the civilized nations could induce their governments to abolish war, they would remove it by all the obstacles now obstructing the progress of mankind.

Such are the general features of his remarkable work. If we remember that it was written in the end of the eighteenth century (the first part in 1793, the second in 1797), amidst the general war in Europe — that its author belonged to a semi-civilized nation, — we cannot see it with indifference. Mr. Mahnofsky's views deserve the attention of this Society and of all the Christian world. His name can be mentioned with the names of St. Pierre, Kant, Bentham, and of others, enemies of war. In perusing his work, we find in him a man of enlightened views. It is evident that his mind was struck with the evils of the system of mutual destruction then prevailing in Europe — that his mind was deeply imbued with the sacred principles of Christianity.

To appreciate better the spirit of the work now lying before us, we translate from it the following page on the mutual prejudices of nations:

> The first source of mutual prejudices of nations is ignorance; they ascribe to foreigners, the most absurd habits, and therefore despise them. I think that to respect each other the nations should only be better acquainted.
>
> The second source of these prejudices is the hatred produced by wars. This hatred, prevailing sometimes for many ages, makes the nations ascribe to their enemies the most abject vices and deny their virtues. It is unjust, because the principal cause of war lies not in the nations but in the governments.
>
> It is remarkable that these prejudices are predominant, not only in masses, but sometimes infect the better educated people, who should know that every nation has some good qualities — that each quality has his brighter as well as his darker side — that the qualities imputed to nations are too general, and that there is no rule without exception to it. Every nation consists of individual men, very often different in their characters. All these things prove the necessity of general union and of mutual aid.

– *Communicated to the Peace Society,*
by Professor Katchenoffsky,
on 18*th* *May,* 1858

INDEX OF NAMES

www.ingramcontent.com/pod-product-compliance
Ingram Content Group UK Ltd.
Pitfield, Milton Keynes, MK11 3LW, UK
UKHW041853031026
15587UKWH00006B/1209/J